Adult education and the postmodern challenge

DATE DUE

Demco, Inc. 38-293

Adult education and the postmodern challenge

Learning beyond the limits

Robin Usher, Ian Bryant and
Rennie Johnston

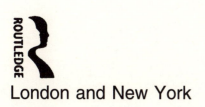

London and New York

First published 1997
by Routledge
11 New Fetter Lane, London EC4P 4EE

Simultaneously published in the USA and Canada
by Routledge
29 West 35th Street, New York, NY 10001

Reprinted 1999

Typeset in Times by
BC Typesetting, Bristol

Printed and bound in Great Britain by
Biddles Ltd, Guildford and King's Lynn

British Library Cataloguing in Publication Data
A catalogue record for this book is available from the British Library

Library of Congress Cataloguing in Publication Data
Usher, Robin
  Adult education and the postmodern challenge: learning beyond the
limits/Robin Usher, Ian Bryant, and Rennie Johnston.
      p.   cm.
  Includes bibliographical references and index.
  1. Adult education–Social aspects. 2. Postmodernism and
education. 3. Adult learning. I. Bryant, Ian.
II. Johnston, Rennie. III. Title.
LC5225.S64U75   1997
374´.1–dc20   96–21559
                                                      CIP

ISBN 0–415–12020–9 (hbk)
ISBN 0–415–12021–7 (pbk)

Contents

Introduction

This book started life as a proposed second edition of *Adult Education as Theory, Practice and Research: The Captive Triangle* (Usher and Bryant 1989). Although it evoked strongly polarised feelings amongst its readership, *The Captive Triangle* did contribute to the creation of a change in intellectual climate and outlook in the world of adult and continuing education. Alongside its sometimes fierce critics, there were many who indicated that the orientation and approach we proposed was welcome and stimulating. Many of the ideas and concepts introduced have now been incorporated into the general thinking of the field. In retrospect, we would argue that it was probably ahead of its time when published in 1989, which may, perhaps, explain why there was a tendency to dismiss it as a 'difficult' text (which we admit that it was).

The overall purpose of that book was to examine the relationship between theory, practice and research in adult education. The assumption was that there is a unity between these elements and that the enhancement of practice is best achieved by a recognition of this unity and its consequences. However, the argument put forward was that we are 'captured' by a foundationalist and restricted understanding of the nature of the triangular relationship; so that, for example, we always see theory and research in terms of disciplinary knowledge and therefore as always applied to practice. We sought in *The Captive Triangle* first of all to challenge the notion that adult education as a field of study is founded in disciplinary knowledge. If it is to be understood as a practice, it cannot be reduced to a psychology of learning or a sociology of participation. Second, that it is necessary to provide a different way of analysing the place of 'theory', one which emphasises its purpose as 'reviewing' rather than 'legislating' for practice, a different approach to the theory–practice–research relationship. Third, we wanted to highlight the notion of 'practical' knowledge and 'practical' reasoning, to emphasise that it has its own integrity and could provide an alternative to a technical-rationality model of practice and a positivist paradigm of research.

Much has changed in the world of adult and continuing education since *The Captive Triangle* was written in the course of 1987–8. For example, there have been significant developments in a) policy and practice, such as the spread of vocationalism and marketisation, the pressure for accreditation of learning and the decline of the liberal tradition, and b) in intellectual and conceptual frameworks, such as feminism, critical pedagogy, postmodernism – all of which have had an increasing impact on practice itself. At the same time, there have been significant changes in the understandings of the authors who, in their teaching and writing, have participated in and reflected on the changes.

In general, the difficult territory that we began to explore is now being explored by others, and much that was considered radical and challenging then has now become far less so. We therefore envisaged a need to take account of these changes and investigate areas that are currently problematic whilst still maintaining the critical thrust of the original. We also saw the need for something with a wider scope – which could, for example, encompass such activities as research training for practitioners and such themes as experiential learning and postmodernism. Furthermore, although we have never accepted in their entirety the criticisms of difficult and inaccessible language and discourse made about *The Captive Triangle*, we recognised a need to give more serious reflexive attention to this issue. We therefore suggested a second edition that would encompass not simply minor revisions and up-dating but something much more ambitious in its scope – so much so that it would in fact constitute a new book. Thanks to our publishers, this is how it ended up.

In this successor book, the intention was to maintain a critical anti-foundationalist stance and thus problematise whatever flows from this stance – for example, the technical-rational model of practice and the positivist paradigm of research. However, we also wanted to amplify and broaden certain key themes and issues, such as disciplinary knowledge, which is not so much foundational for practice but a power/knowledge formation, already entwined with practice. These themes include: the increasingly important role of 'governmentality' in the light of the impact of marketisation, competence-based training and vocationalism, guidance and counselling; the need to relate educational trends and policies to changing socio-economic and socio-cultural structures; changing intellectual frameworks, for example, critical pedagogy, feminism, postmodernism and their impact upon educational theory, practice and research.

It is worth here picking up the point about language and accessibility which we alluded to earlier. There is no doubt that this turned out to be a major problem in *The Captive Triangle*, where the density of expression and the highly intellectual treatment of the subject-matter did create problems of reader accessibility. While we do not want to be too defensive about a text that was meant to require interpretive efforts and close reading, we have now become much more fully aware of these problems and have had the time to reflect on their significance. In particular, we are aware that there is a certain incongruity in the quest for a text that empowers but which at the same time disempowers through its inaccessibility. If nothing else, our own commitment to reflexivity requires us to pay close attention to this problem. In this book, writing with clarity and with the needs of reader-accessibility in mind, whilst maintaining the critical and conceptual thrust of our subject-matter, has been an important consideration throughout. However, we have to say categorically that it has been our intention to produce a work of scholarship rather than a manual for practice. This obviously imposes its own inescapable demands. However, questions of practice continue to inform what we have written and we have attempted to present the concepts, ideas, theories and arguments we deal with in as accessible a way as possible. This aim has been helped by Rennie Johnston joining the original Usher/Bryant team, in that he brings with him experience of and engagement in adult education practice that extends well beyond the academy, as well as a long-standing commitment to both accessible education and texts. As a collaborative team, our hope is that both academics and practitioners in the field will read this book and, and at the very least, be stimulated by what it says.

Our original intention had been to retain the theme of *The Captive Triangle*. As our work developed, however, we soon began to feel that this essentially spatial, bounded metaphor was one which did not do proper justice to the things we wanted to say. We therefore adopted the notion of going 'beyond the limits' as our guiding theme. This has helped us to locate our work as critique and at the same time reflects and highlights the transgressive times in which adult education itself is located. Each chapter, to differing degrees, picks up and develops this theme in relation to its specific focus.

We were also very much aware of the need to consider in some depth the contextual or locating background of adult education. Very often, insufficient emphasis is placed on this. Where there is any emphasis, it tends to be through theorisations which still retain a purchase increasingly confined only to the small world of professional adult educators. The consequence has been that, while the field of adult education has been subject to significant changes, there has tended to be a failure to adequately theorise these changes. One of the things we have attempted to do in this book, therefore, is to provide a portrait of changing contexts and their effects. To do so we have made use of the conceptual resources provided by scholars such as Bourdieu and Foucault, whose writings have not until recently been extensively deployed in academic work within adult education and whose relevance has not yet been understood in the field of practice. We have deployed such concepts as 'postmodernity', 'governmentality', 'disciplinarity', 'power/knowledge', 'discursive practices' and 'habitus' to throw light on the changing contexts of adult education. We have used these concepts to elaborate the significance of the move from 'adult education' to 'adult learning' (this being socially and culturally rather than psychologically located), a move which constitutes a central theme in this book.

Overall, the text that we have produced can perhaps be best characterised as a kind of half-way house between a tightly structured book with a coherent, linear narrative and a collection of essays in chapter form. At one level, the book can be read as a series of stand-alone essays. However, we believe that it also has its own particular unity, whose form readers will no doubt discern for themselves. Partly, this situation is an outcome of a tripartite collaboration, with all the difficulties this raises for forging coherence, linearity and univocal meanings. This difficulty is reinforced by an authorial team the members of which have much in common but also much in the way of differences. Consequently, attempting to construct a single voice and a unified meaning has proved to be impossible. However, we see this as a strength rather than a weakness and are enthusiastic about the self-exemplifying possibilities this raises for a text that aims to highlight difference, openness and specificity.

This does, of course, highlight the problem of authorial voice. Clearly, there is no single unified voice to be found in this book. It would be surprising if there were, given the different backgrounds, biographies and interests of the three authors. It is perhaps appropriate to say a few words about this in view of the fact that situatedness and reflexivity are highlighted throughout the text. Although all three of us are adult education practitioners, we approach our practice, for example, from different disciplinary backgrounds – Robin Usher from philosophy, Ian Bryant from sociology and Rennie Johnston from history and political economy. Each author also differs in his conception of the nature and purpose of practice. Each has a somewhat different view of the aims and purposes of adult education and its place and significance in processes of social change. And perhaps most importantly, whilst it is clear that postmodernity as a contemporary socio-cultural and economic condition is foregrounded throughout the book, there are significant differences in the authors' evaluation of different aspects of postmodernity and in their enthusiasm for postmodernism as an intellectual and theoretical position.

At the same time, we do have things which we share. We are, for example, friends and colleagues in the same Faculty of Educational Studies, and we have worked together on various teaching, research and writing projects for at least the last ten years. All three of us share a critical and an iconoclastic view of the orthodoxies and 'sacred cows' of adult education, and we share a desire to deconstruct its dominant discourses. We all recognise that adult education has to change and accommodate itself to the new social phenomenon of adult learning and find a new role within changing contexts. Furthermore, we agreed that, whilst we had no problem in foregrounding the significance of postmodernity, this would not extend to writing this book as a postmodern text! So although the differences between us may have been more publicly prominent, our more implicit commonalities none the less provided a secure base for collaboration – even if this turned out to be a collaboration which recognised and accepted difference and diversity.

The approach that emerged, therefore, was one that could be characterised as having a fair degree of variation. We decided it was best not to seek to impose consistently a clear and coherent structuring theme. As we have hinted, the notion of 'beyond the limits', a loose yet resonant theme, provided a thread which could be deployed and explored very differently in each chapter. Furthermore, although as joint authors we take joint responsibility for all the content of the book, we believe, in the cause of foregrounding textuality and telling the 'true' story of authorial collaboration, that it is appropriate to explain that each chapter was not jointly written in the full sense of the word. Robin Usher took primary responsibility for Chapters 1, 4, 6, and 8; Ian Bryant took primary responsibility for Chapters 3, 7 and 10; Rennie Johnston took primary responsibility for Chapter 2, and with Robin Usher shared responsibility for Chapters 5 and 9. This reflects not only a practical division of labour but the fact that each of us has different interests and expertise. The result is a book which takes a selective rather than a panoptical approach to investigating the field.

The story of our collaboration is fascinating, instructive and probably deserves a book in itself. However, this is not the right place to elaborate further. But one thing which is clear in retrospect is that the more the number of authorial voices the greater the likelihood that what finally emerges will be different in significant ways from what was envisaged at the start of the process. Our original intention, for example, was to structure the book in three parts – theory, practice and research – with three chapters in each part. Clearly, this was a reflection of our continued immersion in the metaphor of the triangle. We began to realise that the rigidity of the metaphor was matched by the rigidity of the structure. We therefore abandoned this in favour of a more open structure, and all that can still be discerned as traces of the original structure are the three chapters on research. Within the other chapters there is an inmixing of theory and practice, since we took the view that a structural separation had neither textual nor intellectual justification.

At this point, it is appropriate to provide short summaries of each chapter so that readers can get some idea of what lies ahead. In general terms, it is possible to see the first three chapters as focusing on the changing contexts of adult education and in particular on why it is more appropriate to talk of 'adult learning'. The next four chapters take up more explicitly the notion of going beyond the limits in different ways and to differing degrees, which challenge certain adult education orthodoxies and attempt to provide alternative readings which we believe are more resonant for changing contexts. The final three chapters deal with research, focusing on a critical macro-analysis of mainstream paradigms, a review of alternative approaches and a more micro-analysis focusing on the role of the socially located self in the research process.

Chapter 1 is contextual in that it is intended to provide a 'backdrop' of the contemporary socio-cultural and economic scene for the rest of the book. It analyses some of the key features of modernity and post-modernity, with a particular emphasis on the nature of knowledge in the postmodern and the relationship of knowledge as 'efficacy' to consumption and consumer culture. The aim is more adequately to locate adult education on the contemporary scene. An important aspect of this is the phenomenon of 'adult learning' which, it is argued, should no longer be seen in psychological or institutional terms but in relation to its meanings within the social practices of the postmodern. There is a foregrounding in this chapter of the need to come to terms with the changing contemporary situation and with new theorisations of the contemporary. It will be argued that adult educators particularly need to rethink their location in the modernist educational project if they are to respond properly to the new forms of adult learning and the increasing diversity of adults engaged in learning.

Chapter 2 focuses on citizenship and its relationship with adult education where the latter, through the nature and structure of the curriculum, has played an influential although largely unacknowledged part in citizenship formation. There is a critical exploration of the approaches to citizenship, whether explicit or implicit, of different adult education traditions – liberal, radical, and community. This provides the basis for an analysis of contemporary influences on education for citizenship, with particular emphasis given to how an educational approach can engage with the interconnections between private and public, personal and political. It concludes by identifying an agenda for adult learning that engages with citizenship in the context of an uncertain and changing postmodern world.

Chapter 3 examines a generally accepted position, originating with Durkheim's influential sociology of education, of how educational practice works in terms of meeting society's 'needs' through the operation of certain governing principles. Such a theory, generally endorsed and institutionalised by the state, is considered limiting in that it is politically accommodative and tells us very little about how practices such as education actually work. Foucault's and Bourdieu's notions of 'governmentality' and of 'habitus', respectively, are explored in order to develop a critical purchase on the complexities of power/knowledge formations in which all practices, but especially those within education, are implicated. Two case examples of the operation of power/knowledge within education at an institutional and individual level are considered in the light of concepts which enable a move beyond the limits of conventional understandings of how the disciplines taken to be foundational for practice actually work.

Chapter 4 remains with the foundational theme by taking as its starting-point the place of a subject discipline such as psychology as the basis for educational practice. Whilst recognising that it cannot provide a foundation without imposing severe limitations on practice, the discussion centres on the notion of 'disciplinarity' – the entanglement of educational practices with disciplinary knowledge in the service of regulation and self-surveillance. In this chapter readers are introduced to Foucault's concepts of 'discursive practices', 'power/knowledge' and 'confession'. The argument put forward is that disciplines do not just describe and explain states of affairs, e.g., with respect to teaching, learning and adulthood, but actually constitute (form and shape) these as 'objects' of powerful discourses. Thus, a discipline (a theory or body of knowledge) 'disciplines' and cannot be separated from the regulatory and normalising practices with which it is associated.

Chapter 5 focuses on conceptions of the self and the implications of these conceptions for the way experience and experiential learning is constructed in adult education discourse. Whilst recognising the contribution that a particular formulation of experience and the notion of experiential learning has made to the enhancement of practice and the empowerment of learners, a new foundationalism is introduced when 'experience' is conceived as the 'raw material' of learning. This is examined in terms of how selves and subjectivity are constituted as the agents and agency, respectively, of experience. We would also take a different approach to experiential learning by placing less emphasis on essentialism, psychologism and individualism and more on locating both selves and experience in the contemporary socio-cultural context. In this way, it becomes possible to relate experiential learning to contemporary trends such as marketisation, vocationalism, the growth of the New Right and the new middle class, new social movements, the emphasis on education as consumption and as a positional good, and the social practices associated with these trends. This opens up the possibility of thinking differently about selves and experience where the meaning and significance of experiential learning is related to the social practices of postmodernity.

Chapter 6 is the one which perhaps draws most from *The Captive Triangle*. It is in a sense a continuation of the discussion initiated in Chapter 4 of the latter. There is a revisiting of the traditional and, from the viewpoint of practice, unhelpful separation of theory and practice and the notion of practitioners' 'informal theory' first formulated there. This provides a basis for an ensuing discussion which marks a radical departure from the intellectual framework deployed in *The Captive Triangle*. The emphasis remains on the theory–practice relationship but now there is a movement beyond resolving this in a philosophical way, for example, by deploying a hermeneutics of practice, to a more grounded resolution where the theory–practice relationship is itself seen as part of a 'meta-practice', a contest over the meanings of what a particular practice is about, how it should go about fulfilling its aims and who should be dominant in defining the meaning of practice.

Chapter 7 examines the limitations of Schon's modelling of the process of reflection-in-action by means of a critique both of the theory of reflective practice and his methodology of unpacking the process itself. Case examples are presented in the form of extracts from interviews with experienced practitioners working in adult education, with the addition of a reflexive commentary in which the interviewers (two of the present authors) address the problem of reflexivity that is notably absent in Schon's own accounts. His model is found to be limiting in that it is critically aware neither of the situatedness of his practitioner case subjects nor of his own situatedness as a theorist. At the same time, the limiting features of the present authors' own practice as academic researchers is used as an opportunity for opening up critical interpretive spaces for extending an understanding of a process that moves practice into new territory.

Chapter 8 examines the mainstream approaches to research in the social sciences generally, and in education in particular, in terms of three influential paradigms or traditions of research, namely, the positivist/empiricist, the interpretive/hermeneutic, and that which draws on critical theory. Whilst recognising that there is now a considerable body of critical comment relating to the problems of the positivist/empiricist paradigm, it is still the case that approaches to doing research based on this paradigm continue to exert a powerful influence, particularly with bodies and agencies who fund research. The epistemological assumptions which underpin this paradigm are therefore still worth problematising. At the same time, this can only be done properly if these are compared and contrasted with the assumptions underpinning those alternative paradigms which many consider to be more appropriate for carrying out educational research. This also provides the space for critically examining the epistemological bases of interpretive/hermeneutic and critical theory approaches since it is all too easy simply to assume that because they are anti-positivist they must therefore be unproblematic and therefore automatically more appropriate.

Chapter 9 deals with two approaches to research which move beyond the conventional limits of mainstream research traditions. Emancipatory research, an approach to research that is influential in radical and community-based adult education, highlights the ethical and political dimensions of an approach that is geared explicitly towards empowerment. By foregrounding these dimensions, we question the conventional inter-relationships between researchers and researched, knowledge and power, and theory and data. Furthermore, the emancipatory focus raises key questions for researchers regarding participation, ownership and voice. We then move on to consider a postmodern approach to research – or perhaps less an approach to research, more a way of questioning the structuring assumptions of any research text. To ask postmodern questions is to foreground the textuality of research, and thus the constructed and constructing nature of research. It is also to recognise that there is always a reflexive element in the research process, a reflexivity that raises questions about the power relations and the place of the researcher inscribed in the text of research.

Chapter 10 extends the analysis of the self to consider its location within the experience of doing research. The place of writing in research is generally understood to be a technical and transparent matter of reporting outcomes in methodologically approved ways within a text constructed through the conventions of narrative realism, an approach which problematises neither the authorship nor the authority of research. The depiction of the self in *The Captive Triangle* is revisited and found to be too limiting in that it fails to address the dynamics of doing research in a critically reflexive way. The idea of a research trajectory is introduced as a way of engaging with the issue of writing the self in research. Drawing on recent work in critical ethnography and postmodernist interpretations of practice as text, we explore the ways in which research is informed through the power of methodology and show how this may be 're-formed' in order to give voice to researchers and researched alike. Two case examples are offered which illustrate possibilities for teaching and learning about the practice of research as simultaneously one of writing the self and the world.

The background which has informed the writing of this book is our feeling that throughout the field adult education roles and purposes are being increasingly questioned. Some would argue that this is a perennial condition for adult education, and that it is something which should not be the cause of undue concern – perhaps adult education thrives best in an atmosphere of uncertainty and lack of clear direction.

Adult education currently finds itself in an ironical situation. On the one hand, more and more adults are engaged in learning programmes. The dream of adult educators that lifelong learning should become a universal condition is now closer to realisation than ever before. This, however, makes problematic the institutionalised forms that adult education should take. As many commentators have noted, whilst the significance of adult learning has increased to the extent where its importance in both personal and social life is unparalleled, adult education finds itself increasingly unable to justify its position as an autonomous institution responsible for organising that learning. To the extent that adult learning has been individualised and privatised, it has become part of the 'culture market' and the 'market culture' which characterises postmodern times, albeit a market which *excludes* as well as includes. The upshot is that adult education is now one amongst many cultural producers in a situation where there is little clear differentiation between education, leisure and entertainment – and where it has to sell its products by being better at meeting the desires of consumers. At the same time, with the decline in universal ideals and grand narratives, with the scepticism about the possibility of progress through collective action and all-embracing ideologies, the relevance that adult education has traditionally claimed of providing a means of supporting and fulfilling the Enlightenment project seems to have less intellectual or practical relevance.

In this book, we make no pretence at resolving this situation, although we do make some tentative suggestions about possible ways forward. Our focus is that adult educators in their theorising have failed adequately to account for these changes and consequently this has had unfortunate effects in practice. In the current situation, there has been an oscillation between nostalgia for a mythical Golden Age and a mindlessly enthusiastic embracing of the market. The failure to understand and get to grips with the postmodern challenge means that we have neither adapted to nor properly exploited the tensions and ambiguities of postmodernity. This prompts either a) a knee-jerk rubbishing of postmodernism, and/or b) a pessimistic assumption that nothing critical or oppositional is possible without universalistic and collectivist concepts and programmes. We have tried to steer a course between these new binary oppositions and to show how the contemporary condition, although complex and ironical, is far from being hopeless.

Chapter 1

Adult learning in postmodernity

Adult education is inevitably affected by the uncertainty that characterises the contemporary situation. Increasingly, difficult questions are posed about what constitutes the field of adult education and what are its values and purposes – all this at a time when a greater number of adults, from a diversity of backgrounds, enter an increasing variety of programmes. The difficulty in coping with the current uncertainty is compounded by the nature of the contemporary situation, which is itself difficult to characterise and interpret. Whilst there is general agreement that we are witnessing profound economic, technological and cultural changes, there is less agreement on whether these constitute a continuation of modernity, a phase of late modernity where already existing trends are intensified, or whether we are now in a condition of postmodernity, a radical break consequent on the failure of modernity.

The only thing that does seem reasonably certain is that adult educators are finding it increasingly problematic simply to take refuge in the certainties of the past. As we move from the 'field' of adult education to a 'moorland' of adult learning, so the guiding paradigms of adult education, its theory, purposes and practices, need reconfiguring and new conceptual resources are required to make sense of the contemporary conjuncture and of the place of adult education within that. It would be difficult to argue that adult education can sustain itself as it is presently constituted in the face of the challenges posed by late modernity/postmodernity.

Thus, in the first part of this chapter we present an analysis of some of the key features of modernity and postmodernity with a view to highlighting significant contemporary socio-economic and cultural changes which have begun to impact on adult education. We go on to consider the nature of knowledge in the postmodern and then relate this to consumption and consumer culture. The aim is more adequately to locate adult education in the contemporary socio-economic and cultural environment and by this means to examine the nature and consequences of changes from adult education to adult learning. This chapter, therefore, will attempt to elucidate the significance of contemporary adult learning, but will focus not so much on the process of adult learning or what it involves in terms of provision. Rather, the emphasis will be on the significance of adult learning in terms of its *significations* in the contemporary conjuncture and within contemporary social practices. We will argue that adult learning has tended to be defined through an adult education discourse where it signified learning outside educational institutions but still within the framework and purposes of the modernist educational project. Increasingly, however, 'adult learning' is now beginning to signify learning which may be inside or outside educational institutions but not within that project and not necessarily bounded by what educators would define as 'appropriate' and 'worthwhile'. Within this changing context of adult learning, we hope to point to ways in which adult educators need to review their purposes and practices, to review their ideas of what is appropriate or worthwhile.

THE SOCIO-ECONOMIC DIMENSION OF MODERNITY AND POSTMODERNITY

Modernity is normally understood as a historical period with its origins in the Enlightenment and continuing to the present day. The Enlightenment saw the beginning of a process of modernisation, of socio-economic and cultural change and disruption marked by 'industrialisation, the growth of science and technology, the modern state, the capitalist world market, urbanisation, and other infrastructural elements' (Featherstone 1991: 60). Alongside these developments went such cultural changes as secularisation and an emphasis on personal identity and individualistic autonomy.

Postmodernity (or, as some would say, 'late modernity') is associated with such contemporary trends as the growth of service-sector employment, 'post'-industrial social formations and post-Fordist models of production. A revitalised and reconfigured capital accumulation based on globalisation and the progressive integration of national economies through market mechanisms is its most predominant socio-economic feature. These changing forms of production have been brought about by the transnational flexibility of capital and, to a lesser extent, labour markets, coupled with new forms of communication and information technology.

Markets for goods and services have become volatile and fragmented, with customised design and specialised market niches displacing established forms of Fordist mass-production for mass markets. With this contemporary form of flexible capital accumulation have come post-Fordist forms of work organisation and management – flatter management structures, team-work, quality assurance procedures, a decline of centralised trade union bargaining power and, perhaps most significant of all for adult education, a demand for a multi-skilled work-force. With the changes in products, services and working practices has come a reconstruction of the workplace (for example, the contemporary emphasis on the 'workplace as a site of learning') and the social definition of skills (for example, skills become 'competences'). However, alongside these dynamic changes in workplace culture and practices, there is also an increasingly fragmented and unequal, core–periphery labour market where those without skills, cultural capital, access to information or market power can usually expect only a living and working existence on the margins. In recognising the power and contemporary primacy of the market, it also has to be emphasised that markets, for all their flexibility and dynamism, do not distribute goods according to need and do not protect the vulnerable (Abel Smith and Titmuss 1987). This has clear implications for citizenship and for the role of adult learning in promoting and sustaining it within this changing socio-economic context – a problematic which will be explored further in the next chapter.

The 'techno-scientific' revolution, i.e., recent developments in information technology, the media, transportation and advances in communications, inseparable from the process of globalisation, has been a significant factor in all these changes. This revolution, in conditions of flexible capital accumulation, has resulted in the reorganisation of space–time at many levels and in many ways. In particular, two seemingly paradoxical yet interlinked features are noteworthy. Space–time compression creates the contemporary phenomenon of a global integration which is at the same time coupled with an increased emphasis on 'place' and identity.

The integration and globalisation of the market produces both homogeneity and heterogeneity. Parallel and related to the spread of Western institutions and culture, globalisation produces pressures for local, substate autonomy and identity. With a globalised economy which homogenises comes an emphasis on the uniqueness and difference of place and the advantageous conditions specific places can offer for free-floating capital. The same paradoxical process is emerging from globalisation in the cultural sphere. The development of communications in its widest sense, from travel to the increasing reach of the electronic media, underpins global integration. Urban and suburban landscapes become more identical, with familiar icons such as McDonald's golden arches ubiquitously present and with certain media images instantly recognisable in every corner of the globe. The world enters our homes in the media we engage with and the products we consume – a process of 'global cultural convergence, the production of universal cultural products and global market consumers' (Kenway et al. 1993: 118). At the same time, however, globalisation induces effects of cultural specificity. We are all, for example, familiar with the media explosion generated by deregulation and greater accessibility to the means of communication. There is 'a renaissance of place-bound traditions and ways of life' (ibid.), a new sense of pride and value in the recognition of difference and the revival of hitherto suppressed identities. The globalisation of culture, then, far from repressing the local and the specific, actually stimulates it. What results is a paradoxical situation where, on the one hand, global marketisation devalues community and communitarian values whilst, on the other hand, globalisation's effects of specificity and difference enhance these values, albeit in a reconfigured form.

This is reinforced by the changes in cultural forms which have accompanied changes in the economy. In the realms of culture narrowly defined, e.g., music, art, architecture and film, modernist seriousness and the search for deep hidden meanings is interwoven with postmodern playfulness, 'surface', eclecticism and self-referentiality as the possibility of providing secure meanings and firm foundations is overwhelmed by a proliferation and mixing of constantly changing signs and images – Pavarotti performing in Hyde Park and the use of classical music in advertising are but two contemporary examples. At the same time, the aesthetic values which previously pervaded only the arena of high culture and the elite associated with that culture now pervade everyday life and equally, everyday life now invades high culture (Lash 1990; Featherstone 1991; Harvey 1991). More significant is the changing place of culture generally to the economy and the social formation as a whole. As Lyon (1994) suggests, the cultural and the aesthetic displace or are valued more highly than the economic and the functional, with the latter no longer the dominant central axis of economic activity.

Thus, the hitherto tightly defined boundaries between the cultural and the economic begin to break down with a consequent proliferation and fragmentation and an emphasis on the celebration of difference and a foregrounding of multiple identities. In effect, boundaries do not operate in quite such an exclusionary and exclusive way. This is not to say that they have ceased to exist but rather that under challenge and contestation both from new forms of capital and from alternative, including oppositional, groupings, some boundaries have shifted and others have become more permeable.

Thus, the culture industries, e.g., entertainment, the media and increasingly education itself, have all become significant in contemporary social formations and are implicated in the growth of a consumer society. In postmodernity, there is a valuing of consumption and the consumer. A culture of consumption coupled with marketisation becomes central to the economy as a whole. Modernist centres of production – the factory, the assembly line, large-scale manufacturing – are being increasingly displaced by centres of consumption – financial services, small-scale specialised enterprises, shopping malls and superstores, entertainment complexes, heritage and theme parks. Here lifestyle concerns manifested through consumption become significant. The influence of fashion, image and 'taste' pervade an increasingly all-embracing consumer culture where seductive images, particularly of the different and the exotic, both incite and realise desire. Choices about the clothes we wear, the food we eat, how we decorate our homes, the places we travel to, are a realisation of taste, and for all social groups 'taste' is educated through the media, advertising, etc. as well as, although perhaps increasingly less, through conventional modes of education and training.

When cultural change becomes so closely linked with economic change, the resulting emphasis on the individual as a consumer means that socio-cultural distinction overlays socio-economic division. Lifestyle becomes as, if not more, important than class position. Even those with little or no cultural capital are swept up in a culture of consumption, saturated with images and dreams of the desirable and where enterprises such as national lotteries seem to provide the only possibility for desired lifestyles. It is here perhaps more than anywhere that adult education's hitherto guiding paradigms are proving to be most inadequate. Learning through life and lifelong learning have become not simply an aspect of economic instru-mentalism nor an assertion of enlightened humanism but also a way of constituting meaning through consumption. When consumption becomes a matter of meaning, those with the necessary cultural and economic capi-tal no longer consume for the sake of utility or need alone but to signify difference, to say something about themselves and to identify themselves in relation to others. A desirable lifestyle is no longer about consuming in order to be the same as others but rather about consuming in order to be different. In other words, it is difference, rather than goods and services *per se*, that is consumed.

POSTMODERNISM AND INCREDULITY

In a culture of consumption where the emphasis is on lifestyle and where the state redraws traditional boundaries of responsibility, choices in the direction of lives become more and more the responsibility of individuals. Given the explosion in the availability of goods, services and information, and given the significance of lifestyle choices in the constitution of personal identity, making choices becomes both necessary and yet at the same time increasingly difficult. Reactions to this situation are many and complex but clearly, existential anxiety and concern is likely to be significant. But one of the characteristics of postmodernity is that this is not the only possible reaction. In the postmodern, with fixed reference points and solid groundings becoming increasingly detached and shaky, the difficulty becomes something to be accepted rather than regretted; it becomes troub-lingly pleasurable in opening up possibilities for constituting identities.

The emergence of postmodern identities is also due to the valorisation of difference and the recognition of the significance of the particularities of differences. The white Western male cultural assumptions found within modernist discourses have been problematised by, among other things, consideration of the importance of gender, sexual, ethnic and racial differences. New ideas and fresh conceptualisations, new discourses such as feminist, postcolonial, gay, and green discourse have been found necessary to help explain the contemporary condition. However, this foregrounding of difference should not merely be construed as a facile celebration of pluralism, an openness which serves to more effectively conceal the workings of globalised power. A diversity of meanings, lifestyle choices and identities still has to be seen within a network of power relations; to have difference recognised within the relations of everyday life still involves struggle and contestation against dominance and subordination.

The discourses and practices of modernity are characterised by an emphasis on progress and a faith in rationality and science as the means of its realisation. This faith, with its promise of inevitable human betterment, is the feature of modernity which is perhaps most intensely questioned in the postmodern moment. Lyotard (1984) refers to the idea of human betterment and social progress through the application of reason and scientific knowledge as one of the 'grand narratives', the higher-order forms of legitimisation which in postmodernity are increasingly greeted with 'incredulity'. The notion of 'incredulity' is important and needs further elucidation. In one sense, it is a scepticism that results from the discrepancy between modernity's ideals and promises, as enshrined in the grand narratives, and the actuality of the oppression and destruction which characterises the contemporary world. As Burbules (1995) points out, 'incredulity' is an inability to believe. We can no longer bring ourselves to believe in the grand narratives. We cannot take them at their word because if we do they become monolithic and hegemonic, totalising power-plays concealed in the cloak of universality, value-neutrality and benevolent progress. Rather than true accounts, we now see them simply as interesting stories, even though there will be different degrees of investment in them. It is difficult, as adult educators, for example, are finding, to completely disinvest from them because although our confidence in the grand narratives is not what it was, we seem to have few alternatives. Postmodernism cannot provide an alternative grand narrative. In this sense, modernist grand narratives continue to remain indispensable. Think, for example, how difficult and indeed artificial it is, despite our scepticism, to avoid talking in terms of 'progress', particularly if we are adult educators.

In other words, modernist discourse provides ways of talking and knowing which we cannot readily dispense with. But although postmodernism cannot provide an alternative, the postmodern attitude does at least enable us to recognise this. We recognise both the indispensability of modernist discourse and its power, and it is precisely because modernist discourse is so indispensable that it is so dangerous. Through the intellectual resources provided by postmodernism we see the need to critique that which we cannot do without. Hence, we are brought back to ourselves, as postmodernist critique becomes self-critique and a dissolving of self-certainty. Postmodernist incredulity, therefore, is not so much aimed at modernist discourses and grand narratives as such, but at our own modernist pre-understandings.

Postmodernism enables a *questioning* of the scientific attitude and scientific method, of the universal efficacy of technical-instrumental reason, and of the stance of objectivity and value-neutrality in the making of knowledge claims. This is not so much a matter of *rejection* but rather of recognising that these are claims not truths, claims which are socially formed, historically located cultural constructs, thus partial and specific to particular discourses and purposes. Postmodernism, therefore, neither rejects nor refutes modernist conceptions of science or reason. In this sense, it is neither anti-rational nor relativistic. It makes no claims to a superordinate truth, nor does it seek to establish an alternative and superior position by means of irrefutable logic or definitive explanation. Postmodernism's incredulity marks a doubt which, unlike Cartesian doubt, is not a doubt in the cause of attaining certainty. As Burbules argues, rightly in our view, it is about doubting whether we should be doing more and more of what we have always done, even when it might have brought benefits. That's the whole point about 'progress'. We can accept that progress has occurred in certain areas, for example, better health through the use of antibiotics, whilst at the same time doubting whether more of the same will automatically continue to do so. Morss (1995: 123) points out that 'science is no longer treated as the search for answers to problems that arise outside science'. We can accept that science has brought about betterment in many areas of life but doubt whether more applications of science will solve all problems or continue to make life better.

Burbules locates this doubt in three key sources. First, the growing awareness, through globalisation and space–time compression, of the diversity and incommensurability of the cultural forms that shape and sustain groups and individuals. As we become aware of and in closer contact with diversity we recognise that it is difference rather than sameness which is most significant and that indeed sameness can only be maintained through the repression of difference. We also recognise, therefore, that the only way to unify this diversity is through violence and oppression and consequently we have become sceptical of modernist projects that seek to do so. Second, we become sceptical of Utopian projects that promise universal betterment. In promising an end to oppressive power, they often merely enshrine power subtly yet more firmly through surveillance and regulation, through manipulation of body and soul. The web of interactions and contingencies through which life is played out involves unequal power relations regardless of emancipatory and benevolent intentions.

Third, we recognise both the mediating and formative power of language and discourse and the 'textual staging of knowledge'. Postmodernism's deconstructive thrust foregrounds and challenges the place of the binary oppositions which structure thought. Communication, justification, explanation, truth-telling, it is argued, are achieved within discursive practices. Since discourses are diverse and non-congruent, overlapping and discontinuous, there will always be a limit to any particular discourse as a standpoint. Not only, therefore, can no discourse hope to capture unambiguous truth, but there is no Archimedean point from which any one discourse can speak, no definitive discourse or 'final vocabulary'.

Postmodernism as an intellectual movement has undoubtedly raised fierce passions, with partisans and opponents tending to adopt entrenched positions. These are not debates which we intend to enter. Rather, and more helpfully in our view, we prefer to see postmodernism as expressing a certain mood or attitude. Burbules argues that this can be best understood in relation to three narrative tropes. These narrative tropes, or ways of telling a story and hence ways of being, thinking and acting, constitute the means by which we cope with the contemporary condition of postmodernity and are themselves an index of the postmodern. In particular, they are the means by which we cope with the incredulity towards the very modernist discourse and mind-sets which we find virtually impossible to dispense with, of a way of critiquing that still has to deploy the resources provided by that which we wish to critique, ways of problematising in the words of the language that one is problematising.

The three tropes are the ironic, the tragic and the parodic. Burbules characterises the ironic as taking back with one hand what is given with the other. The ironic works in the realm of allusion and reversal. It is the mark of statements which appear to have a single definitive meaning but which also suggest multiple meaning possibilities. In effect, it is the refusal, by means of serious 'playfulness', to be tied to any position that claims to be definitive or 'natural'. The tragic is the troubling recognition that the need to critique our own pre-understandings, although necessary, is no easy task. To embrace uncertainty, to doubt comforting foundations, to question the efficacy of hierarchical opposites is difficult in practice, especially when certainties, foundations and opposites are enshrined in our practical discourses. To speak and act through the tragic is to recognise that all attempts at radical transformation are ambiguous in their outcomes even as, and especially as, attempts to transform are recognised as desirable and worthy. It is a way of recognising that there are limits to what we, as educators, can do. The parodic, finally, is located in the realm of the playful or the ludic, both in the sense of game-playing and play as performance. The parodic foregrounds subversion, a refusal to take 'sacred' positions and 'articles of faith' seriously and at their own self-important valuation. This is a self-exemplifying subversion which punctures pretensions by apparently playing the game but doing so in an exaggerated and reflexive way.

Whilst it is undoubtedly the case that these narrative tropes emphasise the playful and the playfully subversive, it would be simplistic to conclude, as some critics of postmodernism have done, that the postmodern mood or attitude is unserious and flippant. On the contrary, to coin a phrase, this is no laughing matter. As Burbules (1995: 8–9) points out, 'these tropes can be seen as ways of making somewhat coherent and liveable what remains a conflicted unstable outlook, an outlook of sustained tensions and disenchanted hopes'. He argues that what is provided is an aesthetic rather than a logical coherence, a way of telling one's story and of creating an identity where apparently contradictory and self-undermining positions are embraced, where uncertainty and ambiguity are recognised and accepted as inevitable features of a conflictual and uncertain world, but where this presents not only limitations but also possibilities.

CHANGING CONCEPTIONS OF KNOWLEDGE, CHALLENGES TO MODERNIST EDUCATION

To recognise the significance of language, discourse, socio-cultural located-ness and power in any knowledge claim is therefore also to question the modernist notion of universal and transcendental foundations and thus of canonical forms of knowledge. There is, instead, a *decentring* of knowledge where modernist certainty is undermined, with consequent uncertainty pervading thought action and identity. This is another aspect of fixed references and traditional anchoring points disappearing. In postmodern conditions, knowledge is not only constantly changing but is becoming more rapidly, almost overwhelmingly, available, mirroring a world of rapid change and bewildering instability.

The postmodern incredulity about grand narratives leads to a scepticism both about the transcendental and universal foundations of knowledge and the claim that certain kinds of knowledge have canonical status. This has paradoxical educational consequences. On the one hand, it has contributed to an erosion of the 'liberal' curriculum and an emphasis on learning opportunities that optimise the efficiency of the economic and social system. On the other hand, the decentring of knowledge has resulted in a valuing of different sources and forms of knowledge and a corresponding devaluing of specialist discipline-based knowledge. The emphasis on experiential learning is one example, although its apparent break with modernity is attenuated by its modernist self-understandings. What these consequences have in common is that they both reflect and give rise to greater uncertainty and conflict over the power and purpose of education.

The decentring of knowledge is accompanied by a decentring of the self. We mentioned earlier the influence of consumer culture. Postmodernity has been described as a condition where the commodity has become culturally dominant and where the dominant commodity form is the image (Kenway *et al.* 1993). The communication revolution creates a situation where people become engulfed by images, to the point where the distinction between reality and image breaks down in a condition of hyper-reality (Baudrillard 1988). The hyper-real is a world of constantly proliferating images or simulacra (copies detached from their original but which still have meaning independently of their original) which become a desirable reality to be consumed. In this situation new forms of experience proliferate, experiences that are not rooted in a stable and unified self. Hence, there is a continual shaping and reshaping of subjectivity and identity. In postmodernity, sensibilities are attuned to the pleasure of constant and new experiencing where experiencing becomes its own end (autotelic) rather than a means to an end (instrumental), a way of cultivating the desire for a constant making and remaking of subjectivity and identity.

Modernity is characterised by a search for an underlying and unifying truth and certainty, a search for a definitive discourse that makes the world and self coherent, meaningful and masterable. In modernity, although the self constantly experiences a sense of discontinuity and fragmentation, this is regarded as an unnatural condition, a source of disquiet and anxiety, to be remedied by life-planning, therapy, counselling and perhaps even engaging in educational activities – all of which are seen as a means of enabling a pre-existing coherent and authentic self to be uncovered. As we have noted, postmodernism views the world as 'irreducibly and irrevocably pluralistic, split into a multitude of sovereign units and sites of authority' (Bauman 1992: 35). The modernist search for a true and authentic self and the fulfilment of a pre-given individual autonomy gives way to a playfulness where identity is formed (and 're-formed') by a constantly unfolding desire that is never fully and finally realised. The unified, coherent and sovereign self of modernity, the firm ground for the fixing of identity, becomes a multiple and discontinuous self, traversed by multiple meanings and with shifting identity. In the postmodern, one does not experience in order to enumerate the knowledge gained or to become a 'better' person or to better become oneself. Or if one does, it is not in order to achieve some externally defined goal but rather to try on a new identity. Experience is itself the end, leading to further experience. It is the very openness and unteleological quality of experience which is desirable.

As the means by which knowledge is generated and transmitted through dedicated institutions, educational discourses and practices have had a powerful role in the development, maintenance and legitimisation of modernity. Education has traditionally been the site where ideals of critical reason, individual autonomy and benevolent progress are disseminated and internalised. It is here that the project of modernity is most obviously realised. This project, embodied in the grand narratives, emphasises mastering the world in the cause of human betterment by means of 'objective' knowledge and rational scientific approaches. In modernity, mastery is progress, progress mastery, where individual enlightenment, social and material development, individual emancipation and liberal democracy are seen as mutually interactive and reinforcing.

Although there have always been profound disagreements over curricular means and the particular forms education should take, educational practices are legitimised and shaped by grand narratives of progress and emancipation through the mastery of knowledge and knowledge that masters. The project of modernity can be seen, therefore, as a kind of benevolent and generally implicit social engineering where progress has a certain meaning and functions both as a pre-given end which education strives for and as the norm by which it is judged.

A good example of this is liberal adult education. The condition of postmodernity and the impact of the postmodern mood of scepticism about modernity has helped to render liberal adult education problematic and has contributed to the state of crisis which liberal adult educators feel. They are concerned about the erosion of opportunities to learn for its own sake without the intrusion of vocational and instrumental goals and beyond this to the loss of a commitment to social purpose and transformation. Historically, however, the apparently non-instrumental nature of the liberal tradition in adult education has its basis in the aristocratic values and patriarchal position of the cultured 'gentleman of leisure'. It is actually possible to argue that liberal adult education is instrumental – not perhaps in a narrow sense, but in the sense of being directed towards the fulfilment of the project of modernity. Here, the role of education lies in shaping a certain kind of subjectivity, a self with certain qualities and attitudes rather than a self with certain kinds of work-oriented vocational skills. Liberal adult education, particularly in terms of its emphasis on 'serious', academically based study, did not so much provide 'learning for its own sake' but a training for a certain kind of citizenship. It was an important instrument in the formation of the 'liberal' citizen, individualistic, rationalistic, with a faith in benevolent progress through science and 'truth'.

Adult educators have therefore participated in fulfilling the project of modernity and in particular the task of forming and shaping a certain kind of subjectivity and identity. The voluntary nature of participation in adult education has played a vital role here. Its goals, definition of needs, curriculum, pedagogy and organisational forms have been implicitly structured by the social engineering of the project of modernity. In effect, it has functioned as one of the carriers of the message of modernity. The grand narratives are inscribed in the very practices of adult education, whether in its liberal or radical variants. Thus, the contemporary sense of crisis experienced by many adult educators can be seen as a microcosm of the more general crisis of modernity, as a symptom of the postmodernist incredulity and doubt which we have noted earlier. But also, as we noted then, the crisis is one of self-doubt, a questioning of self-certainty, a critique of that which has formed adult educators and which they cannot readily do without.

Clearly, therefore, education generally does not fit easily into post-modernity, nor can it adapt easily to the postmodern mood. One reason for this is that the decentred self, the more fluid positioning of subjectivity, challenges both the assumption of the bounded 'natural' self with an inher-ent potential and the goal of personal autonomy which is at the heart of modernist education. If the self is socially and discursively constructed then the individualistic assumptions underlying dominant forms of educa-tion are undermined. As we have already noted, in the postmodern there is a celebration rather than a suppression of difference and a refusal to accept the white, male middle-class self as the norm. Postmodernism suggests that autonomy is not something to be attained 'self-ishly' but relationally, through a recognition of difference where difference is not defined as deficit.

Second, in questioning the status and indeed the very existence of foun-dational knowledge there is also a challenge to scientific rationality, to existing concepts, structures and hierarchies of knowledge and to the part education plays in maintaining and reproducing these. If there are no sure foundations and no Archimedean points from which knowledge is gener-ated and assimilated but instead a plurality of partial knowledges, then the very foundations of discipline-based education are themselves under-mined. Without foundations and an absolute faith in scientificity, the certainty and determinacy for which modernity strives is no longer so certain, and with this a curriculum based on the dissemination of 'true' and certain knowledge becomes highly problematic. This is not a recipe for chaos or for letting in oppression by the back door, rather it highlights the contested nature of knowledge and the need for knowledge which is locally grounded and efficacious in relation to local struggles.

Third, the undermining of the modernist project in relation to education undermines the grand narratives of progress and hence the meaning of progress which that narrative embodies and disseminates. As we have noted, progress means change that fulfils certain pre-defined ends. In the project of modernity, progress is judged by such things as greater mastery of the physical and social world, the growth of scientific knowledge, the spread of a particular kind of rationality and the development of a certain kind of person. Whatever fulfils these ends is deemed 'good' i.e. progres-sive; everything which does not is 'bad' i.e. retrogressive or 'irrational'. But the most important aspect, and one which has the most significance for education generally, is that the modernist project tells us *in advance* what is universally good for us, what we should be aiming for and how we can best attain it. In other words, modernist progress is both teleo-logical and totalising. Anything which does not fall under these definitions becomes a feared and rejected other to be ignored, marginalised, derided and suppressed. The postmodern mood or attitude subjects this modernist notion of 'progress' to a critique that highlights the possibility of change without teleology. This makes it possible to conceive of change outside the totalising modernist project. Here, change at either the personal or the social level can take a multiplicity of forms and fulfil a variety of ends, or even simply be its own end.

CONSUMPTION AND KNOWLEDGE IN THE POSTMODERN

The economic, technological and cultural changes which we have referred to as 'postmodernity' or the 'postmodern condition', and the incredulity which characterises the postmodern mood have also contributed to a changed postmodern condition of knowledge (Lyotard 1984). Lyotard argues that the difference between modern and postmodern conditions lies in the purpose of knowledge. In modernity, the generation and dissemina-tion of knowledge is justified in relation to the grand narratives and in terms of its contribution to the pursuit of truth, liberty and the betterment of humanity. The grand narratives legitimise rationality, disciplinarity and the canons of scientific investigation and are also the basis for the develop-ment of state-supported educational practices and of educational institu-tions, curricula and pedagogy that embody and disseminate these grand narratives. As we have noted, they are now proving increasingly unsustain-able, their own legitimacy open to question. We referred to them then as 'interesting stories', albeit stories which are still powerful. Lyotard refers to them as now having the status of a language game in a world charac-terised by a multiplicity of language games. The rationalist and humanistic discourses that try to justify only certain forms of knowledge, certain universal moral stances, and their accompanying educational practices themselves increasingly come into question, challenged by a postmodern condition of 'decentred' knowledge, where the power and purpose of modernist education, including adult education, no longer seems so un-problematic.

In postmodernity, knowledge has different purposes. Given that it is no longer so closely related to legitimising grand narratives, these purposes are complex and to some extent contradictory, a reflection perhaps of the ambiguous tendencies characterising the postmodern. However, one clearly discernible tendency (and one which is often emphasised to the exclusion of any others) is to do with knowledge being valued for its 'performativity'.

This is usually taken to mean that the purpose of knowledge is the optimising of efficient performance. This is the most influential way of understanding 'performativity', although, as we shall see later, it is by no means the only way. This contemporarily influential view of knowledge is closely linked to the post-Fordism and the information-communications revolutions we discussed earlier. As far as the latter is concerned, Lyotard has highlighted the crucial role of computers and information technology. He argues that computers have their own logic and increasingly come to determine what is to be counted as knowledge. One consequence of this is that knowledge becomes assimilated to 'information' that can be conveyed through electronic media. It is also part of the process whereby knowledge becomes commodified – 'an informational commodity indispensable to productive power' (Lyotard 1984: 5).

Educational processes become individualised, reconstituted as a market relationship between producer and consumer. Knowledge is exchanged on the basis of the performative value it has for the consumer. Hence the contemporary demand for education that is 'value-adding'. The marketisation of knowledge in the form of information spreads from the commercial realm into educational practices. Educational institutions increasingly find it difficult to claim a monopoly in the generation and dissemination of knowledge. When knowledge takes the form of information, it circulates through networks that evade the control of educational institutions (Plant 1995). Moreover, educational institutions become part of the market, selling knowledge as a commodity and increasingly reconstructing themselves as enterprises dedicated to marketing their commodities and to competing in the knowledge 'business'. Not only do they become geared to producing the personnel of post-Fordism, they are themselves expected to behave in post-Fordist ways (Ball 1990).

The valuing of knowledge in terms of its performativity suggests that there is a co-implication of contemporary discourses of individualistic learner-centredness and current trends towards the marketisation of learning opportunities. Given this situation, it is hardly surprising that 'a vast market for competence in operational skills' is created (Lyotard 1984: 51). Hammersley (1992: 172) argues that this represents a shift for educators from a professional to a market orientation – 'the professional orientation views the occupational task as a sacred calling requiring a cultural outlook rather than mere technical expertise'. In other words, for Hammersley, utility displaces vocation, technique drives out calling. The activities of professionals become, and this is obviously significant for the situation adult education practitioners find themselves in, increasingly governed by managerialism and the criteria of efficiency and effectiveness. Skilled performance embodied in 'competences' becomes an increasingly significant part of the agenda and an increasingly important and valued outcome of learning.

At the same time, it would be mistaken and oversimplistic to not take account of other trends. As education in the postmodern becomes detached from legitimising grand narratives, it becomes increasingly implicated with specific cultural contexts, on localised and particularised knowledges, on the needs of consumption and the cultivation of desire and on the valuing of a multiplicity of experience as an integral part of defining a lifestyle. In modernity, education is concerned with shaping a certain kind of disciplined subjectivity and the pursuit of certain pre-defined goals; in postmodernity knowledge is valued for its 'interest' and its role in supporting the play of difference.

This is probably an appropriate point to bring these two tendencies together and complicate the picture even more by introducing consumption. We have alluded to this earlier in referring to the culture of consumption that is a feature of postmodernity. Now we need to discuss this culture in further detail. There is a problem here, however, in as much that consumption is not high on the adult educator's list of 'good things' to be involved with. Surrounded by an aura of disapproval and with connotations of the frivolous and the oppressive, consumption is something to be criticised rather than something to be taken seriously. We reluctantly accept that consumption figures importantly in people's lives but we also wish that it did not and we tend to account for its importance in terms of the language of manipulation and false consciousness. Furthermore, if adult educators do take consumption seriously, the implication is they have ceased to be concerned with oppressed groups and have compromised their commitment to social purpose. The argument goes that, since oppressed groups do not have the means to consume, then consumption can only have a disempowering significance in their world. Whilst there is much truth in this argument, it is ultimately simplistic and indeed patronising in its view of oppressed groups. Although it is certainly the case that not all may consume equally, it is also the case that all are affected by consumer culture and consumerist discourse and images. Furthermore, this is not to be accounted for simply by pointing to manipulation and the inducing of false consciousness, since this explanation neglects the dimension of desire in consumption which even oppressed groups are not immune to. There are many examples of oppressed groups who see empowerment in terms of the increased consumption of desired goods and images; as adult educators we ought to recognise this and at the very least not deny it.

Perhaps the failure of adult educators to foreground the place and significance of consumption in contemporary society is yet another example of how theory in adult education lags behind the development of theory in the wider social field. Postmodernism as an intellectual movement has generated a rich literature on the nature and significance of consumption in postmodernity which we can only briefly touch upon here. Bauman

(1992), for example, talks of the development of a post-full-employment consumer society that characterises postmodernity as a new type of social system. He argues that consumer behaviour rather than work or productive activity has become the cognitive and moral focus of life, the integrative bond of society. In the West, capitalism rather than operating through repression works through the idea of the individual freedom to consume. The historical emphasis on self-denial or deferred gratification associated with the settled bourgeoisie and the legitimising power of the grand narratives has become displaced by the pursuit of desire through the consumption of commodities and services.

Postmodernity and contemporary capitalism encourage and require consumption and people who develop their identities through consumption (Urry 1994). There is an emphasis within consumer culture on tendencies which favour the aestheticisation of life. The goal of life becomes the endless pursuit of new experiences, values and identities (Featherstone 1991). Harvey (1991) points to a postmodern aesthetic which celebrates difference, ephemerality, spectacle, fashion and the commodification of cultural forms. Thus, in the postmodern there is an emphasis on lifestyle which is not one particular style but a whole range of practices which privilege the eclectic and the aesthetic. Where, as in the postmodern, everything is 'up for grabs', the distinction between high and low culture melts and everything becomes available for raiding, appropriation and recycling. Furthermore, certain sites become centres of aesthetic consumption – urban areas, re-developed and gentrified, shopping malls, museums, theme and heritage parks – all providing spaces for new experiences and the forming of new identities. Postmodern lifestyle requires certain dispositions and sensibilities, an openness to emotional and aesthetic exploration which goes with the aestheticisation of life. Emphasising self-expression, consumer culture publicly suggests that we all have room for its cultivation, whatever our age or class origins.

As we have noted earlier, consumption is not so much about goods and services *per se* but about signs and significations. Consumer objects function as a classification system that codes behaviour and differentiates individuals. They become markers of difference. According to Bourdieu (1984) consumption, or the active use of goods and services, enables people to establish and demarcate a distinctive social space. Consumer culture therefore becomes an economy of signs used by individuals and groups to communicate messages about social position and worth.

It is easy enough to see adult education as the supplier of the multi-skilled post-Fordist worker. Yet this would be simplistic, since there is also a need to examine the consequences for adult education of the consumer culture we have been describing. Field (1994) has pointed to a number of factors which emphasise the need to take proper account of this. First, long-term changes in affluence have enabled an increasing number of adults in Western society to exercise choice in the purchase of goods and services – how they spend their money and how they use their time. Second, the notion of citizens as consumers stands at the heart of contemporary policy developments. This is part of an ideological shift where the supply of adult education is governed by a consumer orientation and a growing private sector of providers. Linked to this is the widespread development of video and audio cassettes and increasingly sophisticated multi-media programmes available commercially which provide adults with a range of self-study options previously unavailable. Third, educational activities have become consumer goods in themselves, purchased as the result of choice, by free agents (adults) within a marketplace where educational products compete with leisure and entertainment products. As we have already noted, the boundaries of leisure, entertainment and adult education activities blur as, for example, people increasingly learn from television programmes aimed at entertaining, and educational activities geared to consumer satisfaction produce outcomes previously associated only with leisure and entertainment.

Fourth, and getting back to a point made earlier, consumer culture is marked by individuation and it is this which also characterises contemporary trends in adult learning. In order to explore the changing relationships between consumption, individuation and adult learning, we need to look much more closely at areas such as personal development and cultural creativity. The fact that there has been a growth in activities related to the fashioning of a new identity – assertiveness training, slimming, bodily well-being, creative writing, interpersonal skills, counselling, rebirthing – is no coincidence, yet formally organised adult education has tended to regard these activities as 'unserious' and second rate, worthy only of inclusion in the curriculum for their income-generating power rather than their educational purpose.

Finally, as Field rightly emphasises, there is a need to take on board the notion of educational events as enjoyable experiences. This is not easy for adult educators to do, despite the rhetoric of 'learning is fun' commonly found in adult education. To talk about educational events being enjoyable experiences is to foreground the place of play and desire, and learning as the fulfilment of desire – in other words, learning as autotelic as against, for example, the instrumental search for enlightenment or some other educationally pre-defined end. It is to see learning as something to be consumed, an object of desire implicated with pleasure rather than discipline. This is the basis of a learning approach to life disembedded from modernist assumptions about education.

Whilst the language of consumption undoubtedly jars amongst adult educators, patterns of participation in adult education and the increased significance of adult learning cannot be understood without reference to it. We need to recognise that boundaries have become blurred and the attempts to speak the language of the uniqueness of adult education's offer has become increasingly irrelevant. Whatever adult education does offer, it now has to compete for the consumers' income and their scarce leisure time.

More than this, however, taking account of consumption means that we have to consider the education of adults in the context of a cultural economy of signs where consumer choices are social communicative acts and where education is increasingly used by adults as a marker. It becomes an expressive means of self-development, a central part of the process whereby individuals differentiate themselves from others. For adults, therefore, it is only important for learning to be considered education if to be an 'educated person' is important to their identity, if it acts as a means of distinguishing themselves from others and of identifying themselves with other educated persons.

One thing which emerges very clearly and very significantly from this is that consumption is a complex and multi-dimensional process which can be active and generative as well as passive and reproductive. Consequently, we would argue that it is no longer possible to understand contemporary adult learning without a conception of the part played by consumption and consumer culture. In particular, we need to understand the significance of the cultural meanings of consumer behaviour, the role that consumer choices have in certain social practices where meanings and identity are developed. In general terms, this is an argument for locating adult learning within a socio-cultural paradigm of postmodernity. Mainstream adult education paradigms, with their foregrounding of inherent adult characteristics on the one hand or their exclusive emphasis on production as the site of learning, are beginning to have limited uses as explanatory and curriculum-planning devices.

To illustrate this point more fully we shall relate consumption to certain contemporary social practices, all of which involve instances of adult learning. First, lifestyle practices. These work through an expressive mode of learning. Learning is individuated, with an emphasis on self-expression marked by a stylistic self-consciousness. Aestheticisation (the self-referential concern with style and image) and the constant and pleasurable remaking of identity necessitates a learning stance towards life as a means of self-expression and autonomy. Every aspect of life, like every commodity, is imbued with self-referential meaning; every choice an emblem of identity, a mark of difference, each one a message to ourselves and to others of the sort of person we are. As we have noted, consumption is a signifier of difference – of the need to make oneself different and to identify with those who are different. Lifestyle practices, given the emphasis on novelty, fashion, taste and style, are practices of consumption and moreover of a consumption which is potentially unending, since as desire can never be satisfied, there is always the need for new experiences and new learning.

Second, confessional practices. These work through the bringing forth of one's self which becomes an object of knowledge, with one's inner life the terrain to be explored. The assumption is that there is deep hidden meaning buried 'inside' which, once discovered, opens the door to happiness, psychic stability and personal empowerment. The emphasis is on talking about oneself, being open, being prepared to share with total strangers the most intimate details of one's 'private' life. At the same time, there is an increasing emphasis on the notion of 'inner power', of the release of one's inner creative potential. The burgeoning and very popular literature of a self-help kind, as well as a plethora of courses, seminars and workshops (many offered by adult educators), is an indicator of the widespread incidence of confessional practices.

It is through these practices that one is supposedly enabled to gain knowledge of the inner self, the better to enhance one's capacities and in this way become adapted and well-adjusted – in other words, to be 'at one' with one's self and one's environment. Again, this is a process where one is never done – one can never know all there is to know about one's 'hidden' inner self, one can never finally realise all one's inner potential – there is constant need to change in order to adapt a changing self and a changing environment. Once again, then, there is a lifelong process at work here. In confessional practices, it is the self that is 'consumed' in a process based upon a neverending fascination with the self, its deepest secrets and its hidden potential. Difference is signified in terms of an open, well-adjusted, fulfilled and empowered person, 'in touch' with self as against those who are out of touch, repressed and incapacitated. Confessional practices clearly demonstrate a situation where work, leisure and education overlap and where the distinctions make no sense to those engaged in these practices. In the sense that confessional practices are implicated with the achievement of an empowered and capable self, it has relevance to work contexts, providing a direction for leisure and is something achievable through adult education within or outside educational institutions.

Third, vocational practices, to which we have to some extent alluded in our earlier discussion of the marketisation of knowledge. These work through adaptation to the needs of the socio-economic system. The emphasis is on a predisposition to change and to not seeing particular skills as something to be owned and defended. Here, what is consumed is predefined and 'relevant', i.e., applicable knowledge and skills which are disposable and ephemeral. Here then, consumption signifies difference (in relation to others) in the sense of being motivated, trained and effectively positioned in the market in order better to consume.

Fourth, critical practices. These work through the foregrounding of action in the 'here and now' as against theorising or contemplation or waiting for the right moment. They are located in a multiplicity of sites and can take a myriad of forms. They are not confined to educational institutions, although these can be sites of critical practices. At the same time, critical practices do not occur within the productive order alone. Critical practices often involve struggles against the dominance of consumption, particularly against the waste and pollution which is an inevitable feature of a consumerist economy, but they do this by utilising techniques of ludic subversion and the creation and manipulation of seductive images. Indeed, it could be argued that they do this through 'image' and the significations of, and investments made in, particular images, e.g., Greenpeace's image of a David taking on the Goliath of nuclear states and multinational capital. Furthermore, the postmodern mood or attitude is characterised by a reflexivity about contemporary 'risk' society, particularly in the threat of nuclear war, pandemics and environmental degradation. We have alluded to this earlier when we discussed the incredulity that characterises the postmodern mood. This reflexivity has led to popular campaigns such as the boycott of Shell for its plans to dump the Brent Spar oil platform in the North Sea and of French goods over nuclear testing in the Pacific. People have developed 'the capacity to reflect upon environments, to develop the kinds of understanding by which they know what unspoilt places should look like' (Urry 1994: 146). Here is a postmodern critical practice brought about through consumption (travel, tourism) and made possible by space–time compression. What this also shows is the very breachable and dynamic line between critical and lifestyle practices, and more generally between the playful and the serious.

A strong case could be made, therefore, that consumption in postmodernity is an active, generative process. It is embedded in a variety of social practices that involve adult learning, thus it cannot be argued that all that is going on is simply a matter of passive and alienating consumption of goods, services and images. Furthermore, although all these practices involve adult (and indeed lifelong) learning, this has a different signification within each practice. Of course, what we have described is probably not 'lifelong learning' as it would be understood conventionally by adult educators. This returns us to our original problematic. Adult educators tend to see 'lifelong learning' in a transcendental and largely psychologistic way. They thus fail to locate it in contemporary social developments, a failure which is largely attributable to inadequate theorisations about the social field in which adult education is located.

This now brings us back to the postmodern condition of knowledge. Earlier, we pointed out that there was a powerful tendency to see this condition as one where knowledge was valued for its performativity. The latter has been mainly understood as signifying 'efficiency', but another and perhaps more fruitful alternative is to see performativity as 'efficacy'. Doing this enables us more adequately to relate knowledge to the social practices we have been discussing. Thus, in lifestyle practices efficacious knowledge is that which helps to create and re-create identity and difference; in confessional practices it is that which helps provide access to inner life and potential; in vocational practices it is that which enables advantageous positioning in the market.

Critical practices, on the other hand, pose certain problems in relation to this way of understanding knowledge. It would be possible to argue that in critical practices efficacious knowledge is that which facilitates action for change. But this is somewhat simplistic. Here, we can turn for help to Newman's account of what he terms 'postmodern social movements'. According to Newman, these involve a form of cultural activism that is:

> a phenomenon peculiar to today, reflecting the dislocation, the search for an intensity of present experience (to be found in performance), a form of service to others based on the consultancy model . . . and a reaction not against one identifiable oppressor or category of oppressors but simply against organisation and unwanted control.
>
> (Newman 1995: 12)

The characteristic of such movements is that they do not posit a single pre-defined desired future; hence they are neither teleological nor totalising. These postmodern social movements embody critical practices that are not directed towards a universalistic 'cause'. These are practices which are rather rooted in shared interest, dismay or disquiet about the present, a reaction against current events rather than a common support for some particular end. Activists in critical practices do not seek to build structures nor do they feel the need to cleave to prescribed ideologies. They are motivated by a sense of injustice but see themselves as activists in a generic sense, not activists for a particular single cause. They work, not through conventional political and community action methods but by surfacing local and very often subjugated knowledge and getting people to think about their situation through role-play, workshops, street theatre and popular carnivals – in effect, through *performance* – performance which might often be transgessive, e.g., the 'zaps' of ACT-UP and the bare-breasted marches of Lesbian Avengers.

Performativity, therefore, does not necessarily simply mean 'efficiency' in the reproduction and maintenance of a market-dominated capitalist system. Whilst there are certain practices where performativity is linked in this way, there is also, as we see, scope for critical, oppositional practices. These, however, are not the practices of the traditional, modernist Left. Performativity means 'efficacy', but efficacy has a particular signification in the critical practices of postmodern social 'movements'. It is not the efficacy of commitment to totalising projects of transformation, rather it is a more modest yet no less effective efficacy of 'giving voice' to specific, sub-jugated knowledge, of empowering through a learning that is both partici-pative and performative. Here then, is another example of the significant place of 'serious' play and ludic subversion that is so characteristic of the postmodern condition and mood. Furthermore, it is clear that critical practices in the postmodern do not posit idealised futures which only serve to oppress through their very totalising unattainability. The critical practices we have outlined overlap with lifestyle, confessional and even vocational practices. They are firmly located in marketisation and the contemporary culture of consumption. They do not dichotomise themselves from these, indeed, to a large extent they use the techniques of the market; they work through the culture of consumable and desirable images. They recognise their 'tragic' immersion in the conditions of the present. But they do this reflexively, ironically and parodically, performatively subverting that which is their very condition of possibility.

THE CHALLENGE OF ADULT LEARNING

Postmodernity has provided spaces for rising social groups such as the new middle classes, for new postmodern social movements and for hitherto oppressed and marginalised groups such as women, blacks, gays and ethnic minorities to find a voice, to articulate their own 'subjugated' knowledges and to empower themselves in a variety of different ways and according to their own specific agendas. In this situation, education stops being a univocal, predictable reality and consequently it makes no sense to speak of it simply as either functioning to reproduce the social order or as implicit social engineering, whether this be for domestication or liberation. The very binary opposition of domestication–liberation becomes questionable and loses some of its structuring power. Linked with this is the impact of a reconfiguration of education away from its institutional and provider-led location.

The postmodern emphasis on ephemerality, fragmentation and reinvention links with certain notions of a democratic education and education for democracy – the taking into account, without suppressing difference, of a diverse range of interests and locations within the social formation (Westwood 1991). It is precisely the instability introduced by cultural change that provides a means of challenging dominant values and norms of knowledge. By undermining the certainty surrounding canons of knowledge, universal messages and the efficacy of enlightened pedagogues, opportunities are presented for diversity and for new and innovative practices which switch the emphasis from 'provision' to learning opportunities, from the student to the learner. For those with a commitment to the fields in addressing inequality and oppression, contemporary uncertainty and diversity can be both a condition for and an outcome of rethinking the challenge of marginalisations in a situation of new and multiple forms of lifelong learning.

Educational forms, including those of adult education, are increasingly becoming more diverse in terms of goals, processes, organisational structures, curricula and pedagogy. This both reflects and is a contributor to the social phenomenon of dedifferentiation, of which the condition referred to as 'adult learning' is an aspect. Dedifferentiation implies a breakdown of clear and settled demarcations between different sectors of education and between education and cognate fields. Consequently, education is not so narrowly construed; for example, the distinction between education, leisure and entertainment becomes blurred. Furthermore, education can no longer claim a monopoly over learning simply because it is a formally constituted field, since potentially any activity in any context could claim to involve learning and hence be deemed 'educational'. The notion of 'adult learning' foregrounds the simultaneous boundlessness of learning, that it is not confined by pre-determined outcomes or formal institutions, and its inherent discursive and socio-cultural contextuality.

Reconceptualising 'adult education' in this way affirms the significant place of 'learners' as against the institutional form or the discursive tradition. It is to position adult education as part of the more open and expansive 'moorland' of learning rather than as an all-embracing yet bounded field. Perhaps, more significantly, it is also to problematise the powerful dichotomy of needs and wants that adult educators seem to find difficult to do without. In this dichotomy, wants are what learners have, needs are what adult educators think they should have. Conventionally, this is justified on the grounds that education must have a moral purpose, that educators must know what this purpose is and that it is their duty to ensure that what is learnt and how it is learnt is shaped by this. Whilst no one would seriously argue that education can be purposeless, there is a problem in so far as it is by no means axiomatic that educators alone should dictate what these purposes are. In one sense, this is a problematic which is well known in adult education, as is attested by the privileging of experiential learning over discipline-based learning. But this is not really a solution since it misses an important feature of the problem, which is the inevitable boundary-maintenance and policing which is a consequence of privileging educationally defined needs over wants. Educational activities are based on a faith in progress and betterment, on judgements that some things are more important to learn than others. Even though diversity and difference may be valued, education in the modernist mode converges on the same, endeavouring to make everyone alike. Notions of progress, rationality, privileged knowledge and values, and normalisation is in-built into the educational event.

The consequence is that wants are inevitably cast as the villain of the piece, irrational manifestations of desire and products of false consciousness. Needs, on the other hand, are cast as heroic, rational, truth-seeking and emancipatory. Yet it is clear that this dichotomising of needs and wants is itself tied in with a modernist discourse which privileges the 'enlightened pedagogue' and the role of education as the vehicle for realising the modernist project. 'Adult learning' does not, therefore, simply signify 'out of school' or 'outside' the formal educational institution, the widening and increased incidence of learning opportunities, but more significantly the lessening of the power of the educator to define what constitutes worthwhile knowledge and serious learning, a questioning of the role of normalisation and a refusal to acknowledge that learning must always be shaped by the values of a particular conception of progress.

The modernist notion that educational discourses, forms and practices have to be shaped by a set of invariant and universal norms and goals is now giving way to the recognition that these are dynamically implicated in diverse cultural contexts. Education escapes the boundaries traditionally delimiting it from the wider social formation and dividing it within itself. In the process, what a 'learning opportunity' is and who legitimately provides such opportunities is problematised and reconfigured.

Equally, instead of everything being delimited and reduced to the 'same', e.g., to liberal adult education, to experiential learning, to education for liberation, to the creation of the rational goal-directed individual, the trend is becoming one where educational forms are seen instead as expressing 'difference' in their diversity and providing spaces for a diversity of voices. Whilst it is easy enough to mock this by pointing to the oppressive features of vocationalising trends and the current emphasis on adult education as a business, it is important not to downplay the significance of the increasing diversity, multiplicity and dedifferentiation which characterises the contemporary landscape of education and the reconfiguring of learning opportunities for adults.

In this context, it is impossible to ignore the impact of new forms of provision and delivery. One aspect of this is increased prevalence of open and distance learning (ODL). Here, the postmodern phenomenon of space–time compression has meant that learners and providers become increasingly available to each other on a global scale (Edwards 1994). ODL provides a ready means for satisfying the diverse desires of a more diverse range of adult learners. Without the need for attendance at specific places of learning at specific times, the relationship between learning, face-to-face interaction and pre-planned curricula is fractured – in this process, it is the learner (as against the 'student') once again who is foregrounded. At the very least, ODL poses the need to re-evaluate ways in which learners are engaged. When linked with developments in the communications revolution, such as the increasing scope and use of the Internet, it is clear that dominant conceptions of knowledge, curricula and pedagogy are in drastic need of rethinking.

For many adult educators it is precisely these trends that are most worrying. Yet this ignores the significance of the massive increases in participation by adults in diverse settings and diverse forms of learning that are currently taking place. At the same time, it could be argued that adult educators are being unreflexive about their role, particularly within the academy, in sustaining the inequalities and exclusions of modernity. Gore (1993) argues that all pedagogies, whether liberal or radical, are framed within modernist 'regimes of truth' articulated in terms of universal macro-level explanations and centred on conceptions of teleological progress and goal-directed rational selves. From the perspective of these regimes, much of the learning currently engaged in by adults can only be deplored as contrary to the 'true spirit' of adult education or as 'uneducational' and therefore beneath their concerns.

Again, we can turn to Burbules (1995) for help. He argues that postmodern incredulity requires us to change our conception of education and educational activities. First, education involves an engagement between teachers, learners and knowledge. Since this engagement can lead to dependency, there is a need for critical distance. This means that teachers need to problematise their conventional role as 'enlightened pedagogues'. They need to avoid taking themselves too seriously even when they are engaged in education for social transformation. Burbules suggests that speaking and acting through the ironic, the tragic and the parodic might provide one way of doing this.

Second, education must inevitably have purpose and direction. But purposes should not become easy teleologies, they should not be held slavishly and/or with an expectation they must always be fulfilled. We should leave ourselves open to the unexpected, the tangential, the countervailing. A sense of direction need not always be implicated with notions of linear, unidirectional growth consonant with a particular yet universal conception of 'progress'.

Third, we need to cultivate a high tolerance for difficulty, uncertainty and error. We should not see difficulty so much as the challenge of a problem to be overcome but rather of a problem never fully resolved. Equally, uncertainty is not a passing state of puzzlement but an acceptance of the provisional and contingent in what we believe and do, whilst error is not simply falsehood that will be replaced by truth but more an unacceptable version of an idea or value that is entangled with other ideas and values we are not prepared to abandon. Burbules argues that difficulty, uncertainty and error are not necessarily flawed states to be overcome but ongoing conditions of the educational process itself, indeed, educationally beneficent correctives to arrogance and complacency.

Finally, although education implies within its own definition that one cannot be 'educated' for the worse, in effect, therefore, that education necessarily must be for betterment, it does not follow that there is only one kind of 'betterment' and that we always know what it is in advance. Rather than emphasising 'betterment' in a teleological sense, Burbules suggests that education might more aptly be seen as a process involving disenchantment or disillusionment. Although we would consider it a strange education indeed that did not involve the gaining of new insights and understandings, these gains might well be ambivalent, partial and pro-visional. Education is still education even if it involves losses as well as gains. We need to recognise that betterment is never unalloyed and that present successes may in the future become tragic or laughable errors.

AN UNCERTAIN PROSPECT

As adult educators prepare to abandon the security of the bounded 'field' of adult education for the rugged and open 'moorland' of adult learning Burbules' arguments are likely to have a fruitful resonance. To deplore, as so often happens, the trend towards an increased diversity of learners, new sites of learning and new forms and contents of learning only serves to increase the marginality of adult education even as adult learning in all its various manifestations is given greater prominence. Perhaps adult edu-cators need to recognise the significance of partial perspectives rather than striving for all-embracing knowledge and universal 'messages' – a need to be both 'more modest about the autonomous contribution they can make to social problems and less convinced of a role as the messenger for all-embracing liberating ideologies' (Jensen and van der Veen 1992: 285).

As Edwards (1994) points out, when students are positioned as consumers demands are made on educational providers which they find difficult to cope with. The very notion of 'student' is reconfigured as indeed are notions of what constitute 'provision' and 'providers'. When students become 'learners' changes follow in both the control and content of curricula. That learners should make choices based on desire (including the desire to be optimally positioned in the market) rather than a search for enlightenment and the mastery of a canon of knowledge can no longer be automatically considered perverse and uneducational. To do so is to claim that this is not what education is 'really' about and this itself is based on the assumption that there is an ideal model of education and that education is itself directed by a set of transcendental ideals. It is to see adult learning from a purely educational frame of reference as the systematic selection and delivery of learning experiences predefined by the professional educator. But the postmodern attitude would argue that this is a dangerously oppressive totalising discourse which assumes learning is a 'gift' bestowed by enlightened pedagogues. Whilst, as adult educators, we might well want to foreground the empowering potential of education, we need to see educational forms contextually rather than transcendentally, and we need to reassess the place of pedagogues within this.

The contemporary diversity of adult learners and the multiplicity of sites of learning is very often seen as problematic, as a 'dilution' rather than an enrichment of the learning environment. The demands for greater professional competence and acceptability tend to be constructed as a loss of social purpose and as a threat to a critical and emancipatory engagement rather than a response occasioned by changing times and changing conditions. As the boundaries that traditionally defined adult education break down and become increasingly problematic, the defensive concern over adult education as a bounded field or even as a 'profession' under threat looks increasingly misplaced as the focus shifts to practitioners working 'professionally' with adults, whoever and wherever they may be, and within a variety of learning situations, both inside and outside formal educational institutions.

Chapter 2

Adult learning for citizenship

Education for citizenship is concerned with the knowledge, skills, attitudes and values necessary for citizens to participate meaningfully in society. This chapter will attempt to sketch out what a contemporary adult education for citizenship might look like. We will tackle this by first analysing and deconstructing different historical approaches to citizenship, whether implicit or explicit, within adult education. We will then try to reconstruct an agenda for adult learning for citizenship which draws from this analysis of competing traditions but relates it to more recent educational debates and developments in the context of an increasingly complex and rapidly changing world. As part of this process, we will adopt two central themes: the relationships between *the public and the private* and *the personal and the political.*

Historically, much of the Western world's post-war debate about citizenship has been framed by Marshall's three identified dimensions of citizenship: the civil, the political and the social (Marshall 1950). Civil rights have consisted of individual legal rights, for example, to a fair trial and to hold property; political rights have been seen in relation to the right to vote and to participate effectively within a democratic nation-state; and social rights have been linked to social entitlements, for example, to health, education and unemployment benefits within the context of a welfare state. These rights have in turn underpinned developments in education for citizenship, whether as an explicit curricular focus, as in 'civics' or 'political education', or as part of a 'hidden curriculum' which has operated in different ways both within schooling and in the context of more diverse adult education practice.

But the world is changing: in economic terms, with the globalisation of capital and the pre-eminence of market considerations; in social terms, with the polarisation and fracturing of the labour market into a core/periphery/unemployed model, the increased questioning of the welfare state and the emergence of a socially excluded 'underclass'; in political terms, with the decline of the nation-state, the growth of international issues and interest groups and the problems of stateless people; in cultural terms, with a wider acknowledgement and assertion of cultural diversity and pluralism amidst a new global emphasis on consumption; and in terms of knowledge, with a questioning of the grand narratives of science, rationality and human betterment and a postmodern emphasis on local narratives. These developments challenge many of the Marshallian assumptions: full employment, the sexual division of labour in the public and private domains, the predominance of the nation-state, the inevitable evolution of modern(ist) progress. They also raise further questions about cultural dimensions to citizenship: identity, difference and cultural pluralism. All these factors have implications for the link between learning and contemporary citizenship.

The relationship between education and citizenship raises the fundamental and long-standing debate about the overall purpose of education, a debate which has centred on the two apparently opposite aims of socialisation: fitting people into social roles and functions, and individuation, enabling them to think for themselves and so be self-directing. Such oppositions are familiar to adult educators, most notably expressed by Paulo Freire when he poses the alternatives of education for domestication or education for liberation (Freire 1972). Indeed, within the discourse of adult education, conflicts between liberals and radicals, academic knowledge and community action have revolved around different ways of interpreting and resolving this difference. Such polarisations have served to permeate the discourse of adult education with a whole litany of further dualities which can be unhelpful in practice: those between rhetoric and reality, theory and practice, education and training, experiential and disciplinary knowledge, and so on. Such oversimplifications have often served only to reify certain ideological positions and so lock educators into inflexible and unreflexive stances.

A problem with an opposition like education for domestication versus education for liberation is that, for progressive educators, it can often produce a disabling oscillation between Utopianism and despair, as education repeatedly promises to liberate the creative human talents of people and then consistently fails to do so (Gilbert 1992). This opposition is unproductive in practice as education inevitably involves elements of both subjection and autonomy. Socialisation and individuation are not direct opposites but linked – the whole process and outcome of 'thinking for yourself' arises out of social and intellectual engagement which, in turn, involves the learning of skills, techniques and information as well as participation in debate and decision-making. The key point at issue here is a recognition that education is an apparatus for instituting the social, not for eliminating it. The purpose of education is less a matter of liberation or domestication than negotiating the terms of participation in a learning process and a society in which subjection and autonomy coexist. What matters most for educators are the principles and contexts that inform the conduct and organisation of educational engagement. These need to be investigated further in any exploration of the meanings and possibilities of education for citizenship.

The rapid socio-economic, political and cultural developments within an increasingly diverse and uncertain world clearly influence the knowledge, skills, attitudes and values a citizen requires to participate in a contemporary democracy. However, in an adult learning context, the terms of engagement will also be influenced by different traditions within the discourse of adult education. Thus, before identifying an agenda for adult learning for citizenship within today's world, it may be instructive to look back critically at different historical approaches to adult education and see what can be learnt from their approach to citizenship.

ADULT EDUCATION TRADITIONS AND CITIZENSHIP

Any educational endeavour implies a certain type of citizen and a certain type of citizenship through the curriculum it constructs and the values it espouses. A central task in reviewing different adult education approaches to citizenship is to try to be more explicit about what this involves. We will seek do this in relation to three different traditions within adult education: the liberal, the radical and the community.

A dominant influence on the formation of adult education, certainly in English-speaking countries, has been the *liberal tradition*. This has taken a number of forms and directions according to its national and cultural location (Taylor *et al.* 1985; Duke 1992). Fieldhouse's summary of its basic values provides a useful baseline from which to understand and appraise its approach to citizenship:

> The notion of 'liberalism' in English adult education implies a democratic, dialectical and non-utilitarian approach. It is democratic rather than authoritarian with students enjoying the right to choose what and how they study. . . . It is dialectical rather than propagandist, with a total freedom of discussion of all subjects. And it is non-utilitarian, non-vocational in that it is concerned with the education of the individual either for personal intellectual advancement or to make the individual a better citizen.
>
> (Fieldhouse 1992: 11)

These liberal values have certainly underpinned much of a liberal adult education tradition whose concept of adulthood stresses the individual's potential for ever-increasing autonomy and social agency. Based on fundamental liberal conceptions of education as initiation into disciplinary knowledge, leading in turn to education of the free and rational person and education for critical awareness, adult learning has been seen as a means towards both self-actualisation *and* the development of an informed and critically aware citizen. The liberal approach has been probably the most extensive influence on adult education in Western societies and it has played an important part in expanding individual access to higher education, wider academic knowledge and hence social mobility. However, it has clear limitations in both its implicit and explicit approach to education for citizenship. Some of these limitations are associated with its epistemology and some to the very meaning of 'free' and 'rational' within a liberal ideology.

In terms of knowledge, a liberal adult education emphasis on 'education for its own sake' has served at one level to institutionalise a conventional division of 'non-vocational' curriculum content into either a range of 'practical', 'recreational' and 'domestic' subjects or more recognisable 'academic' territory. This has had the conservative effect of only replicating the traditional low- and high-status knowledge divisions of the school curriculum (Rogers 1992), which have served to maintain and reinforce an elitist differentiation between those learner/citizens who can be academically 'liberated' and those who are more suited to be practically and, in the case of women, literally, 'domesticated'.

Even its more specific attempts at education for citizenship have been constrained by two overlapping factors. The first has been an approach to political education which has failed largely to acknowledge that:

> Knowledge as such is not power: power requires the will to act and action skills. Classes on political ideologies . . . or political issues . . . too often end up as debating societies, sharpening the wits but unrelated to anything members will do when the class is over.
>
> (Ridley 1983: 13)

and the second encompasses the realities of a social and cultural location where:

> people interested in political or public affairs are disproportionately male, middle-aged and middle-class; they are home-owners, well-educated, and members of voluntary organisations; they are predominantly white.
>
> (Hampton 1983: 29)

Liberal adult education's democratic and dialectical approach to study has been largely restricted to the realms of the classroom. In its concern for individualistic civil and political citizenship at the expense of wider social and cultural dimensions, it has failed to connect the private to the public, the personal to the political, in any convincing way. The main impact of such a liberal education for citizenship has been to help maintain and reinforce a common culture based on sameness that was largely conservative, limited and exclusive; and in so doing, to identify difference as a deficit (Keddie 1980).

A liberal position assumes a rational, autonomous citizen within a certain kind of consensual liberal democracy. In this context, liberal adult education has been seen to rely too much on a modernist conception of the enlightened subject with an agency largely unrestricted by wider socio-economic conditions and constraints. This tendency not to problematise the social and economic dimensions of citizenship raises important questions about a social situation where adults clearly possess significantly different amounts of economic and 'cultural capital'. As Giroux puts it, without an understanding of the political and economic context of inequalities, the result of a liberal emphasis on democracy:

> is often little more than a simple-minded celebration of individualism and citizenship, taking for granted the ability of the capitalist state and its attendant market logic to address the suffering of subordinated and marginalized groups.
>
> (Giroux 1989: 55)

Within liberal adult education, individual rationality has not been subject to wider scrutiny within a societal context where the ruling forms of capitalist organisation impose their own form of economic rationality, as highlighted by Marcuse in the 1960s:

> The means of transportation and communication, the commodities of lodging, food and clothing, the irresistible output of the entertainment and information industry carry with them prescribed attitudes and habits, certain intellectual and emotional habits which bind the consumers more or less pleasantly to the producers, and through the latter, to the whole.
>
> (Marcuse 1970: 26)

Liberal values have often all too easily been overwhelmed by the economic imperatives of capitalism. In this context, liberal adult educators have tended to indulge in overoptimistic readings of the micro–macro societal relationship and wishful thinking about the role of education in changing society, a stance which, in effect, has served mainly to support the socio-economic and political *status quo*.

If a liberal adult education approach to citizenship has been limited and inadequate because of its lack of recognition of structural factors in creating and maintaining social inequality and its adherence to ideas of uncritical social agency, what are the possible alternatives to this and what implications does this have for education for citizenship? An alternative 'radical' approach to adult education has been a central focus on *class, inequality and social reproduction*. Jane Thompson identifies a central strand of thought in such a position when she states unequivocally that:

The liberal hope of changing the context and process of education to make it more responsive to the needs of the disadvantaged is a vain one without corresponding and significant changes in the organisation and control of economic life.

(Thompson 1980: 96)

Influenced by social theorists like Bowles and Gintis (1976), Althusser (1977) and Bourdieu and Passeron (1977), who emphasised the structural determinants of class and thus the labour force, subjectivities and culture, such an approach was able to critique the dangers of adult educators adopting an oversimplistic needs-meeting ideology and hence (often inadvertently) colluding in the social and cultural reproduction afforded by the formal education system. Such a perspective has been successful in injecting into adult education discourse a necessary element of macro-structural analysis to offset the more optimistic micro agency of an individualistic liberal adult education approach.

Moreover, it has built on the epistemological traditions of radical thinkers like Tom Paine and earlier radical social movements to reject any ideas of value-free, non-utilitarian academic knowledge and replace it with an emphasis on 'really useful knowledge'. 'Really useful knowledge' is neither predominantly academic nor primarily domesticating. Rather it is practical, political and dynamic, it engages directly with the lived experience of the unequal and oppressed, it is 'knowledge calculated to make you free' (Johnson 1988). At issue here is the nature and power of different conceptions of knowledge and its role in maintaining or transforming social relations. In contrast to a liberal approach, a radical adult education perspective has reasserted a much broader political and social dimension to citizenship within an overall class analysis of society.

Radical adult education strategies were developed outside of educational institutions and in association with a variety of social movements. Radical adult educators included Ashcroft and Jackson in Liverpool and Coady and Horton in North America, with the latter's work very much focused on citizenship, civil rights and the active involvement of racially oppressed groups (Brookfield 1983: 106–17; Crane 1991; Peters and Bell 1991). Whereas Horton and his colleagues at Highlander favoured a community-based praxis which allied their own broad socio-economic critique to a prolonged listening and 'tuning in' to the concerns of local people, the educational approach of other radicals tended to be more prescriptive.

The educational strategy advocated by Ashcroft and Jackson in Liverpool in the early 1970s was explicit and unequivocal, that the starting point for working-class adult education should be the recognition that exploitation was the central feature of class society and that the purpose of education was to confront the student with his/her class position as a necessary first step towards learning for action (Ashcroft and Jackson 1974).

This approach met with some success in the 1970s and beyond. Nevertheless, such a radical adult education perspective raises a number of important questions in relation to education for citizenship. In its focus on 'really useful knowledge', it appears to offer a more grounded, democratic and active approach than that of the liberal tradition, and it certainly addresses the problem of the 'thoughtless action' which can take place in community work. However, an attendant danger is that of imposing a very specific, exclusive and unreflexive definition of 'really useful knowledge'. In the Liverpool context, Ashcroft and Jackson's assertion of 'theory' amounted in some ways to a 'banking approach' to knowledge and the construction and perpetuation of a false dichotomy between socialist 'rigour' and 'community' relevance.

This class-based focus on public, political life could be seen to set up a new kind of elitism, only compatible with a very specific form of 'economistic' democracy rooted in the patriarchal traditions of 'old' social movements like trade unions, the churches and socialist societies. It was in great danger of ignoring the historical situation that:

> the working-class has never been a single unitary subject but has been simultaneously fractured by skill, gender, ethnicity, region and the cultures engendered by these divisions.
>
> (Westwood 1992: 234)

and so was likely to exclude the interests and culture of a wider, more diverse range of citizens within the community. In direct contrast to the liberal tradition, in its approach to citizenship it privileged the public over the private and the political over the personal.

Radical adult educators were successful in promoting a more socially critical and socially purposeful approach to education for citizenship. However, the radical approach's overreliance on the notion of 'false consciousness' and the universal 'truths' that adults need to absorb, understand and internalise before they can become proper citizens, succeeded only in replacing the grand narrative of liberal humanistic progression and emancipation with just another grand narrative, that of orthodox Marxism. It is perhaps not surprising that this vanguardist approach has foundered in the face of rapid socio-economic change, increasing cultural diversity, the emergence of new social movements and the ideological onslaught of the New Right.

In the light of the liberal approach's tendency towards uncritical agency and the radical perspective's inclination towards monolithic determinism, a *community* adult education approach perhaps offers a way forward that takes account of both structure and agency. It holds out the prospect of relating to the civil, the political, the social and the cultural dimensions of citizenship. A community adult education approach attempts to combine the critical structural analysis of the radicals and a more specific social purpose of liberal adult education which aims at:

> providing individuals with knowledge which they can use collectively to change society if they so wish, and particularly equipping members of the working class with the intellectual tools to play a full role in a democratic society or to challenge the inequalities and injustices of society in order to bring about radical social change.
>
> (Fieldhouse 1992: 11)

Community adult education attempts to move away from grand narratives and universal truths and offers the prospect of a meaningful, dialectical link between the private and the public, the personal and the political. It promises a reference point that goes beyond the concerns and remit of the individual citizen, an understanding of economic inequality, social diversity and cultural pluralism, an interest in and acknowledgement of the empowering potential of community-based knowledge and experience and a focus for local educational action within which to develop a more participatory education for citizenship.

At its best, a community-based adult education has taken account of local inequalities, celebrated cultural differences, initiated new educational processes and forms of participation for non-participant adults and developed a dialogue and educational way forward with a variety of learner citizens in a locality. Building on the ideas of Illich and Freire, Tom Lovett, in his early work in Liverpool, was able to devise a specifically non-institutional and non-hierarchical 'network approach', requiring new roles for an educator in engaging and supporting adults in the local community and this in turn has prompted a growing adult education focus on outreach work (Lovett 1975). More recently, Ward and Taylor have used a community orientation to revise their understanding of social purpose adult education in recognition of five aspects of social structure which reproduce inequality, namely education, gender, race, age and geography (Taylor 1986: 4). In addressing these at a community level, they adopt two central guiding principles: the necessity for in-depth, preliminary groundwork and dialogue to ascertain the real, felt needs of specific target groups in the community and the development of community-based provision related to emerging local issues rather than conventional academic 'subjects' (Taylor and Ward 1986: 172).

While community adult education has provided a more comprehensive theory of educational agency in the face of difference and inequality, the potential for a more active and participatory education for citizenship centred on community life, community voice and community issues and a more imaginative educational process, it has still been seen to suffer from some of the shortcomings of the liberal tradition. Several radical critics of community adult education (Cowburn 1985; Westwood 1992; Thompson 1993) have noted that, despite the outreach methods, community development approach and non-formal focus, the content of the education offered in most community adult education provision has often been very similar to that in a liberal adult education programme. The only significant difference perhaps has been a greater professional preoccupation with, and investment in, education of a compensatory or 'remedial' nature designed to meet the perceived needs or deficiencies of those deemed to be, in some way, 'disadvantaged' (Thompson 1980). Indeed, this very situation may be the result of an over-professionalised, community-based needs-meeting approach which amounts only to the 'domestication' of a Freirian agenda and its reduction to a mere method stripped of its essential ideological underpinning (Allman 1987; Westwood 1992). The rhetoric of community outreach, community participation and community needs obscures the fact that the needs of local populations have been very largely defined by professional educators with an ambivalent, but still primary, loyalty to and dependence on the educational establishment (Jeffs 1992). Indeed, a romantic 'community' localism often serves only to make more palatable an educational approach which has been increasingly controlled from the centre (Vincent 1993).

A key consideration here is the whole construction and meaning of community, and the way romantic, mutually supportive *Gemeinschaft* characteristics are attributed to communities, despite clear evidence to the contrary. In the past, Keith Jackson has criticised the assumptions of much community adult education in both the UK and the USA, asserting that:

> What must be challenged is its quietism; its acceptance of the circumstances it describes to which adult education must adjust. The concept of community has always been used in social policy to divert such a challenge.
>
> (Jackson 1980a: 42)

Notwithstanding the more informed and critical approaches of, for example, Lovett, Ward and Taylor, and in spite of an articulated commitment to the 'disadvantaged' and a pluralist society, the historical practice of community adult education has often been to construct a homogeneous 'locality as community' with ostensibly shared values and beliefs. In a UK context, for example, Sallie Westwood has diagnosed that the historical and ideological context of much of community adult education has been such that:

> The contradictions and fractures of gender, ethnicity and age divisions, to name the most important, melted and were not constructed as a central part of 'communities'. Thus, community was located within a

consensus constructed around the hegemony of white Englishness and homogenised as the 'community' becoming itself the subject/object of educational intervention.

(Westwood 1992: 234)

Indeed, this has also been the history of 'community college' initiatives in a variety of countries in the North and the South, where the discourse of community adult education or non-formal education has been incorporated into and overwhelmed by that of conventional schooling. In curricular terms, this has meant at worst, second-best education and at best, second-chance education. In advanced capitalist countries, a community orientation has too often meant no more than a localised marketing and consumerist focus on a predictable and largely reproductive curriculum, sometimes accompanied on the fringes by occasional multicultural celebrations and festivals.

Although community adult education promises a focus on community issues, culture and knowledge, and a more active and participatory education for citizenship, it has often delivered less than it promises, foundering on its proximity to mainstream education, professional colonisation and an unwarranted *Gemeinschaft* view of community which privileges consensus and sameness over structural inequality and difference. It is not surprising, therefore, that under the influence of New Right marketisation, community in education has often been reduced to an unproblematic aggregation of individual choices, and education for citizenship has meant little more than a limited extension of consumer choice and rights for some – in effect, knowledge and power have been individualised and privatised.

CITIZENSHIP AND EDUCATION IN A POSTMODERN WORLD

Each of the liberal, radical and community traditions within adult education have had their own distinctive approach, implicit or explicit, to education for citizenship, and some of their respective strengths and limitations have been identified and analysed above. While this analysis clarifies the discursive influences of different traditions within adult education, it locates them very much within a modernist framework and suggests none of the traditions offers a convincing way forward for education for citizenship within the context of a rapidly changing, postmodern world. A new approach to education for citizenship may need to be explored.

Before exploring the possibilities for a new education for citizenship, it is necessary to look briefly at different current conceptions of citizenship within an increasingly diverse and uncertain world. Although traditional

Left–Right distinctions are perhaps less useful in analysis than they once were, it can still be said that citizenship is viewed differently along the political spectrum. Those towards the Right construct the citizen as consumer within the ambit of a market economy and look to detach the active, enterprising and self-reliant citizen from *dependence* on the state. As Apple portrays it:

> the common good is now to be regulated by the laws of the market, free competition, private ownership and profitability. In essence the definitions of freedom and equality are no longer democratic but *commercial*.
>
> (Apple 1993: 30–1; emphasis in original)

Here, empowerment is viewed primarily in individual, economic and consumerist terms and responsibilities are couched in terms of self-help and a paternalistic and apolitical voluntarism.

In contrast, those towards the Left attempt somehow to link individual civic and political rights to wider social, economic and cultural rights and to understand the concept of the active citizen in the light of the growth of new social movements. Empowerment is to be understood and pursued, and responsibilities exercised, within an acknowledged context of inequality and in relation to a mutuality of purpose which underpins an established civic-communitarian tradition (Hill 1994: 13). In reaction to the social, economic and moral fragmentation resulting from the 'possessive individualism' of the marketplace, there is once again a concern with 'community', but now acknowledging the politics of difference and identity. There is also an emphasis on 'thinking global and acting local' in a context where citizenship rights include the continuing world-wide struggle for equality of gender and race, for conservation and the more equitable distribution of the earth's resources (ibid.: 25).

Educators clearly need to take stock of these changing global circumstances and different constructions of the citizen. In so doing, they need also to acknowledge the hegemonic influence of New Right thinking on current educational theory, policy and practice, where the needs of the economy have precedence, market solutions are the rule and educational consumerism flourishes. In this context, predominant adult education concerns of the 1970s for social improvement, social critique and the encouragement of a critical citizenry appear to be increasingly irrelevant and anachronistic in relation to the two prevailing forms of education identified by Dale as 'education in the national interest' incorporating a vocationally dominated curriculum and 'education in the private interest', to prepare a population of 'possessive individuals' (Dale 1989: 104).

Within this hegemony, significant features of the liberal adult education tradition have been incorporated and reconstituted into a new adult education orthodoxy with an emphasis on consumer choice, learner-centredness, personal competence, individual progression, even empowerment, within a free market system. Brookfield identifies 'hegemonic concepts' in the current literature and rhetoric of adult education world-wide, namely self-directed learning, meeting felt needs and valuing learners' experiences. At the same time, he also conducts a critical analysis of how their general use and application serve to leave:

> unchallenged the philosophy and culture of laissez faire capitalism in which individuals, communities and 'races' are pitted against each other in a war of advantage which is portrayed as natural.
>
> (Brookfield 1993b: 67)

An important reaction to the above hegemonic trend is that of critical pedagogy. Born out of a determination to counteract both the conservatism of New Right 'cultural restorationists' and the deterministic pessimism of reproduction theories, critical pedagogy holds out the promise of hope, liberation and equality in education as a means of forging a new radical democracy. Deriving its theoretical foundation from first-generation Frankfurt School critical theory, critical pedagogy's primary reference point is schooling. It assumes that, if the experience of schooling is changed, then students' lives and hence civil society will also change for the better. By enabling students to focus on their own lives and explore their cultural experiences, meanings and identities they can develop the critical tools to oppose the oppression of, for example, racism, sexism and classism, and help to transform schooling and hence society into more equitable and democratic forms.

More recently, the focus of critical pedagogy has begun to move beyond a predominantly school orientation to take account of the broader educational contexts and intermeshing of the political, the cultural and the educational addressed by Freirian pedagogy. This focus has also been influenced by the critiques, perceptions and alternatives of feminism and postmodernism. In relation to citizenship, Aronowitz and Giroux frame the educational issues thus:

> for educators the modernist conception with enlightened subjects, when coupled with the postmodern emphasis on diversity, contingency and cultural pluralism, points to educating students for a type of citizenship that does not separate abstract rights from the realm of the everyday, and does not define community as the legitimating and unifying practice of a one dimensional historical and cultural narrative.
>
> (Aronowitz and Giroux 1991: 82)

For Giroux, education for citizenship incorporates a number of different and overlapping political, socio-economic and cultural dimensions. Citizenship must extend the conventional idea of the political to take account of a pluralist and postcolonial democracy and, amidst growing fears of the development of an underclass, advance the notion of rights to participation in the economy. In cultural terms, it needs to take account of horizontal links between citizen and citizen, involving a politics of differ- ence and identity which recognises diversity but tries also to identify common interests. The emphasis of critical pedagogy on the politics of identity and difference, the language of possibility, prospects for 'voice' and social empowerment and, indeed, the emancipatory potential of new social movements is powerful and attractive to educators looking for refer- ence points for a critical education for citizenship which also takes account of social and cultural change. However, the translation of these from argu- ments and goals into actual practice remains problematic.

What advocates of critical pedagogy are in danger of doing is over- polarising the debate in setting out to replace the 'domestication' of current schooling and education with the 'liberation' of critical pedagogy. Here, it is clearly not enough to assert or desire fundamental changes in educational and political philosophy and practice without relating these to contemporary educational contexts, the political realities of existing educational policies and practice and the predominant cultural influences on the lives and interests of different learner/citizens. In constructing and developing a new education for citizenship, a key question is how adult educators are to acknowledge and respond to the existence of a changing and fragmenting postmodern world, yet, at the same time, challenge a new educational orthodoxy which can reduce adult learning to an uncriti- cal, unreflexive and essentially privatised servicing of the economic, social and cultural needs of capital and the social and political *status quo*.

Rather than getting trapped within utopian oppositions to the educa- tional *status quo*, it might instead be instructive to:

> make allowance for the complex and unstable process whereby dis- course can be both an instrument and an effect of power, but also a hindrance, a stumbling block, a point of resistance and a starting point for an opposing strategy.
>
> (Foucault 1981: 101)

With this in mind, adult educators cannot merely wish away current emphases in education on, for example, consumerism and vocationalism but rather use them as *starting-points* for further constructive *exploration and negotiation* within a new critical context.

ADULT LEARNING FOR CITIZENSHIP

In reviewing and developing a contemporary politics of citizenship, Hall and Held make the important point that we must address not only the previously-acknowledged barriers to full citizenship constituted by class and inequality, but take increasing account of questions of membership

posed by 'the diverse communities to which we belong, the complex interplay of identity and identification in modern society, and the differentiated
ways in which people now participate in social life' (Hall and Held 1990:
176). Chantal Mouffe takes this one step further when she argues that 'a
democratic idea of citizenship must find a way of constructing the public
and the private that does not relegate all differences, diversity and plurality
to the private. . . . Democratic politics has to make room for particularity
and difference' (Mouffe 1988: 30).

A more explicit linking of *the public and the private* may offer a way forward for adult educators who recognise that notions like justice, liberty,
democracy and citizenship have contested, not univocal, meanings, and
who want to take account of the diversity of postmodern society yet also
look beyond the private sphere to the exploration of some kind of
common good and common interest. A useful reference point here for
adult educators trying to shape an education for citizenship may well be
to follow C. Wright Mills and try to relate 'personal troubles of the
milieu' to 'public issues of social structure' (Wright Mills 1959: 8). Wright
Mills differentiates between 'troubles' which are private matters where
individual values appear to be threatened and 'issues' which transcend the
local and the particular and are public matters where public values
appear to be threatened. However, he also shows how they can be inextric-
ably linked. As an example of this, he cites unemployment as a classic case
where 'both the correct statement of the problem and the range of possible
solutions require us to consider the economic and political institutions
of the society, and not merely the personal situation and character of a
scatter of individuals' (ibid.: 9). Certainly, in addressing unemployment in
a contemporary context, there is plenty of evidence that adult educators
across the globe have come to understand more readily and in greater
depth the complex economic and social interrelationship where private
problems connect with public issues and so to concur with a growing
body of social commentators and politicians in recognising that mass
unemployment and its attendant social and economic divisions and problems are in no-one's long-term interests, irrespective of the logic of the
marketplace.

In a postmodern world, it is clear that a large number of public issues
cut across traditional class and community boundaries – the responses to
a variety of environmental threats right throughout the world or to indigenous land rights in North and South America, South Africa, Australia
and New Zealand are good examples of issues where individuals with
different backgrounds and differing private interests collaborate in the
interests of the common good, where citizens' rights and responsibilities
are seen to be closely interconnected. This development further highlights
a situation of considerable significance for adult educators where, in
contrast to the conventional wisdom of the liberal and radical traditions,

there are clear links between the *personal and the political*. That 'the personal is political' has long been a rallying call for feminists in responding to the historical relegation of women to the private realm in politics, economics and education and the subordination of the oppressions of, for example, gender and race within an undifferentiated, class-based model of societal oppression. For educators, a growing recognition of the interrelationship of the personal and the political allows scope for an educational contribution to forms of practical resistance to the prevailing socio-economic system where there are:

> a proliferation of new points of antagonism, new social movements of resistance organised around them, and consequently, a generalisation of 'politics' to spheres which hitherto the left assumed to be apolitical; a politics of the family, of health, of food, of sexuality, and of the body.
>
> (Hall 1981: 63)

In attempting to link more clearly the public and the private, the personal and the political, adult educators may need to move beyond the polarities and certainties of 'domestication' or 'liberation' and begin to map out an educational process that engages with current educational orthodoxies yet sets these in a critical and forward-looking context. In reconstructing an education for citizenship within a postmodern world, adult educators could usefully explore and problematise different meanings and dimensions of citizenship in relation to key contemporary developments in social and educational life. An agenda for an adult learning for citizenship might be *experiential learning, consumerism, literacy, vocationalism and empowerment*.

Experience and learning from experience have long been valued, particularly in the radical tradition of adult education, as an important epistemological counter-weight to codified academic knowledge delivered from above and as having some critical connection with 'really useful knowledge'. In more recent times, the contemporary approach of *experiential learning* has gained much wider credence and use within a more mainstream approach to adult learning, both in liberal and vocational contexts. In both instances, the location of experience is important. It could be said that the radical approach was in danger of placing undue emphasis and reverence on the undifferentiated experience of working-class adults. However, in contemporary society, the counter-dangers are that in a liberal teaching/learning context, teaching can be collapsed into a banal notion of facilitation, where student experience can become an unproblematic vehicle for self-affirmation and self-consciousness (Aronowitz and Giroux 1991: 117); and in the context of the accreditation of experiential learning, experience can be decontextualised and commodified as a means of integrating the individual into a more formal educational or employment system and a technology of control (Bryant 1994).

If an educational focus on experience is to avoid the worst of these extremes and move beyond both the anecdotal and the prescribed, it needs to locate individual experience within a wider critical social context. With this in mind, student experience and 'voice' should not be taken at face value but educational efforts made to problematise, locate and evaluate them. This can further be illustrated in relation to one of the growing emphases in postmodern society highlighted by critical pedagogy: the politics of identity and difference.

In contrast to liberal adult education privileging of the autonomous rational subject located within a certain type of consensual liberal capitalist democracy, critical pedagogy has focused on the politics of identity and difference as a key reference point for education for citizenship. Such an emphasis has been seen to be much more than a reaffirmation of liberal pluralism – as part of a postcolonial pedagogy it has taken due account of the effects of the Eurocentric, imperialistic and racist discourse of modernism in order to combat actively the 'culture of silence' this can engender amongst the unequal.

A key issue for educators in focusing on identity and difference, relating 'personal troubles' to 'public issues', is the extent to which human experience in general and learning experiences in particular are mediated and shaped by the power relations which exist in society (Wildemeersch 1992: 24). This involves a close study of the interrelationship of micro education practice to macro political analysis. In their teaching of a course on 'Race, Community and Society', Brah and Hoy develop a critical approach to experiential learning which neither privileges nor uncritically validates 'authentic' experience, nor does it locate it exclusively within the blanket of 'false consciousness'. They aim to help their students towards an understanding of how their different experiences and perspectives as, for example, black and white, working-class and middle-class women, are shaped by social conditions: 'Each of us, though unique as individuals, are positioned within society alongside hierarchies of power constructed around such factors as class, caste, racism, gender, age and sexuality' (Brah and Hoy 1989: 71).

Such an approach may point the way towards developing both a more critical approach to experiential learning and an investigation of key issues like identity, difference and student voice that are grounded in the specific experience of learner/citizens rather than existing primarily at some abstract level. Indeed, in this context, there might well be merit in some kind of accommodation and negotiation between academic critique and deconstruction, with their attendant dangers of paralysis and disablement, and the more grounded and practical approach of experiential learning, involving as it often can, an over-romanticised and uncritical view of the common-sense and contradictory voices of learners.

In further interrogating modernist conceptions of citizenship, in taking account of the complex interrelationship of identity and difference and in envisaging a more democratic and pluralistic concept of citizenship, another key focus might be on *consumerism*. Once again, the task for critical educators is to move beyond pure reaction to a narrow consumerist focus in education. At one level, educators may need to recognise and critique the commodification and unequal impact of consumerism on society and education and, at another, to acknowledge its increasing significance within a postmodern emphasis on desire and pleasure, and explore the implications of this for citizenship and citizenship education. Certainly, an educational focus on consumerism needs to move well beyond the limitations of circumscribed commercial choice. One more exciting and expansive possibility is that an educational focus on consumerism can provide a 'voice' for minority groups and interests and this can be pursued around the politics of consumption.

Much recent educational effort has gone into the encouragement and development of student 'voice'. Advocates of critical pedagogy combine critical analysis productively with a rationale for practice which makes the important political point that:

> voice provides a critical referent for analysing how people are made voiceless in particular settings by not being allowed to speak, or being allowed to say what has already been spoken, and how they learn to silence themselves . . . voices forged in opposition and struggle provide the crucial conditions by which subordinate individuals and groups reclaim their own memories, stories, histories as part of an ongoing attempt to challenge those power structures that attempt to silence them.

> (Aronowitz and Giroux 1991: 101)

As part of an education for citizenship, critical pedagogy has emphasised the need to deconstruct 'authoritative voices', those who claim to speak for or on behalf of others. However, within the context and constraints of the classroom, its proponents have often struggled with the complexities and difficulties of doing this in practice, of taking proper account of the personal investments that different people have in their particular identities and positions. In this context, there has been much debate on and agonising over trying to make practical sense out of number of key issues: reconciling the balance of power between 'empowering' teacher and student; the dangers of vanguardism inherent in any idea of 'correct readings'; the different strategies, including silence, which students adopt in response to the rhetoric and methodology of critical pedagogy; and the dynamic

interplay between classroom participants and their multiple and contradictory subject positions (Ellsworth 1992).

Adult educators may have an advantage in this respect in that outside
the more regulated and controlled territory of mainstream schooling, and
within an increasingly diverse consumer society, they may have more
scope to encourage, promote and respond to the 'voice' of a variety of
non-mainstream groups and individuals. In envisioning and fostering a
new approach to citizenship in a rapidly-changing world, much rhetorical
capital has been made out of the emancipatory potential of 'new social
movements' which combine a critical, global analysis with a more localised
focus for action. The argument is that such movements, coalescing around
concerns of feminism and anti-racism as well as peace, environmental
issues, gay rights, 'grey' issues and other alternative identities, visions and
lifestyles have the potential to organise at a local level around issues of
(social) consumption in respect of, for example, housing, education and
health. With their insider understanding of cultural diversity, identity and
different subjectivities, their commitment to promoting the 'voice' of different minority interest groups and their concern for social and cultural
empowerment, they are interested in a more broadly based citizenship
which challenges the prevailing cultural hegemony of Western liberal
democracies.

The question is how and to what effect adult educators can engage with
these new social movements in the development and negotiation of education for citizenship. In relation to social movements that highlight cultural
diversity, issues of identity and different subjectivities, there is an opportunity to build the link between the personal and the political into a wider
focus on education for the socially conscious, active citizen which focuses
on the interrelationship of rights and responsibilities. Within an increasingly differentiated consumerism there is an opportunity for adult educators to work with and respond to the particular demands, interests and
circumstances of new social movements. This holds out the prospect of a
more critical and participative approach to the conventional educational
wisdom of needs-meeting and a way of connecting the agendas of new
social movements to wider social, economic and cultural inequalities, the
polarisation of the marketplace and the complacency and dangers implicit
in a 'culture of contentment' (Galbraith 1992).

A key issue in developing education for a democratic and pluralistic
citizenship is that, as well as a recognition of difference and diversity,
there needs also to be a focus on common reference points and common
interests. Raymond Williams, recognising that any educational curriculum
amounts to a compromise between an inherited selection of interests and
an emphasis on new interests, has long since argued for the replacement
of established hierarchical and divisive educational traditions, not by the
'free play of the market' but with 'a public education designed to express

and create the values of an educated democracy and a common culture'
(Williams 1961: 152–5). Adult educators have a role to play in promoting
a common culture which does not involve convergence to the same culture;
which is based not on where people come from but what they do now and
how they relate to each other. They can help to focus on an education for
a citizenship which respects differences yet also stresses democratic participation and accountability and the need for communication between all
parties.

This raises the central question of *literacy*. Within the discourse of adult
education, approaches to literacy have often been framed in terms of
'domestication' or 'liberation'. However, these polarities can obscure the
need both to have access to culturally valued knowledge *and* to view it
critically – Donald expresses this as both the institution of structures of
cultural authority and their negotiation (Donald 1992: 151). The way forward may lie somewhere between a liberal adult education initiation into
disciplinary knowledge and the polarised oppositions of 'purist' versions
of Freirian literacy or 'really useful knowledge'. It is too much of an over-
simplification to replace the traditional authority and dominance of the
canon only with that of the 'politically correct'.

While culturally valued knowledge and the way it serves to sustain
unequal social relations and disadvantage needs to be understood critically, this does not mean its complete rejection and replacement only by
a second-best community or experiential knowledge. Certainly, in this
respect, Gramsci (1971) was only too aware of the power embedded in
and exercised through language, literacy and education to reject disciplinary knowledge and mainstream culture before he tried to explore
and understand them more thoroughly. If we accept the argument stated
earlier that education is an apparatus for instituting the social, then the
approach to literacy within a democratic education should be more about
the terms in which learner/citizens participate in social and cultural transactions. In this context, Jeanne Brady offers a way forward in suggesting
a combination of three forms of literacy: functional, cultural and critical,
where functional literacy moves beyond the predominantly instrumental
and utilitarian; cultural literacy facilitates communication across borders
and lines of cultural difference; and critical literacy enables 'a critical reading of how power, ideology and culture work to disempower some groups
of people while privileging others' (Brady 1994: 143).

In continuing to explore an education for citizenship which focuses on
aspects of a common culture, another central reference point might be
'work'. An emphasis on *critical vocationalism* could form a starting-point
for a process that acknowledges and problematises the current vocational
emphasis of 'education in the national interest' and also seeks to help
learner/citizens engage critically and productively with their private interests in securing and retaining work and gaining personal meaning and

worth from it. In place of the crude socialisation processes into workplace discipline and an enterprise culture or an uncritical assertion of human capital theories, there might be an emphasis on a democratisation 'in work' and 'of work'.

Within work, Donald advocates that a critical vocationalism would focus on 'what concepts, knowledges and intellectual skills would be necessary for understanding how industries and economies work' and could lead to a more informed, skilled and participatory work-force as a precondition for both industrial democracy and improved economic effectiveness (Donald 1992: 62–3). Here, there may be possibilities for a more vocationally orientated education for citizenship which takes account of difference and diversity as well the inequalities inherent in production and consumption. While there is a real danger of wishful thinking in terms of the democratisation possible in relation to a new industrial world of 'flexible specialisation' and 'post-Fordism', there may nevertheless also be democratic opportunities as well as possible worker safeguards and benefits arising from the consequent loosening of hierarchical management structures. Certainly, there appears to be some prospect of this in the developing social and economic policies of expanding international socio-political-economic groupings like the European Union. A critical vocationalism offers the possibility of new forms of participation and engagement 'in work' as part of an education for economic and social citizenship. Its also raises the question of 'empowerment' within a new understanding 'of work'.

Empowerment is a central area of contestation in a rapidly changing society. The New Right has latched on to empowerment at an individual and economic level, appearing to offer a limited but attainable empowerment. This contrasts very clearly with the prospect of the wider-ranging, less tangible, social empowerment held out by Freire and successive advocates of a broader-based critical pedagogy. There is clearly a significant difference between the idealistic social empowerment that is central to a Freirian approach and the much more circumscribed personal empowerment achievable within the narrowly defined competence and vocational instrumentalism that is closely associated with serving the needs and interests of capital. In more recent times, Freire and his allies within critical pedagogy have sought to retreat from the totalising, often patriarchal narratives of modernism, oppression and emancipation to take account of the critiques of feminism and postmodernism (Freire 1993) and recognise how inequalities of power are mediated by different subjectivities and situations with respect to differences of, for example, gender, race, class and sexual preference. The development of a 'postmodernism of resistance' (Giroux and McLaren 1994; McLaren and Lankspear 1994) is an attempt to retain the social vision of Freire but also to move away from the dangers of previously identified tendencies towards theoretical vanguardism and the crude binarism represented by the stark alternatives of education for domestication or education for liberation.

But what kind of empowerment is possible as part of an education for citizenship? This can best be explored in relation to educational approaches to work. The individualistic empowerment offered by vocational competence and consumerist acquisition may be modest and circumscribed, at times even illusory, but it is demonstrable and achievable, for some at least. In contrast, social empowerment is more critically constructed and far-reaching but less readily identifiable and hence less easy to pursue as part of education for citizenship. Empowerment clearly needs to have situated meaning in direct relation to the living and working contexts of adult learner/citizens. There may be some merit in trying to combine aspects of both approaches to empowerment, in linking the economic to the social and cultural.

A key area which affects everyone, is central to the idea of citizenship and allows meaningful connections between the societal macro and the educational micro, is the changing nature of work. As the global labour market fragments into a volatile mix of core workers, peripheral workers and the unemployed, one way that an empowering education can try to address the economic and welfare rights of citizenship is through developing a new focus on education for work. This need not be an educational approach which takes for granted or accepts uncritically the interests, norms and requirements of capital. On the contrary, it can help to re-address the whole concept of 'work' and a social wage, and view productive work as covering a very wide range of activities from further education, voluntary work, community action, caring, housework, part-time paid work, casual work, self-employment, co-operative work through to more conventional full-time paid work. Such an approach can address the immediate lives and concerns of learner/citizens at a micro, private level, while, at the same time, posing macro public questions about life, work and citizenship. As Mechthild Hart puts it in her recent resurrection of adult education social purpose:

> Instead of simply adjusting people to the hierarchical and divided reality of work, adult educators need to ask the question of how we could and how we should work in a manner that contributes to the maintenance and improvement of life rather than profit.The question of how we should work is also the question of how we should live . . . the insane separation of work and life impoverishes both, making the former deadly and the latter empty. In fact, it destroys life.
>
> (Hart 1992: 200–1)

A broader, more critical economic and welfare focus in education for citizenship in relation to work can help to extend and challenge the more circumscribed economic empowerment associated with the discourses of competence and consumerism at the same time as giving more specific meaning to the idea of pursuing social empowerment for learner/citizens. Indeed, a new concentration on the whole area of productive or socially useful work appears to be an area which could bring a greater unity of purpose to a wide variety of different interest and identity groups, with a vested interest in challenging the prevailing nostrums of economic rationalism. This might even involve some kind of alliance and common cause between revitalised and changing 'old social movements' like trade unions and the churches and a variety of developing 'new social movements' (Johnston 1994; Newman 1995).

CONCLUSION

In this chapter we have tried to identify a role for adult learning in the development of a new education for citizenship within a postmodern world. In doing so, we have developed a critique of the approaches to citizenship of different historical traditions within the discourse of adult education and have suggested that a key focus for citizenship education should involve a closer exploration and linking of the private to the public and the personal to the political.

In identifying what a future adult education for citizenship might look like in practice, it is not possible to be too specific due to the uncertainty of postmodern change and the situatedness of practice. Nevertheless, it is useful to point to curricular indicators, issues for resolution and areas for leverage in the development of an approach to adult learning which engages with citizenship.

First, it should relate to a citizenship that includes not only individual civic and political rights but connects these to rights and responsibilities that also encompass the economic, social and cultural. A curricular focus within adult learning needs to take account of a lifelong learning process which takes place on multiple sites, acknowledges different identities, celebrates cultural diversity and makes room for all voices. Key issues here are the nature and accessibility of lifelong learning. It should be not be constructed as the mere handmaiden of capitalism, fostering a largely adaptive and circumscribed curriculum, but needs to be available to all, in a variety of ways and at a variety of levels. This whole issue may need to be tackled in relation to the identification and promotion of a common culture which recognises difference within communality, which stresses what people do and how they live rather than where they come from, and which concentrates on how they can best communicate, participate and be mutually accountable across economic, political and cultural barriers. As such, this is bound to involve a critical understanding and exploration of the extent and impact of the inequalities of economic and cultural capital on the learning process.

An important further principle to inform any future adult learning for citizenship is that it is open-ended. It should not be a tool for social engineering. Rather, it should be influenced, but certainly not determined, by the 'truths' of disciplinary knowledge, the aspirations of 'really useful knowledge', the authority of the teacher and the goals of economic competence. However, it should also acknowledge localised and particular knowledge, skills, attitudes and values, and recognise the importance of lifestyle and desire in shaping the learning motivation of adults in any negotiation of the curriculum.

Lastly, it should neither tacitly accept the *status quo* nor try merely to 'wish away' contemporary developments in society. Instead, it should try to link wider social and educational aspirations to the starting-points afforded by a contemporary emphasis on experiential learning, consumerism, literacy, vocationalism and empowerment. In this way, it will be able to outline and develop an educational process that engages with current educational orthodoxies yet sets these in a critical, constructive and dynamic relationship to the diverse requirements of citizenship in a postmodern world.

Chapter 3

Governmentality and practice

What do we normally mean when we think of a practice like education as being 'governed'? We may be referring to some guiding values or regulating ideals that frame the practice of teaching as a whole or to a consensual system of professional norms that are more or less self-regulating and steer specific conduct, however imperfectly, in given directions. Reference may also be made to sets of formal rules and regulations, policies and procedures, which are somehow handed down and require practitioners to behave in certain ways. It is not difficult to identify such prescriptions and their sources. We can point, for example, to statutory laws and contractual obligations which authorise corporate and individual conduct, as well as to institutional regulations and other more local administrative requirements, and think about 'practice' as disciplined performance or responsible professional activity working within such codified policy parameters (Becher and Kogan 1992). Such a view regards practice as governed by a system of external and internal controls. However, it is not merely by reference to the obvious existence of these instruments of control that one is able to answer the question 'How is my practice governed?' A more complete answer needs to go beyond the written and unwritten rules of practice and its operating values to address both the formation of practice requirements and their effects. The question as posed is actually a question about metapractice, i.e., it is a question of 'How, in practice, is my practice governed?'

In this chapter, the metapractice question is approached by looking a number of ideas which have contributed to an understanding of the way in which education is governed. One idea which can be taken to represent an archetypically 'modernist' theory of education is that of the French sociologist Emile Durkheim. Durkheim was responsible for constructing a realist pedagogy claiming to have a scientific foundation at a time of great upheaval in the organisation of his country's educational system. His educational theories resonate with many present-day common-sense ideas concerning what education is or ought to be about, particularly those concerning discipline and the purpose or function of education in meeting society's needs. Durkheim's compatriot, Michel Foucault, offers a reading of how practices such as education are 'governed', and in particular an understanding of practice as a disciplined performance, which has itself been read by some interpreters as a 'postmodernist' rejoinder to more conventional educational theories (Usher and Edwards 1994). Foucault's idea of government is not one of sovereign authorisation imposed from without but of 'governmentality' from within and to which we all contribute as practitioners. This local dynamic of governmentality is further explored by drawing on Bourdieu's idea of 'habitus' as a set of dispositions which embody practice.

Two case examples of the operation of governmentality in relation to adult and continuing education – at institutional and individual levels – will be presented in order to illustrate the ways in which the practices of those who are working in this field are constituted. The first examines evidence from so-called institutional 'mission statements' about continuing education; the second draws on a study which looks at how the competences of adult learners are constructed.

DURKHEIM

Two of Durkheim's major professional concerns were fused in his educational theories. They are a) the establishment of sociology as a recognised science of society and as an independent academic discipline, and b) the promotion of national re-integration through secular education. In seeking a rational foundation for pedagogy, he tried to develop a set of sociological principles to inform practice. According to Lukes, Durkheim 'believed that the relation of the science of sociology to education was that of theory to practice' (Lukes 1973: 359). He regarded pedagogy as a 'practical theory' seeking 'to combine . . . all the data science puts at its disposal, at a given time, as a guide to action' (ibid.: 111). For Durkheim, sociology was pre-eminently the science of social facts, and it was these 'facts' in relation to education that he set out in a series of lectures to student teachers.

Social facts set limits to conduct and hence can be said to 'govern' practice. The task of sociology is to establish what the social facts are in a given domain. Its procedures are considered to be no different to those of the physical and biological sciences in determining the facts of the natural order. Durkheim's educational project rested on a belief in the existence of an overarching moral order and that sociology's purpose was to reveal the nature of morality as a system of collective beliefs and to identify the components of normal behaviour therein. Once revealed, practice could properly develop in recognition of the need to maintain social sentiments.

Central to Durkheim's sociology of education was the need for both teachers and learners to acknowledge that, as members of society, they operated within an ever-present, continuously enacted moral order. Morality was not to be seen as a system of rules which could be derived from philosophical principles, e.g., theories of natural rights, utilitarianism or Kantian imperatives, but as intrinsically authoritative in being embedded in social norms. Correspondingly, Durkheim rejected pedagogical appeals based on an abstract, asocial 'inner nature' or those which referred to any kind of a priori educational ideals. A realistic, rational pedagogy sees education as a 'social fact' within which legislators, administrators, teachers and parents have to make choices. A theory of education cannot be constructed in idealist terms, since systems of education are 'the product of a common life' (Durkheim 1956: 66) and will vary between societies and be 'normal' within any given one.

As a science of the moral order, sociology identifies 'the sprit of discipline' as a major element of morality. This has several aspects: first, it is discipline which assures regularity of conduct; second, discipline promotes the collective ideal of attachment to social groups; third, discipline provides us with knowledge of the reasons for our conduct and the autonomy of enlightened acceptance. Discipline is society's message to its members as if from a commanding father enjoining us, in the name of reason and the knowledge of how society works, to do our duty. For Durkheim, concerned as he was with social integration and with countering the fractiousness of an increasingly differentiated society, a restoration of the spirit of discipline within a unified secular educational system was essential. Discipline, therefore, quite properly limits individual desire and, with reference to the collective goals of activity, it is 'the condition of happiness and moral health . . . this capacity for self-control is itself one of the chief powers that education should develop' (Durkheim 1961: 45). Moral discipline is therefore a normalising force, or 'the way in which nature realises itself normally' (ibid.: 51). To teach morality is thus to explain by employing the instruments of science itself as a moral force, an agent for the achievement of collective reason.

Since the family is seen by Durkheim as being inadequate for the task of training children to meet the demands of society, being too local and particular a grouping, the state must take on that role – first by supplying sufficient teachers who are trained to recognise and transmit society's moral imperatives. If successful, the discipline of the classroom will then be carried forward into later life, so that the duties of the adult become 'the civic or professional obligations imposed by state or corporation' (ibid.: 49). The function of education is to explain how society works and thereby instil feelings of collective responsibility in children. The 'profession' of education sits between individuals and the state as a corporate body or 'buffer' which represents the interests of learners to the state and the state's interest in developing society's collective sentiments within learners. However, Durkheim's position with respect to the extent to which the state ought to direct actual teaching practices is somewhat ambivalent. On the one hand, he says that:

> it is up to the State to remind the teacher constantly of the ideas, the sentiments that must be impressed upon the child to adjust him to the milieu in which he must live.
>
> (Durkheim 1956: 79)

and also that:

> Since education is a social function, the State cannot be indifferent to it. On the contrary, everything that pertains to education must in some degree be submitted to its influence.
>
> (ibid.: 80)

On the other hand, the state is seen as having a more limited role. As an embodiment of the collective conscience:

> The State can only consecrate it, maintain it, make individuals more aware of it . . . respect for reason, for science, for ideas and sentiments which are at the base of democratic morality. The role of the State is to outline these essential principles.
>
> (ibid.: 81)

Since education is principally a matter of moral authority and since the best teachers, from society's point of view, are those who represent and transmit the spirit of discipline at its heart, they are not so much to be directed by the state as informed by a sociologically founded pedagogy. Pedagogy is seen by Durkheim as 'a certain way of reflecting on the phenomena of education' (ibid.: 92) and as requiring a certain mental disposition among practitioners. Hence 'pedagogy depends on sociology more closely than on any other science' (ibid.: 114). Pedagogical ideals are expressed through and explained by social structures, and not derived from principles of human nature. Though the 'end' of education is the constitution of social beings and not a realisation of their 'inner nature', Durkheim is prepared to concede that the 'means' also belong properly to psychology (e.g., in addressing questions of intelligence, character and individual development).

The government of practice is more directly addressed in a parallel series of lectures to those on education, published as *Professional Ethics and Civic Morals*. Here, Durkheim reiterates his belief in the state as the highest embodiment of society's collective conscience (1992: 79–80). He attends to the problem of the management of the state, its authority as government and, given that modern societies exhibit a high degree of social differentiation, how discipline can be embodied and not just imposed. Earlier, in *The Division of Labour in Society* he had affirmed that 'To govern our relations with men, it is not necessary to resort to any other means than those which we use to govern our relations with things' (1964: 36).

Durkheim's answer to this problem, in short, is that government is only possible and socially acceptable through a knowledge of how society operates, i.e., by means of a sociological understanding of group practices. This understanding, society's self-representation through sociology, would reveal how professional and occupational associations exemplify social solidarity and act as an intermediate stratum between individual and state. Durkheim's corporatist view of the professions was explicitly *not* extended to business and the market, which he took to manifest socially disintegrative tendencies. The state is not to be seen as a representative of an abstract 'general will' nor as a protector of 'natural rights', but in terms of how it actually works in representing collective sentiments to its constituent groups.

How then does it work ? According to Durkheim:

> Each occupation, indeed, constitutes a milieu sui generis which requires particular aptitudes and specialised knowledge, in which certain ideas, certain practices, certain modes of viewing things, prevail.
>
> (Durkheim 1992: 117)

He now affirms an extensive and proactive role for the state. It is to intervene in all areas of society. Indeed, it must:

> enter into their lives, it must supervise and keep a check on the way they operate and to do this it must spread its roots in all directions . . . it must be present in all spheres of social life and make itself felt. . . . Nowadays we do not admit that there is anything in public organisation lying beyond the arm of the State. In principle, we lay down that everything may for ever remain open to question, that everything may be examined . . . in this enlargement of the field of government consciousness . . . we see yet another distinguishing feature of democracy. . . . All these deliberations, all these discussions, all this enquiry by statistics, all this administrative information put at the disposal of government councils, and which go on increasing in volume, all these are the starting point of *a new mental life*.
>
> (ibid.: 65, 84, 88, 92; emphasis added)

In these latter comments, as well as in the earlier ones on discipline and normalisation, Durkheim anticipates the themes of governmentality and habitus which are to be taken up by Foucault and Bourdieu respectively. His positivist sociology in general and functionalist account of education in particular are now seen as naive. It is important to recognise, though, that Durkheim was not just engaged in analysing social practices but helping to constitute them in a particular way. It was part of his admittedly political project to do so. In particular, the effect of his theorising is to render a practice such as education more 'governable' in relation to the requirements of society and the state. He sets out the 'facts' of a consensual moral order which, it is claimed, can be discovered scientifically so that practice can be appropriately guided; and these 'facts' become part of the knowledge of a practice through which it is governed. Durkheim's programme for rationalising education by means of a sociological discipline is a pre-eminent modernist example of the management of desire, so that the subjectivities of teachers and their students can be accommodated to the requirements of a supposed overarching moral order. Positivism may have been discredited as formal theory, but its cultural contribution to a valuation of practice, its inherent conservatism and legacy in the state's sentiments concerning education remain.

FOUCAULT

Foucault offers a way of analysing practices by introducing the idea of 'governmentality'. His approach is to take practices apart and examine the detailed mechanics of how they work. The short answer is that they do so by 'working their authors'. Foucault's writings represent a critical extension of Durkheim's idea of normativity and embrace a consideration of practices' internal dynamics. His focus is on the processes of 'normalisation' whereby practices are sanctioned, not by an external authority or an appeal to collective sentiments, but by mundane acts of self-authorisation which sustain the practitioner as a compliant identity, a self-policing individual. So, governmentality is manifest in all routine activity, even at those points where one might as a practitioner question the operation of specific rules for appropriate conduct; it is part of a practice's own self-consciousness. The effect of governmentality is that it constitutes the subjectivity of individual practitioners. One *becomes* the way one is identified and identifies oneself. Practice is governed by an ever-moving agenda to which one contributes as an author, but which can never be solely one's own and for which there is no single authoritative source. There is no single identifiable locus of control. Foucault does not see practices as governed from outside but from within, driven as it were by a continually circulating capillary power.

Drawing on his studies of imprisonment, Foucault's model for self-policing practice is the Panopticon. 'A particular rationality accompanies the panoptic technology, one that is self-contained; and untheoretical, geared to efficiency and productivity' (Rabinow 1984: 20). This is the 'mentality' of 'governmentality' whereby 'a vast documentary apparatus becomes an essential part of normalising technologies' (ibid.: 22). In any professional practice, but particularly education, the principal business is the circulation of text. Practitioners are defined and governed, i.e., normalised, through a never-ending process of inscription. We are all party to the

reproduction of such technologies in the continual generation and amend-
ment of texts in our daily practice. This is not simply a question of
having to deal with paperwork, which is often viewed as an impediment
to practice – something that one has to get out of the way before the
'real work' can begin. For Foucault this is not the case. Documentation
is a metapractice which records and accounts for our practice.

One of the problems of coming to grips with Foucault's ideas on 'governmentality' is the conventional view we have of government as the
operation of the state over and above society, imposing a politics, an
ideology 'from without', as it were. In challenging modernist political philosophy as an explanation of government, Foucault argues that we do not
need a theory of how the state works or what it represents in order to
understand how practices are governed. He invites us to consider the all-
pervasive character of 'governmentality' as something that, in constituting
our subjectivity and in shaping and reproducing our practice, we contribute to directly. Disciplines are crucial in this context; they occupy a
strategic place as discursive forms of the 'will to truth'. 'Every educational
system is a political means of maintaining or modifying the appropriation
of discourses, with the knowledge and power they bring with them'
(Foucault 1972: Appendix). Disciplines, in Sheridan's words, 'bind individuals to certain types of enunciation' (Sheridan 1980: 127). If we think
for a moment of our own practice as educators, we now have many ways
of enunciating that practice that could not have been foreseen or spoken
of twenty years ago. We are in the Panopticon – incorporated, surveyed,
assessed, evaluated, bottom-lined.

Speaking of the programmatic character of the Panopticon, Foucault
notes that 'we are dealing with sets of calculated, reasoned prescriptions
in terms of which institutions are meant to be reorganised, spaces
arranged, behaviours regulated' (Burchell, Gordon and Miller 1991: 80).
This programming depends upon the operation of a particular form of
rationality – 'governmentality'. It is an instrumentalist view of how things
work administratively (ibid: 100). Foucault is important for the way in
which he links the operation of power to the constitution of subjects –
for example, the way in which adult learners have come to be constituted
for the purposes of certification.

How are subjects made? By dividing practices – the subject is objectified
by a process of division either within himself or from others (Rabinow
1984: 8). The process of division is accomplished by modes of classification
and categorisation employed as much by academic disciplines in the name
of understanding as by administrations for the purposes of disposal. And
by confessional practices – whereby subjects are active accomplices in
their own self-formation. Foucault is not interested in the truth or falsity
of what disciplines have to say so much as discovering how they achieve
their discursive effects. He rejects questions of sovereign norms in favour

of those about mundane administration. Government is about the means of marshalling resources in order to know more about a population, to subject it to an all-encompassing gaze and to have it keep a watchful eye on itself. He brings the matter down to our daily practices and routine collusions. Foucault makes much of the ambiguity of the notion of 'subject' as one who both knows (as the carrier of experiences) and is known (as a product of discourse) in particular ways. Governmentality operates through various disciplinary practices which control by means of knowing ever more, i.e., through 'power/knowledge'. This is especially evident in the practice of the examination (not just in the sense of sitting exams, but through a multiplicity of procedures for overseeing and rendering accountble the actions of subjects). So the analytic grid of power/knowledge (Marshall 1990: 23) supplies a framework for exploring particular educational practices. We are now required, as a condition of practice, to constitute education and ourselves in particular ways, to continually rewrite the texts of our practice and to be constantly monitored while so doing.

The idea of examinability joins dividing and confessional practices. The examination reveals and marks what is 'known'; it is a technique that is not just divisive, but one which works to constitute subjects' own selfhood in the guise of a confession – this includes even the apparently liberating and progressive use of the idea of 'reflective practice' as self-examination. Hoskin remarks that 'Foucault himself named examination (which we can now see is a quintessential educational practice) as the key that simultaneously turns the trick of power (discipline) and knowledge (the disciplines) in the modern epoch' (Hoskin 1990: 51).

Governmentality is thus concerned with the operation of local practices. It is exemplified by a discourse which supposes that anything can, and everything should, be managed. In continuing education for professional development, for example, emphasis is placed on 'self-management'. Courses which address problems of practice are described as 'stress management' or 'time management', etc. We have now become used to these descriptions, but from Foucault's perspective they are not just descriptions. They are examples of something more significant. Micro-technologies of control and normalisation 'bring together the exercise of power and the constitution of knowledge, in the organisation of space and time along ordered lines, so as to facilitate constant forms of surveillance and the operation of evaluation and judgement' (ibid.: 31).

The key to governmentality is 'the self-regulating capacities of subjects, shaped and normalised through expertise' (Miller and Rose 1993: 75). It is governmentality that constitutes subjects as 'competent', 'deserving', 'credit-worthy' or 'experienced'. The operation of governmentality is apparent through 'programmes of conduct which have both prescriptive effects regarding what is to be done . . . and codifying effects regarding what is to be known' (Foucault 1991a: 75). We can see examples in education of how experience is hijacked as currency. Practical guides to the conduct of accrediting prior experiential learning (APEL) see its value in cash terms, as a way of 'spending' credits. The only experiences worth having are those which are so accredited. As Challis, for example, assures us, the system can only work if experiences are 'brought into the planning equation' (Challis 1993: 20). Furthermore, the key to APEL is seen to be the management of evidence of competence – the only 'evidence' that matters. Experience is delivered as competence in the guise of educational choice.

But as Edwards and Usher view it, 'competence-based education and training can . . . be seen as a strategy of governance' (Edwards and Usher 1994: 2). The governance of adult education works, not so much because we have submitted ourselves to any new regime of 'truth' but rather because we are implicated through our practice routines in its continual creation. We are all partial authors of the current 'truths' of our practice. The effect of governmentality is to make our practices more programmatic, which is to say subject to systematic analysis and prescription. Ineffable qualities – 'experience', 'competence', even 'quality' itself – are operationalised. Such practices crystallise into institutions, they inform individual behaviour, they act as grids for the perception and evaluation of things (Foucault 1991a: 81). We 'know' about experience, competence, etc. through systems of encoding and by knowing how to deal with them (subject them to measurement, assessment, evaluation). This is operational or programmatic knowledge. Such core dimensions of subjectivity are rendered into 'things' and become the means by which they are administered.

In reconfiguring discipline, Foucault has moved a long way from Durkheim who, as we have seen, had himself hinted at a new mental environment within which practice was required to operate. But, for Durkheim, this mentality supplied only the external parameters for practice adjustment and were not intrinsic to the practices themselves. Nevertheless, his scientism and corporatism contributed directly to that new mentality, to become part of the governmentality of practice. Following Foucault, we can see the effects of governmentality in the domestication of practice – of how it works 'in practice' through confession, examination and discipline to govern itself.

BOURDIEU

Bourdieu makes three important contributions to a postmodern understanding of how practices are governed through activities of self-domestication. First, he introduces the notion of 'habitus' to explain how practices come to be at home with themselves. Second, he examines practices in relation to their 'field' of operation. Third, he brings to the fore the discursive arena of practice fields and thereby emphasises the constitutive effects of the language of practice. Unlike Foucault, who claimed not to be theorising about practice in any formal sense and certainly did not wish to be associated with any particular academic discipline, Bourdieu is content to be a sociologist – but a particular kind. He offers a reflexive, anti-foundational micro-sociology of practice and is very much aware of his own metapractice in writing about practice. His own texts can be read as 'moves' within a disciplinary field to reorient the analysis of practice.

The personal and routine effects of governmentality within practice can be appreciated by examining Bourdieu's idea of 'habitus'. Practices are embodied skills, represented in the habitus. 'The habitus is a set of dispositions which incline agents to act and react in certain ways. The dispositions generate practices, perceptions and attitudes which are "regular" without being consciously co-ordinated or governed by any "rule"' (Thompson 1991: 12). It has the following features: a) habitus is the product of experiences and mundane processes of learning which become embedded and embodied as 'second nature', b) dispositions are structured through the conditions in which they are acquired, c) habitus is durable and not amenable to conscious reflection, and d) habitus is generative and transposable; it can spawn different practices in sites away from that of its acquisition. We can think of habitus as a system of affective, cognitive and bodily orientations. Through habitus, we 'produce on the appropriate occasions skilful social activity that embodies, sustains, and reproduces the social field that in turn governs this very activity' (Dreyfus and Rabinow 1993: 37). Such governing determines 'what possibilities show up as making sense' (ibid.). In effect, habitus sets the horizons of practice. It is the dynamic of the habitus which shows us both how practices are formed and how they work. As Brubaker puts it, 'the habitus determines the manner in which problems are posed, explanations constructed, and instruments employed' (Brubaker 1993: 213).

Habitus provides us with tacit understanding and a sensibility about how to act in practice. As Bourdieu himself remarks, 'I have put forth a theory of practice as the product of a *practical sense*, of a socially constituted "sense of the game"' (Bourdieu and Wacquant 1992: 120–1). The link between habitus and 'field' is that practitioners inhabit fields and generally feel quite at home there. So at any given time, the habitus operates within a 'field' of practice or across a number of fields.

Particular practices or perceptions should be seen, not as the product of the habitus as such, but as the product of the relation between the habitus, on the one hand, and the specific social contexts or 'fields' within which individuals act, on the other.

(Thompson 1991: 14)

If the habitus is usually at home within its selected field(s) of practice, there are occasions when this is not the case. From the perspective of the habitus, some fields are just not considered appropriate. For example, we can see a contradiction between the working-class habitus and higher education field so that members of the working class are not naturally disposed to enter higher education, feeling that they do not 'belong' there.

Another important dimension of habitus in relation to fields is that different practices actually 'feel' different and operate their own mix of formalities and informalities, so that one has to become accustomed to particular styles of work in order to understand what is really happening in any one. Within post-compulsory education in general one gets a different sense of what is going on, say, between the sub-fields of continuing professional education, vocational education, community education, university adult education, etc. As a practitioner, one becomes habituated to one's own field of practice and others are sensed as strange, not conducting their affairs as 'we' are disposed to do.

In relation to these examples of habitus as either belonging or not belonging to a field, Bourdieu makes this comment:

> The sense of one's place, as the sense of what one can or cannot 'allow oneself', implies a tacit acceptance of one's position, a sense of limits ('that's not for us') or – what amounts to the same thing – a sense of distances, to be marked and maintained, respected, and expected of others.
>
> (Bourdieu 1991: 235)

So we can say that one of the ways in which practices are governed is by implicit and explicit demarcations between fields. For the individual practitioner, habitus is an 'internalised' and for the field of practice an 'incorporated' culture. Habitus thereby sustains practice without express regulation, through tradition as a mode of transmitting expectations, routine and tacit knowledge in maintaining them. Liberal adult education as a field of practice has a 'tradition', for example, and a particular orientation to practice within which its advocates have been concerned to mark out what is distinctive and worthy of protection.

The third controlling aspect of practice for Bourdieu is language, both in the way it works and is worked. Practices are picked up through language and any practice is taken to be the different ways that language is used therein. Practice fields are discursive communities. The habitus needs to be attuned to the ways that language is used by and uses its field members. It is a governing requirement of a practice to continually reproduce its accepted language forms. 'From a strictly linguistic point of view, anyone can say anything . . . but from a sociological point of view . . . it is clear that not anyone can assert anything' (ibid.: 74). We can see the operation of governmentality in relation to discursive allowances, i.e., of how we can talk about our practice and have it count. Language is symbolic capital and has a variable value. Changes in practice are signalled by changes in language. At the present time, managerial language in education is worth more within the general field than the language of a liberal tradition. One is less likely to find a discourse of empowerment in the vocational training field and more likely to find it within community education or among practitioners working with disadvantaged groups.

Using the 'right kind' of language gives a practice its affordances, i.e., the ability to act appropriately within a field. Any professional practice will operate a language of distinctions which are often fine-grained and important within the field, but unfathomable to those outside. There is a strong tendency for particular practices to be discursively introverted. Those who wish to reach out into other fields or to connect with another's habitus have to find the right kind of language to do so. Governmentality is at work in observing proprieties in language. We may think, for example, of the artfully restrained and frequently euphemistic language of officialdom. Learning any academic discipline, and becoming an accomplished practitioner thereof, is principally a matter of knowing how to use its language 'properly'. Since practice occurs in discursive fields, one needs as a condition of practice to observe the accepted forms within the field. If a habitus is not attuned to the field in which it finds itself, it cannot use and so authenticate the language therein. Rapid changes in the circumstances of practice can result in a mismatch between habitus and field. Many practitioners, particularly in adult education, feel at least uncomfortable and may perhaps be openly at odds with the new managerial language of education. Bourdieu's comment about habitus is relevant here. 'Habitus contributes to constituting the field as a meaningful world, a world endowed with sense and value, in which it is worth investing one's energy' (Bourdieu and Wacquant 1992: 74). Fields are structures of possibility for practice, in which only some possibilities will be realised through their authorisation in language. Between the theoretically possible stances of outrage and silence, it may be claimed that adult education has yet to find an appropriate language, consonant with the habitus of its practitioners, in which to authenticate the field.

INSTITUTIONS AND MISSIONS: A NEW CONFIGURATION OF PRACTICE?

In his examination of the evidence gathered from universities' recent mission statements and their reference to adult and continuing education, Duke (1992) provides us with examples of discursive practice at an institutional level. His study is an illustration of the ways in which a new language enters into the life of (higher) education institutions. The key question is: 'Does that language entail a transformation of practice?'

Duke's approach is to pose the question in another way: 'Have universities become learning organisations?'

Until recently, the relative exclusivity of British universities (the so-called 'elite' model) could be compared to the 'service' model of mass higher education more typical of North America. The former is still largely characterised by practices emphasising selection rather than access; the latter incorporates principles of recurrent education, continuing education and lifelong learning. These principles have been an important part of the discursive field of adult education for a long time, even in Britain, but had hitherto been advocated from outside the mainstream of universities, which saw their mission almost exclusively in terms of front-end under-graduate teaching and research. The power of a discourse depends on the extent to which it can command a field of practice. Within university edu-cation in general, adult education was literally 'extra-mural' and proud of that status. Duke speaks of extra-mural departments' isolation and psy-chological distance, making it 'harder to contribute to university debate about the priorities and mission of the university as a whole' (ibid.: 4), and further notes that 'the liberal adult education tradition . . . denied itself effective dialogue with the universities over any wider re-definition of university mission' (ibid.: 5). Its discourse was not part of the habitus of mainstream practice. Consequently, it has encountered problems within a broader field of practice, for example, in its attempts to extend access to non-traditional students. Duke provides evidence of departments' move away from their naming as 'extra-mural' or 'adult education' and towards 'continuing education' – from 60 per cent calling themselves the former to 60 per cent at least incorporating the latter term during the 1980s. Is this a notional change or does it signal a paradigm shift, a change in the actual constitution of practice? Do university mission state-ments now suggest that it could become so?

To answer this question, we need to consider the circumstances in which these statements have been made. The political environment in which insti-tutions have to act is complex and one which requires a careful reading by the institutions themselves. Practice intentions are constructed in the light of that reading in order that they can be realised through the receipt of necessary resources. Duke reviews the planning statements that universities provided to the government in their bids for funds from 1991 to 1995. The context of the planning statements and the construction of missions is that universities have been required to impose more extensive managerial con-trols, to establish approved procedures for research assessment, staff appraisal, quality audits, etc. and to monitor results. 'Missions' are care-fully crafted projections of practice intentions, providing evidence of what an institution thinks of itself and where it is going. They are authored and authorised with respect to two sets of circumstances. First, the state's belief that the function of the university is to meet society's needs as defined by the agencies of government (and in this belief there are strong echoes of a Durkheimian theme). Furthermore, the 'needs' themselves are defined unequivocally in terms of international market competitiveness. Second, the institution has to attend to the competition for recognition and resources between its constituent academic fields. We can see, then, that missions are constructed with both an inner and an outer eye.

Mission statements 'explain each institution's mission, purposes, strategies and intended means of working' (ibid.: 10). They set a framework for practice and are contrived in the context of seeking funds by finding the right kind of language. As Duke notes, the bidding process was an 'offer to contract' which could not really be refused and had to pass a rigorous test, set in the guise of the government as contractor offering extensive 'advice' to contractee institutions on how tenders should be submitted. He calls the advice given on how to prepare submissions 'rules for this important examination paper' (ibid.: 32) and an example of 'planning to order' (ibid.: 33). The guidance on submitting tenders was couched in terms of cost-effectiveness and accountability.

Institutions have learnt how to make the right noises to government and to pass the test with more or less success. They are still in business, partially reconfigured. At the same time, the voices within and between higher education institutions themselves have begun to change. Duke provides a table (ibid.: 16) to contrast 'old' and 'new' discourse in higher education with respect to values and purposes, and the practices of admissions, curriculum design and teaching, managing resources, measuring and evaluating outcomes. The new discourse of flexible entry, credit accumulation, experiential learning, etc. is rooted in principles of lifelong learning, continuing and recurrent education, and is now being reproduced in faculty reports, research bids, consultations, seminars and staff meetings. At the same time, this is happening within the contexts of an internal and external governmentality of efficiency, cost control, fitness for purpose and the value-added. Yet, the old discourse of selectivity and collegiality is extensively retained. Practices have yet to be 're-normalised' within a contradictory discursive arena. So, in answer to the question regarding whether a discourse about lifelong learning signals a change in institutions' practices, Duke answers 'only partially' and quotes from Knapper and Cropley:

> while lifelong learning is unlikely to produce immediate and radical change in conventional systems of higher education, it makes sense to be on the alert for examples of partial shifts in philosophy and practice that go some way towards fulfilling our goals for this new approach.
>
> (Knapper and Cropley 1985: 86)

The paradigm shift has started, but is not yet complete.

INDIVIDUALS AND PROFILES: GOVERNING THE SUBJECT

We have seen how educational institutions themselves are now governed through having to work within a new mentality of practice. In higher education, practices have yet to be so transformed that one could say that they have been 're-normalised' within a new paradigm. The traditional habitus of academic practice which values the autonomy of particular disciplinary expertise and academic freedom in general remains, and there are many contradictions between a) this habitus, b) the increasingly prescriptive examinability of institutions, and c) a move towards more learner-centred forms of assessment. Here, we consider an aspect of how subjects themselves are 'governed' through education in the name of learner-centredness by the use of the controlling technology of student profiles.

Foucault's power–knowledge nexus is evident in the disciplining of subjects (both teachers and students) through the employment of records of achievement. It is considered eminently reasonable that both teachers and their students should document their activities in order to generate a record which has a cash value, for example, in terms of gaining employment, promotion or progression to further study. In this context, profiling – i.e., registering achievements in the form of demonstrable competences – is theorised and practised as being 'progressive', as the auditing of the learning process to which it would be improper to object. Therein lies the power of a commonsensical discourse, since nobody wants to be thought of as being 'incompetent' (Edwards and Usher 1994).

In a study of the introduction of profiling within a community education centre, Thorpe (1993) looks at how teachers and students in selected vocational and non-vocational courses are persuaded into this practice. He notes that profiles have been theorised as follows:

> Student profiles are capable of giving much more information [i.e. than examination results] about the skills, knowledge and experiences obtained by the student.
>
> (Broadfoot 1986: 30)

> Profiles are able to draw on evidence as alternatives or additions to examination results, and can therefore reflect a wider range of achievements and experiences. A profile offers a fuller, more rounded picture of the individual.
>
> (Hitchcock 1986: 2)

There is a twofold impetus to profiling. In the absence of any published scheme relating to adult education, the idea of profiling builds on that of records of achievement in schools. As a centre manager, Thorpe has an important agenda – to satisfy the requirements of output-led funding by marshalling evidence of what students have accomplished in order to demonstrate the value of educational courses as a route to progression in further education or employment. Working with tutors who recognise the complications and vagaries of categorising student learning, he develops a system of computer-assisted profiling in which an item bank of competency statements is constructed. From their knowledge of the students' work in class, tutors then draw on these statements to produce a composite profile by matching items to what has been achieved by each student. Profiling is configured as a computer-assisted listing of acquired skills. It is justified as being a more extensive and less idiosyncratic assessment of capability.

We see in this example, which is now being widely reproduced in the name of efficiency and accountability (of centres to their funding agencies as well as of teachers to their students), a move 'to develop a system which offers teachers a "bank" of *standardised accounts* from which they may select in order to *form appropriate descriptions of students*' (Thorpe 1993: 70; emphasis added). It is an example of a discursive practice driven by the needs of technology – governmentality by means of normalisation through machine processing.

Thorpe found that the feelings of tutors in constructing profiles, and the reactions of students when they received them, were somewhat bemused. On the one hand, they appeared to appreciate an itemised accounting of what they (the students) could now do, but on the other hand there was a feeling that the whole exercise was rather contrived, as indeed was the case. This example illustrates the point made by Usher and Edwards that 'Power, through knowledge, brings forth "active" subjects who better "understand" their own subjectivity yet who in this very process subject themselves to forms of power' (Usher and Edwards 1994: 89).

The 'truth' of the profile is validated transpersonally, by means of the computer providing an apparently 'objective' output. It is 'powerful' in claiming to allow students to see for themselves what they can do through a supposedly objective and accurate record which enables them to monitor their own progress. The discourse of profiling and competence is mixed with a progressive discourse of recurrent education, and the profile is constructed to be accreditable when required. Profiling practices, and the subjects of profiles, are governed through a process of inscription in which the themes of behaviourism and learner-centredness are co-implicated, 'evoking the need for individuals to take more control over their learning in order that they can become competent members of the workforce. In an era of structural unemployment, this is a very powerful message' (ibid.: 111).

Although we would agree that information technology is a necessary feature of any modern, complex practice, this case nicely illustrates the double-edged and paradoxical nature of power/knowledge within the governmentality of practice. It may well empower teachers, learners and administrators to exercise more control over their work. At the same time, however, subjects and their identities are reconstructed and governed by the very means which promise liberation.

CONCLUSION

Postmodernism challenges the ways in which practices are represented. In this chapter we have looked at a number of aspects of how educational practices are governed at different levels – institutions, academic fields, individuals – by considering the constitutive effect of discourse on practice. Durkheim's sociology is typical of a modernist discourse which sees disciplines as supplying a necessary theoretical (and in his case moral) foundation for practice, but which is not reflexively alert to the constitutive effects of that discourse. Reality is the sociological truth that science reveals. Teachers are licensed by the state as embodiments of the sentiments of the collective conscience and are disciplined by a science which provides the 'truth' of what these sentiments are. There is no tension for Durkheim between practitioners being governed by the state on the one hand and science on the other. By rejecting any specific academic vantage-point, questioning the claims of science and a representational view of government, Foucault is able to interrogate the power of discipline in a wider sense to show how subjects govern themselves in the ways in which practices are discursively constructed and are, therefore, in principle, open to review. Via the notion of habitus and an analysis of the power of discourse in terms of its ability to command a field of practice, Bourdieu offers new insights as to why we are necessarily locked into routines and ways of talking about practice which are difficult to escape from. Duke's study exemplifies cases of 'examinability through mission', wherein institutions are rewarded in terms of resources by making the right kinds of confessions. Thorpe's establishment of computer profiling illustrates that governmentality operates in ways that are simultaneously disciplining and empowering but never neutral or objective.

Since we cannot abstain from talking and writing about practice in some way or another, it is necessary to be alert to the formative affects of language on practice. This includes the everyday and engaged ways in which we describe our affairs to fellow practitioners and others, and also when deliberately and less tacitly theorising about what we do. We have seen how in an important sense, practices are 'governed' by the ways in which they are described. Concepts such as 'discipline', 'governmentality', 'habitus' and 'field' are useful heuristics which, through their deployment in redescribing practice, can also assist in a counter-configuration of practice itself.

Chapter 4

Disciplines and disciplinarity
Knowledge and power

The debate over the proper place of disciplines in adult education is by now fairly well-trodden ground and any return to it can only be justified if a new and different perspective can be brought to bear. We would argue that such a perspective is urgently required as the practice of adult education evolves into a variety of forms, located in a multiplicity of sites and with a diversity of programmes, for example, those which emphasise competency-based and learner-centred approaches. These developments raise anew the place of disciplinary knowledge, whether such knowledge has a foundational place or, indeed, any place at all. In this chapter, we want to argue that for a rapidly changing practice such as that of contemporary adult education, disciplinary knowledge is problematic. However, we also want to suggest that it does not necessarily follow from this that disciplines can be forgotten or removed from the scene. Instead, what needs to be done is a reconsideration of their role and a reconfiguring of their place in the contemporary postmodern scene.

SUBSIDING FOUNDATIONS

The conventional argument about disciplines is that they constitute a knowledge 'base' or 'foundation' that supports a superstructure of practice. The ascription of foundational status to disciplinary knowledge is because of its universality, security and reliability. If we take medicine as an example, scientific disciplines such as anatomy and biochemistry are seen as having a foundational relationship to practice because they seem to provide descriptions and explanations which are secure, reliable and applicable to any situation and upon which it would seem eminently reasonable for practice to be based. In this sense, therefore, foundation disciplines provide the necessary 'theory' part of the theory–practice relationship, but do so at the cost of a radical separation between theory and practice.

The nature and place of disciplines is not an issue originating with or unique to adult learning or, indeed, to education generally. In his now classical formulation, Hirst (1974) drew a distinction between 'forms' of knowledge (equatable to disciplines) and 'fields' of knowledge constructed as integrated composites from the forms. Fields of knowledge are distinguishable in terms of their theoretical or practical orientation. Education is apparently such a field, drawing from the disciplines in a way appropriate to its practical orientation. In broad terms, the argument is that the disciplines tell us *the way the world is*. Education as a practical activity is primarily concerned with acting in rather than knowing the world, although in order to act, knowledge of the world – a knowledge provided by disciplines – is needed. Disciplines, it can be argued, have a foundational position in relation to essentially practical fields of knowledge such as education. The exemplar here is the foundational place of the natural sciences in relation to fields of knowledge with a practical orientation such as engineering or medicine.

In a field of knowledge the knowledge itself originates from outside the field in relevant foundation disciplines. These disciplines are, however, organised and integrated in a way appropriate to the nature of the field – in particular, according to its theoretical or practical orientation. In a practical field, for example, knowledge is geared to practical use and organised in terms of a perceived need for application. It is constituted by its disciplines and organised to facilitate the application of the knowledge contained in those disciplines. However, as Beckett (1995) points out, a practical field is constructed as being in a parasitic relationship to the host discipline(s). Through the mediation of a conversion mechanism, such as a set of principles or rules, disciplines are applied to substantive issues in the practical field but *not* in the terms constituted by the field – rather, the issues are constituted by the host disciplines.

At one level, education would seem to be a practical field of knowledge. Certainly, there has been a strong tendency both on the part of outsiders and of its own practitioners to see it this way, in particular to understand it as a practice based on the foundation disciplines of the social sciences. The problem is, however, that there has been a signal failure to show how these disciplines are appropriately integrated in relation to practice. Bright (1989) has argued that the attempt to configure adult education as field of knowledge in a Hirstian sense has failed miserably. It has proved impossible to build a theory which integrates the various disciplinary strands and which is also appropriate to a practical field. Instead, there has been a 'raiding' of disciplines in a piecemeal, unsystematic way, with doubly unfortunate consequences – on the one hand, a trivialising of adult education and on the other, a 'vandalising' of disciplinary knowledge. Without a means of integrating practice and disciplines, the very notion both of a *foundation* of practice and of a *disciplinary* foundation becomes problematic.

One could go even further and argue that from the perspective of the practice of adult learning to which disciplinary knowledge must relate, the very attempt to think in terms of a Hirstian field is bound to fail (Usher 1989). As we will argue in a later chapter, disciplinary knowledge cannot simply be 'mapped on' or applied to a field of practice. Schon (1983) has argued very strongly that seeing the relationship of theory to practice as one of application presupposes a technical-rationality model of practice. This model works with a particular conception of rationality, an instrumental means–end rationality which is assumed to be the 'natural' and universally appropriate way of linking thought (theory) with action (practice). In all fields of education there are few who would be happy with an unalloyed technical-rationality model. In this sense, we are all Schonians now! However, even the Schonian critique does not bring out all the problems of a foundationalist position.

As Cervero (1992) points out, to argue for theory as a foundation for practice is to privilege a notion of scientifically derived knowledge as not only different from but *better* than knowledge arising from practice. It is also to construct education as an applied science, dealing with objective facts and value-free, concerned only with how 'common-sense' practice can be improved through the application of scientific knowledge. There is a double failure here. First, a failure to recognise that a foundationalist discourse contains a political *epistemology* and second, a failure to recognise the political nature of any educational practice.

If we consider adult education as a field of study it is clear that if this is to comprise disciplinary knowledge, then this has to originate *outside* adult education as a field of practice. Disciplinary knowledge is the outcome of a particular kind of theoretical practice with its own paradigms, methodologies and rules of work. Adult psychology, for example, is not generated within the field of adult learning but within the discipline of psychology. Adult psychology or the psychology of adult learning answers to psychology as a 'science' or theoretical field. Of course, any body of knowledge constituted as a discipline whilst not necessarily recognising itself as a theoretical practice considers itself to be outside and independent of particular practices. As we noted earlier, one of the characteristics of disciplinary knowledge is its universality. A discipline therefore purports to speak authoritatively of all practices within its field of view. This is probably why the only relationship a foundation discipline can have with respect to a particular practice is one of hierarchical application.

There is also a problem with the disciplines which are usually selected as foundational. Let us return to psychology, given that it is the most influential candidate for the status of a foundation of educational practice, including the practice of adult education. Now, unlike the doctor and the engineer, it is difficult for us to argue that there is an equivalent and demonstrable relationship between the disciplinary knowledge of psychology (theory) and educational practice. In the case of engineers, for example, it is possible to say in broad terms that they apply theoretical knowledge to their practice, since this knowledge is both reasonably secure and relatively uncontentious as the operative paradigms, content and methodological procedures of the relevant disciplines command a large measure of consensual agreement. In this sense, it could be said that these disciplines are foundational, even though it is debatable whether they are used in a foundational way. Yet the same could not be said of psychology. For one thing, the descriptions and explanations which psychological knowledge provides of the world and the security of its claims to truth are problematic and contentious issues even within the discipline itself. Psychology is in any event not a unified discipline and many see this is as part of the problem. There are many 'psychologies', each with its own often different perspective and approach where the only point of commonality is that each claims to have access to the truth. There is always a question, therefore, as to which particular 'school' of psychology is more legitimate (scientific?) and therefore properly foundational. Given all this, it could be argued that psychology cannot be an appropriate foundation for any field of educational practice.

Related to this is a problem about the status and implications of psychology's descriptions and explanations of the world. Psychology understands itself to be in the business of discovering universal laws or empirical necessities about the world. However, even the most positivistically inclined would be hard pressed to quote a single instance of such a universal law discovered by psychology. Yet, because of this self-understanding, there is an emphasis on experimentation and generalisation. This is one of the reasons why psychology's knowledge is difficult to apply to a practical field. More significantly, psychology is left between a rock and a hard place in relation to educational practices. If psychology is describing empirical necessities, then there is little that educational practice could do in the face of these necessities other than perhaps to reinforce them. In this situation, however, it might be difficult to claim that such a practice was *educational*, given that education is about planned change. On the other hand, if these descriptions are not universal but culturally and contextually contingent, then they are no longer 'knowledge' in a scientifically recognised sense. It is precisely these contingencies that education is interested in, yet if knowledge of them is not 'scientific' then there are no grounds for claiming that this knowledge is 'foundational'. On the other hand, if psychology does not describe necessities, then there is nothing in psychology that need constrain education. This is unlike the situation in, for example, engineering, where it is unlikely that a bridge could be built whilst ignoring the 'laws' of physics. In this sense it could be argued that psychology cannot have the same status *vis-à-vis* education as physics might have to engineering.

It is, however, psychology's scientist self-understanding which is perhaps its most problematic aspect. The main criticism made of psychology is that, despite the many differences and variations, it is, as a discipline, located in a positivistic/empiricist paradigm which is not only naive and outmoded in relation to the natural sciences but has led to theories and methodologies which militate against their application to education. Psychology, whether behaviourist, cognitivist or psychodynamic, understands itself to be a science, yet as a mode of understanding it originates within particular socio-cultural contexts and is saturated by the values intrinsic to those contexts. These are the values of positivistic natural science, although psychology does not admit the historicity of its values. The result has been assumptions such as abstracted individualism, impersonal and objective procedures and a rejection of the interactivity of the individual and the social. All these however are characteristics of the West's scientised culture of modernity – a culture where certain dominant values are unacknowledged, indeed are reified as objective eternal truths. As a contributor to and vehicle of modernity, psychology denies both its own value commitments and its location in a particular culture.

One possible response to this critique would be that psychology *could* be foundational if it 'got its act together', for example, by becoming more reflexive or by changing its naively scientific self-understanding or becoming more unified as a discipline. However, to accept this position is to *appear* to be critical of psychology as a foundation whilst *implicitly* accepting the notion of a foundation and thus remaining trapped within a foundational discourse.

It might not be too unreasonable, therefore, to conclude that it would be difficult to imagine anything so unsuitable or inappropriate as psychology having a foundational role in *any* form of educational practice. From this, one could argue that the discourse of disciplines and disciplinary foundations is highly problematic and needs challenging. However, it does not necessarily follow that disciplines can simply be dispensed with (by an act of will or even by deploying a logically impeccable critique) simply because they appear to have no place in practical fields such as education. The key issue might be that they have a place, not because it is philosophically justified but because it is to do with the contemporary operation of power. In other words, the question of what the place might be still needs addressing, but it is a question which cannot be resolved simply through drawing on either a disengaged epistemological discourse of 'forms' and 'fields' or by a critique of the deficiencies of the technical-rationality model.

THE POWER OF PSYCHOLOGY/PSYCHOLOGY AS POWER

One critical factor that has to be taken into account is that psychology has undoubtedly been seen as appropriately applicable to education. After all, it would be hard to argue that educators have had psychology *imposed* on them as a foundation. Despite the critique outlined above, it still manages to retain a powerful hold on educational practitioners, policy-makers and 'theorists'. To explore this further we need to go back to Cervero's (1992) argument that epistemology is political and therefore recognise at the outset that psychology is more than just a body of knowledge. Disciplines do exert a powerful influence; it is precisely psychology's claim to know 'scientifically', a claim which despite the critique outlined above is still generally accepted, that continues to makes it powerful. Psychology's claim to scientific status has meant that its methods and subject-matter have been narrowly conceived, yet, in an important sense, it is precisely this narrowness which gives psychological knowledge its power. It helps to substantiate the claim to know the world 'as it really is' and hence provides a warrant to do things in the world in the name of that knowledge.

This obviously adds to the difficulty of critiquing foundational discourse in a way which would suggest an alternative and provide a purchase for practice. Furthermore, and not unrelated, we need to take account of the fact that psychology has become a technology of human behaviour, a body of knowledge that is also 'technically' exploitable and can be used both to regulate and change individuals and relationships. Although psychology to some extent does itself recognise this, it also believes that its purposes are benevolent and enlightening. We would argue, however, that this is itself problematic. Contemporary social critics such as Michel Foucault have questioned the equation of social progress with the growth of scientific knowledge (the more we know the better we will be) and the assumption that such knowledge is logically independent of the social conditions of its acquisition and communication (that, in effect, knowledge is independent of power).

Psychology cannot be taken simply 'at its own word', therefore. It is precisely psychology's 'power' of offering a more rational and efficient approach to organising the educational experience that has made psychology attractive to education. It is precisely this aspect of psychology as a human technology which requires close examination. As we have already noted, it is probably too simplistic to assess psychology purely as a body of abstract theoretical knowledge. Rather, it is best seen as centrally implicated in educational practices. Walkerdine (1995) has suggested that psychology is everywhere, that education, certainly in the form of schooling, and psychology have developed hand-in-hand. She argues that schools are not places where psychology has been *applied* but where certain truths about children are continually *produced*. The 'truths' of psychology provide the 'objective' basis for legitimising certain kinds of educational practice whilst at the same time these practices define the content of student behaviour. The behaviour is in effect the 'evidence' upon which teachers base their judgements and maintain their practice, a behaviour itself the product of a particular set of discursive practices to which the 'evidence' is relative. Ultimately, it is relative to the 'truths' about the nature of the child produced by psychological knowledge. These 'truths', therefore, can be seen not so much as objective descriptions of reality ('discoveries') but first, as constructs relative to a particular culture that embodies certain values and second, as a means of rendering subjects 'knowable' and hence open to intervention.

In the light of this it might not be unreasonable to suppose that disciplinary discourse has a powerful influence in the theorisation and practice of adult education. Disciplines have always played an important part in forming the boundaries of interpretive horizons, particularly in providing conceptual resources that 'in-form' both thinking and doing. Although it would be fair to say that disciplines are not regarded as occupying a place of exclusive importance, the disciplines of the humanities and social sciences are readily enough seen as having a foundational place. Here, we are not referring to foundations in any Hirstian sense but more significantly to *disciplinarity* as a discourse and strategy of governance where disciplinary knowledge is a vital, although perhaps not exclusive, component.

Disciplinarity refers, on the one hand, to systems of rationality where disciplinary knowledge functions to represent segments of the world as domains of thought. However, disciplinarity also involves 'technologies of governance' which function to translate thought (or knowledge) into domains of reality (Miller and Rose 1993). Through knowledge or systematic thought, an aspect of the world is 'domained' into being, made the object of thought, and becomes a 'reality' which can be talked about, systematised, theorised, researched and evaluated. In effect, an aspect of the world is knowledgeably discoursed into being. Once this is done, usually through inscription, subjects within that domain are made calculable and rendered into a site of intervention. Disciplinarity, therefore, describes the condition, as we noted in Chapter 3, where disciplinary knowledge and 'disciplined' action come together and provide strategies of governance.

What is involved here is an interactive process of *representation* and *action*. Foucault coined the term 'governmentality' (an elision of 'government' and 'rationality') to describe this process. Governmentality does not refer exclusively to the state and government as conventionally understood but rather to the calculated supervision, administration and maximisation of the forces, activities and relationships of the whole population. To put it simply, in modern society there is a need systematically to *know* people in order to maximise their productive capacities. Disciplinarity, the generation and deployment of systematic knowledge, is an effect of these wider processes of governmentality.

The place of psychology in any form of educational practice is therefore complex. For one thing, it cannot itself be understood from the level of practice alone. Part of the problem is that it too often is. Practitioners, for example, often feel very uneasy about directly applying disciplinary knowledge to practice. Here, of course, is where a discipline such as psychology (perhaps because of its methodological and content narrowness) appears, in terms of everyday practice, very obviously to fail as a foundation. Practitioners will ask the question 'What can psychology tell us that will help us to be more effective teachers (or curriculum organisers or managers or evaluators)?' Practitioners experience difficulty in seeing its usefulness in this sense because psychology invariably appears remotely 'theoretical'. Furthermore, it quickly becomes apparent when hard questions are asked of psychology that its 'scientific' findings seem to be merely restatements in abstract and quantitative language of the trivial and the blindingly obvious (Kvale 1992).

It would be an exaggeration to say that this is the way all psychology is perceived. Humanistic psychology, for example, has proved to be very attractive to practitioners. In adult education, it has become very much part of an influential andragogical discourse and many unconscious reference points and implicit frameworks of understanding are constituted by its language of person-centredness, self-directedness, empowerment, student-centred pedagogy and its equation of the educational experience, adult learning and self-development. Yet as Welton (1995) argues, andragogy, based on a 'scientific' psychology of adult learning, served to professionalise and scientise adult education. By foregrounding the professional adult educator, armed with scientific knowledge about how adults learn and an expert methodology about appropriate curricula, andragogy 'domained' the adult learner into being in a way which made adults into a site for professional intervention.

Cognitive psychology has also assumed increased contemporary importance, in line, no doubt, with the influence of the cognitive paradigm in psychology itself. In the theory and practice of adult learning, the cognitive paradigm provides an alternative to the maturational paradigm of irreversible cognitive decline. Its attractiveness lies in the optimistic message it conveys that 'ordinary' adults possess the capacity to learn regardless of age, that they are not simply empty vessels rapidly losing their intellectual powers as their brain cells self-destruct! However, what influence it has had may also lie in the way it seems to readily lend itself to an adaptationist strategy. It is only by trying to unravel the strategic elements in the relationship of psychology to educational practices that the place of disciplinarity can begin to be discerned.

Of course, it is very difficult to stop seeing disciplines as foundational, because one's understanding is enfolded in another aspect of disciplinarity, an implicit notion of disciplines as neutral bodies of knowledge that can be applied with enlightening and empowering effects ('knowledge is power'). Even whilst there is an acceptance that disciplines do not always succeed in their self-proclaimed aim of providing knowledge of the world 'as it really is', there is a tendency to see this as a contingent rather than a necessary failure. Furthermore, even whilst there is some scepticism about the scientism of social science disciplines such as psychology, there is a tendency to see them as disconnected from power and as having essentially benevolent effects (if something is true we assume that it is free from power since power is limiting, distorting and located in the realm of 'untruth').

We are captured by an implicit yet powerful image of disciplines as existing in a vacuum, in some kind of transcendental realm of 'theory'. This image is itself a product of our scientific-technological culture of modernity, a culture which, as we noted earlier, is woven into the technical-rationality model of practice. Psychology is heavily implicated in the technical-rationality model by the way it presents itself as a body of neutral 'power-less' knowledge, existing prior to and separate from particular practices. In other words, the 'power' of disciplines stems from them being seen purely as knowledge discourses, at one and the same time 'power-less' and yet empowering.

DISCIPLINARY POWER

The dominant liberal/humanist paradigm in education accustoms us to seeing knowledge as distinct from, indeed as counterposed to, power. As we have already noted, power tends to be seen as 'thing-like', as something that is *exercised*, and as such invariably equated with coercion, repression, distorted knowledge and falsehood. At the same time, knowledge becomes 'powerful' because as truth it seems to faithfully represent the world 'as it really is'. Truth is taken to be the means of liberating oneself and others from power ('the truth will make you free'). Power, therefore, comes to be seen as negative and oppressive, the source of coercion and illegitimate control, whose removal allows individuals to realise their inherent rationality, express themselves freely and realise themselves fully. This conception of power is a crucial feature of the grand narratives of modernity and it continues to provide many of the significations that shape our modern consciousness and practices.

This conception was challenged by Foucault, who argued that power and knowledge, rather than being counter-posed, are inseparable from one another. He argued that power is more like a network; in other words, power is not 'thing-like' but *relational*, it is not a top-down exercise of the powerful against the powerless but is implicitly present in every social transaction. Furthermore, power should not be seen in a negative way as prohibition and repression but rather as active and productive – power creates fields of possibility or, to put it more simply, makes things possible. Power, working correlatively with knowledge, 'brings forth' active subjects, individuals with knowable capacities who better understand their own subjectivity – 'the individual is also a reality fabricated by this specific technology of power that I have called "discipline" . . . power produces; it produces reality; it produces domains of objects and rituals of truth' (Foucault 1979: 194).

In other words, disciplines as systematic bodies of knowledge (representation), are also regulatory regimes of 'knowledgeable' practice (action) through which power is exercised. In order to be regulated, in order to be incorporated into governmentality, the individual has first to be constituted as an active subject. It is disciplinary knowledge which provides the criteria and methods for doing this. The individual, therefore, is both an object of power and an instrument through which power is exercised – 'power is employed and exercised through a net-like organisation . . . not only do individuals circulate between its threads; they are always in the position of simultaneously undergoing and exercising this power . . . individuals are the vehicles of power, not its points of application' (Foucault 1980: 98).

Foucault refers to power and knowledge as being correlative, always found together in 'regimes of truth', the knowledge practices and discourses through which power is manifested and exercised. Knowledge, therefore, does not so much represent the truth of what is but rather constructs what is taken to be true. Knowledge is effective through discourses which provide boundaries for what can be said and done, providing a means of differentiating the true from the false, the sayable from the unsayable.

Furthermore, power does not operate through coercion and repression. Indeed, to coerce and repress signals that power has failed and been replaced by force. Power operates instead through knowledgeable discourses and practices, which normalise, categorise, measure and generally regulate. Individuals are regulated and governance is secured through power/knowledge formations constituted by networks of discursive practices. Disciplinarity works its effects within fields of practice through power which is not so much in the *service* of truth but is itself seen *as* truth.

In a sense, all practices are 'knowledgeable' but only those which claim a necessary relationship with a discipline-validated truth are power/knowledge formations and thus regulatory in their impact. Disciplinary truth and regulatory disciplining power are co-implicated. The double meaning of 'discipline' is not simply a linguistic curiosity but has implications in the 'real'. Disciplinarity encompasses 'discipline' in the sense of regulatory power and 'discipline' in the sense of a body of knowledge. This 'discipline' in both its senses is manifest in the workings of the institutions of modern social formations, including education. Power/knowledge formations produce, in the form of constituted 'objects', subjects who are 'subject' to regulation. 'Discipline' or 'disciplining' becomes a technology of power. It operates 'where power reaches into the very grain of individuals, touches their bodies and inserts itself into their actions and attitudes, their discourses, learning processes and everyday lives' (ibid.: 39). Foucault identifies discipline as a body of knowledge with a system of social control – 'a body of knowledge is a system of social control to the extent that discipline (knowledge) makes discipline (social control) possible and vice versa' (Marshall 1989: 107).

A power/knowledge discourse regulates in two different yet related ways. As we have seen, it empowers by creating active subjects with certain capacities, but this process also disempowers by objectifying subjects. Here, knowledge is an aspect of regulatory power that operates, in the first instance, externally on subjects. At the same time regulation through self-knowledge takes the form of self-regulation. Again, at one level this creates empowered subjects; individuals who are empowered by learning and knowing more about themselves. However, at the same time, subjects are disempowered in the very process of self-empowerment, because this knowledge of self is also the condition of self-regulation. We shall say more about this in a moment.

Disciplinary power, the form of regulatory power found in a modern social formation such as education, functions through practices of observation, surveillance and examination – practices which render subjects 'knowable'. By becoming knowable they become sites of intervention. Through a process of itemisation (making calculable, categorising) and atomisation (dividing-off, differentiating) where 'disciplinary power . . . separates, analyses, differentiates, carries its procedures of decomposition to the point of necessary and sufficient single units' (Foucault 1979: 170), individuality and subjectivity are constructed through the very means of understanding and learning more about individuals, their propensities, capacities and behaviour. These are then *inscribed* in dossiers, files and records of various kinds. As the need to regulate increases, so too does the need to know more about individuals. Hence, the knowledge generated and the categories needed to classify this knowledge increase. Surveillance becomes ever more pervasive and intrusive yet without appearing to be oppressive. In education, this process can be seen in the increased scope and impact of profiling, assessment procedures and mechanisms of evaluation and appraisal. As Foucault (ibid.: 176) points out, 'a relation of surveillance, defined and regulated, is inscribed at the heart of the practice of teaching, not as an additional or adjacent part, but as a mechanism that is inherent to it and which increases its efficiency'.

Disciplines need, therefore, to be seen as integral parts of power/ knowledge formations and the discourses through which these formations are expressed and made manifest. It could be argued that psychology is an example of such a discourse (Henriques *et al.* 1984; Parker 1989). As we have seen, its claim to possess scientifically valid knowledge, its very scientificity, in so far as it is generally accepted, provides both a justification and the means for a variety of normalising and regulatory practices, including schooling and increasingly adult learning in its contemporary vocationalist and competence-based form. Power-knowledge discourses are powerful because they constitute the 'objects of which they speak' through their claim to know those objects truthfully.

As we have already argued, psychology does not, as it claims, discover the adult with ready-made, 'natural' characteristics. Instead, it is psychological 'knowledge' working with and through certain educational practices that constitutes adults as particular kinds of subjects, for example, as the self-actualising, self-directing subject of humanistic psychology or the adaptive, information-processing subject of cognitive psychology.

How are adults constituted as particular kinds of subject? When psychology worked through a biological maturational paradigm, the adult was constituted in terms of irreversible cognitive decline. Nowadays, this paradigm is regarded as plainly false, although only from the viewpoint of an alternative, cognitivist paradigm through which adults are constituted and 'seen' differently. We should not forget, first, that the maturational paradigm was respected and accepted in psychology for a long time and second, that it was part of a network of practices in psychology, education and the wider society which privileged the education of children and formal schooling and consequently marginalised adults by appearing to show 'scientifically' that their capacity to learn was limited by ageing and its associated neuro-physiological changes. These practices were enmeshed within a political rationale where any regulation deemed necessary was thought to be achievable in sites and through practices outside of the educational. Hence, no powerful motive existed for making educational opportunities available to adults or for elevating the status of adult education.

Now, however, a different situation prevails where education of all kinds is considered too important to be left 'untouched' and unregulated. Educational sites are regulated through discursive and material practices, within which psychology plays a vital part. Adult education has now become such a site where the identity of adults can be 'formed' in terms of certain attitudes, skills and competences perceived as functional to the 'needs' of the socio-economic situation.

It is important to emphasise that what is being referred to here is not a process of overt imposition. Rather, it is through the way adults are 're-constituted' by new psychological paradigms that educational sites become sites of formation and regulation. We note that, where previously psychology, under the influence of the maturational paradigm, barely recognised the adult and adult education was considered barely a proper educational site, both have now been accorded significance and 're-cognised' as fit objects of the disciplinary gaze and fit sites for intervention.

The argument, then, is that 're-cognition' and intervention, or to put it another way, theory and practice, are always inseparably linked. Yet there is a paradox here: at the same time as the power of psychological paradigms to constitute adults within a domain of intervention becomes more heightened, the contemporary practices of educational intervention do not simply increase access to learning opportunities but also more significantly function to downgrade the very notion of learning as an initiation into 'worthwhile' disciplinary knowledge. Increasingly, adult learning is equated with 'training', moreover a training defined as the acquisition of pre-defined skills and competences and the development of certain kinds of attitudes defined in relation to the current 'needs' of the economy. This is part of a discourse which presents an analysis of the contemporary where what is foregrounded is socio-economic change, the impact of new technology, the changing nature of employment and the need for national economic competitiveness. Contingent changes are presented as inexorable facts that entail the need for constant change and adaptation on the part of individual adults. The cognitive paradigm is all about individuals interacting with their environment, processing environmental inputs and learning through changing their cognitive structures. The 'environment', on the other hand, is cast as pre-given and as something to which individuals have no choice but to adapt. Adults are therefore 're-constituted' and 're-cognised' with precisely those 'natural' cognitive capacities and characteristics 'needed' for 'lifelong' change and adaptation. It is very noticeable, for example, that the contemporary discourse of competence which emphasises the need for people to adapt to new technology and new work patterns reconstructs a technology of power within the education and training system as part of wider changes in the social formation and does so in ways which construct individuals as solely responsible for their own position in the labour market and their contribution to it. This is a clear case of discursive practices which function to create active, i.e., 'competent' subjects who are yet at the same time 'objectified' and subjected to the regulatory gaze through the very means by which they become active subjects.

We can trace a coming together of what is apparently a pure knowledge discourse (psychology) with certain kinds of contemporary social and educational practices. What is at work here is not a unidirectional causality but rather a dynamic of mutual implication between discourse and practices, linked by power/knowledge, that 'normalises' and regulates adults in the very process of empowering them. This indicates that a discipline such as psychology is not so much powerful because it represses but because it forms a crucial component of a discourse that has the power to 'name' and by naming, to normalise. To constitute the adult in a particular way is to name, or bring into view and define, the 'normal' adult in terms of certain 'scientifically' validated capacities, attitudes and ways of behaving. In this way, a norm of the adult as an adaptive and adaptable lifelong learner is created and sustained.

A norm works by excluding; by defining a standard and criteria of judgement it identifies all those who do not meet the standard. A norm, therefore, both homogenises and individualises. It provides a picture of what an individual is 'good at' and correspondingly where s/he is lacking or deficient. People become subjects by being classified in terms of their capacity to meet norm(s). In effect, they become their normalised capacities and through their capacities or lack of them become fit objects of surveillance and regulation. Normalisation is not a neutral process but its significance and impact lies precisely in the fact that it appears to be neutral. The seeming 'objectivity' of a norm makes normalisation appear to be simply a neutral procedure for scientifically ascertaining people's inherent 'natural' capacities. Normalisation, therefore, is a manifestation of a 'power-less' power, apparently the mere *application* of disciplinary knowledge.

Educational practices both help to create and themselves work through constructed norms. Thus, they are not simply the consequence of the application of norms but, more importantly, the vital means whereby a norm is concretised and 'substantiated'. It is through normalising practices such as the educational that constituted 'objects' are made 'real'. Adults as 'lifelong learners' rather than existing in their own right or 'in reality' are, therefore, perhaps more usefully understood as the constituted effects or 'objects' of contemporary *discursive* practices of normalisation.

The important consequence of this is that adults can become a site for regulation but without this being recognised. As Foucault (1974: 49) points out, discourses in constituting objects 'conceal their own invention', making these objects appear to be discovered rather than constructed. At the same time, discourses conceal their own assumed values by cloaking them in the guise of facts, inevitabilities, common-sense reality and above all 'truth'.

Power/knowledge discourses have two main characteristics; first, because they speak 'knowledgeably', only their empowering effects are visible, and second, they are always seen as being about truth rather than power. As discourses or regimes of truth they are always understood as having empowering effects. Foucault argues that power/knowledge discourses always appear to be discourses of knowledge and truth, with a power only over thought and the mind – the power to 'enlighten' and thus to empower. But more important is their effectiveness in normalising and regulating bodies and subjectivities without seeming to do so. Power/ knowledge discourses are therefore *material* in the sense that they are not merely ideas (or theory) but intertwined with practices which have concrete, 'real' effects.

COMPETENCES AND CONFESSION

As we have seen earlier, Foucault stresses that power is as much productive as repressive. He reminds us that it is most effective when it is productive, when it 'creates' active, knowing subjects. Education, for example, has always been a site for the creation of 'power-ful' subjects, although it does so by also creating a mass of 'power-less' subjects. It is possible to argue that contemporary adult education is now taking its place alongside schooling as such a site. By becoming a site for the production of subjects it acquires the means to put itself 'on the map' in terms of status and resources. Furthermore, with recognition of adult education as a field of study and research, with the legitimation of its knowledge, those who practice within it as researchers, theory-builders and field practitioners can themselves become 'power-ful' subjects whose 'voice' is listened to.

In adult education as a field of study and a field of practice, 'empowerment' is both a crucial and sensitive issue. At one level, it is difficult and very often appears mean-spirited to be critical about empowerment. Even if we are sceptical about, for example, the value of a learning defined in terms of the acquisition of pre-defined competences or adaptation to a pre-given environment, it is difficult on the face of it to deny that to become competent or more adaptable is to become more empowered. Equally, it is difficult to quarrel with practitioners being themselves empowered if this means that they are more knowledgeable and more efficacious in helping adults acquire the skills and knowledge which their environment demands of them.

What seems to be more significant and problematic is the part played by disciplines in 'subjectifying' adults, that is, in making them into active, knowing subjects. Traditionally, this has been a primary concern for adult education, since to be an active knowing subject is to be able to speak with authority, to speak for oneself and to have one's voice recognised as authoritative. In its more radical guises, adult education complained that for too long the educational system at all levels functioned to deny rather than to give people such a voice. Adult education's emphasis on empowerment through self-improvement was part of a mission that sought to reverse this. But, as we have already argued, the deployment of disciplinary knowledge, through its co-implication with power, was also the means whereby adults were more effectively regulated, ironically by becoming the objects of knowledge and research. It was through this process that the possibility arose of adults becoming more effectively subjectified, of becoming subjects that were also 'objects' to be *spoken of*.

There is a complex process at work here. We have been using language, borrowed from Foucault, of 'subject', 'discipline', 'empowerment' – a language, as we have noted already, with a deliberate ambiguity of meaning that highlights the co-implication and entanglement of power with control. The point about these terms is that they have, simultaneously, an active and a passive sense, the sense of being a subject and of being subjected, of a body of systematic knowledge and of a system of regulation and control, of being authorised and of knowing and affirming oneself. But this is not just a matter of language *per se* but of discursive practices. Practitioners in the contemporary conjuncture find themselves at the very centre of these ambiguities and forced to act within them.

These ambiguities are exploited in what Foucault (1988: 14) calls 'technologies of the self', where people can 'effect by their own means or with the help of others a number of operations on their own bodies and souls, thoughts, conduct and ways of being, so as to transform themselves'. To illustrate this we will examine two contemporary practices which in earlier chapters have been referred to as vocational and confessional practices, respectively.

First, within vocational practices we can identify competency-based education and training as the focus of heated debate. Most of this debate mainly concerns whether or not it works, or whether it bears up to a critical philosophical scrutiny in terms of the aims and purposes of education. Drawing on Foucault, it is however possible to see competences in another light, as an element in a contemporary discursive practice which works to regulate and shape through self-regulation; in other words, a discourse that is part of a strategy of governance that both mobilises capacities and produces consent without overt oppression.

There is a significant aspect of this discourse which is often overlooked or, in our view, too narrowly interpreted. Whilst much has been made of competences as an aspect of an instrumentalist and marketistic discourse appropriate for training but not for education, the presence within that discourse of an emphasis on learner-centredness, on non-educational sites as sites of learning, on negotiation of individual learning programmes, has either been read literally or as an ideological appropriation of progressive educational ideals which merely serves to mystify the regressive narrowness and vocationalism of competences.

However, it could be argued that it is precisely through its articulation with liberal/humanist notions of education that this discourse becomes powerful. It is the means by which 'active' subjects are created, motivated subjects seeking to maximise their capacities through the competency system. At the same time, it becomes the means by which a 'humane' power can be deployed where people become 'individuals' responsible for their own market position. As we have noted in earlier chapters, a vocationalist discourse reconstructs a technology of power within adult education and training as part of wider social changes, such as the reconfiguration of capital through flexible accumulation, the moves towards post-Fordist organisations of work and the increased significance of markets and their 'logics'.

The idea of competence to perform a work-role inevitably involves a form of discipline. Educational practices have increasingly become part of a disciplinary framework in modern social formations where people are measured, defined and regulated – made into calculable selves through the processes of itemisation, atomisation, inscription and normalisation we described earlier. The learner's performance is inscribed as competent (or not) and incorporated into a network which documents and charts their progress through various elements, units and levels. The process of continuous assessment, of credit accumulation, constitutes a continuously expanding surveillance of the learner and a continuous disciplining through the goal of competent performance at every stage of the process (Edwards and Usher 1994).

In this process, goals and performance criteria appear simply as objective forms of assessment from which the exercise of power is drained. Their empowering potential lies precisely in their public availability to learners. Learners can attain these goals in their own time and at their own pace. They are not 'kept in their place' through the mystifying and elitist practices of education – indeed, they can achieve the goals in the workplace without even setting foot in an educational institution.

A competence-based system, therefore, cannot be crudely behaviouristic; if it is to function as a modern form of discipline it has to be humanistic as well. Furthermore, both the humanistic and behaviouristic dimensions refer not simply to a vague set of ideas but to specific bodies of psychological knowledge which are an integral part of a competence-based system. Both kinds of psychological knowledge, the behaviouristic and the humanistic, are necessary. Learner-centredness is part of the rationale, evoking the need for individuals to be active, to take responsibility for their own learning in order to become 'competent', to 'own' what they learn and do and to show what they know through behavioural outcomes. In the contemporary economic situation, this is a powerful message. But, in operating within this hybrid yet knowledgeable discourse, learners also become subjects of their own surveillance, sitting in judgement upon themselves, defined through their behaviourally framed competences, disciplined through self-discipline. In the post-Fordist market economy of flatter management structures and more 'human' and self-imposed practices of resource management, a different kind of person, a different subject position, is required – the individual with *agency*, flexible, motivated, with a disposition for change, 'un-ideological', asocial yet respectful of the social order.

Second, confessional practices – here, people are not so much regulated through 'objectifying' power/knowledge discourses but regulate themselves through 'subjectifying' discourses where what is emphasised is the need to talk about and know oneself. This 'talk', where the autonomous self becomes the normative centre of attention and the focus of activity, becomes the means of empowerment. Rose (1990: 115) refers to this as 'living one's life according to a norm of autonomy'.

Foucault developed his concept of 'confession' through his work on modern sexuality. Sexuality in the nineteenth century, far from being repressed, was continually written and talked about. The new discourses of sexuality worked to 'bring forth' the body as an object of knowledge and to regulate rather than repress sexuality. Most important, however, was the idea that talking about sexuality was itself empowering. Freudian psychoanalysis (the talking cure), as a body of knowledge, was a major, although not exclusive, influence in this developing discourse.

The emphasis on 'talk' became part of a confessional discourse centred on the assumption (promulgated by all brands of psychodynamic psychology) that there is a deep truth or hidden meaning within people which, once found, opens the door to personal autonomy, psychic stability and happiness, or at least some degree of well-being (for example, Freud located this 'truth' in the unconscious, Rogers in the 'organismic self'). Foucault argues that confession is so deeply ingrained that we never see it as an effect of power, as a constraint – on the contrary, when it fails to surface we see that as a constraint, as the effect of power.

The contemporary scene is characterised by a number of different forms of confessional practice. One of these is adult guidance and counselling. Again, we can ask what function does guidance and counselling, as a discursive practice, perform. Conventionally, we see guidance and counselling not only as a means of making the education system more efficient by matching learners' needs with provision and jobs but also as a more 'human', democratic and empowering element in the education process. The argument is that the more people are given the opportunity to understand the choices available to them and to make their own more 'authentic' choices, i.e., the more power is given to the learner, then the greater the degree of personal development and self-realisation possible from the educational experience.

It could be argued, however, following Foucault, that guidance and counselling constitute subjects as individuals whose needs can only be articulated through this process. As we have seen, confession works on the basis that there is something to be confessed, a deep truth hidden within subjects which, once discovered, leads to empowerment. Guidance and counselling are forms of confession where the meanings ascribed to self are *already* effects of power – in other words, people need to have already accepted and be located in the appropriate discourse, they have already accepted the legitimacy and truth of confession and the meanings this evokes (Usher and Edwards 1995). Thus, although guidance and counselling helps people make 'realistic' decisions, they must realign their subjectivity within the appropriate psychological and educational decisions in order to make such decisions. It is in the very process of confessing that people are constituted as 'active' subjects yet at the same time are enfolded in power as they become subject to confessional discourses and therefore sites for intervention.

People become constructed through knowledgeable or 'expert' discursive practices, particularly those of psychology. Rose (1994) suggests that we need to rethink the role of psychology. It has been criticised for its individualistic thrust and for helping to bring about a passive social adaptation. Yet psychology has also played a significant part in shaping conceptions of the self, for example, in its representation of the actualising self. The self has been 'domained' into being through discourse or particular ways of speaking about and acting upon subjectivity. In this way, psychology has rendered subjectivity into thought as a calculable and shapeable force. Rose goes on to point out that this is not the consequence of a planned programme or of collusion between experts and the state. Rather, psychology has been effective because it works *indirectly*. Precisely, because it is a *discipline*, it is, as it were, 'distanced' from the action (or particular practices) and in this way it is better able to provide the persuasive truths, alternative images (for example, the 'active and actualising self') and facilitative techniques which reconstruct and realign subjectivity.

We believe it to be of significance that the discursive practices which are currently shaping adult learning constitute adults in such a way as to make them amenable to these technologies of the self. Being an active meaning-giving subject, having knowledge about self and valuing this knowledge as a source of learning, affirming oneself in order to fulfil one's potential – all these are the ascribed characteristics of the active adult as lifelong learner. Adults, then, are being constituted as self-constructing subjects that must talk about themselves and their experience. This self-knowledge becomes the basis of all other knowledge. From this follows a pedagogical emphasis on 'learner-centred' practice, learning based on experience, and learning experientially through negotiated curricula and activity-centred methods, all of which are seen as encouraging autonomy and empowerment.

Thus, the technologies of the self are designed to empower through self-knowledge. Yet, they too are discursive practices and being subjectifying rather than objectifying discourses does not make them immune from the operations of power. They too can feature in the service of regulation and control. In a sense, we position and regulate ourselves more effectively through these subjectifying discourses. We become active knowing subjects but now we subjectify ourselves rather than being subjected by others. We think we have mastered the power that imposes itself from 'outside' only to find that it is now 'inside'. We think we have abolished the power that limits our potential only to find that the power we now have is empty of content. We have the power, indeed the obligation, to exercise our 'freedom', but we are not thereby empowered to effect our social and political environment. We must actively choose to adapt but we cannot choose that to which we adapt. Yet, rather than feeling regulated, we feel we have found an empowering 'truth' because we have the power to talk about our subjectivity and to conceive of ourselves as active and adaptable.

Through self-inspection, self-problematisation, self-monitoring, in other words, through confessional practices, people evaluate themselves according to criteria provided by others. Knowing is also being known. In making their own subjectivity the focal point of their lives people feel they are living authentically and autonomously. Rose (1994) argues that this produces an alignment between political, economic and social goals and individual desires and self-fulfilment. He refers to this as a process where the soul of the citizen enters into the sphere of government. Finding out the truth about oneself becomes personally and economically desirable. As Miller and Rose (1993: 102) point out 'individuals themselves can be mobilised in alliance with political objectives in order to deliver economic growth, successful enterprise and optimum personal happiness'.

Thus, the most effective forms of power are those which are not recognised as powerful but as enabling or 'em-powering'. These forms of power are cloaked in the 'objective' knowledge of expertise and the humanistic discourse of helping and facilitating. Discipline assumes the form of pastoral power which has become particularly influential in adult education, embodied in a wide range of practices such as guidance and counselling, action-planning, recognising prior learning, portfolio-based assessment, learning contracts, records of achievement and self-evaluation.

In both vocational and confessional practices, there is a process of individualisation taking place. At one level, this provides the grounds for a greater sense of personal responsibility and the condition for the recognition and development of personal capacities – in other words, for a constitution of the active subject. Following Foucault, we can argue, however, that this is also a process where new forms of identity are shaped, for example, an identity which displaces more social, communitarian sensibilities, which brings the 'inside' of people into the power/knowledge domains. It is not therefore *without* power but a reconfiguration of the way power is exercised.

THE PLACE OF DISCIPLINES

A clear conclusion that emerges is that disciplines, because they are implicated in power/knowledge discourses, cannot be separated, either epistemologically or ontologically, from educational or indeed from wider social practices. This is why a philosophical critique of foundationalism, despite its seeming plausibility, ultimately gets us nowhere. The 'problem' of foundationalism in general and of the foundation of any particular practice in disciplines cannot simply be made to disappear through presenting a superordinate truth derived from philosophical analysis. As we have seen, this is because disciplinarity is always *already* present in educational practices. There is no ground which can be occupied which is not already implicated with, if not captured by it. Hence, the technical-rational position where disciplinary knowledge (theory) is *applied* to practice is clearly problematic. In terms of our discussion, it is clear that what is problematic is its separation of theory from practice and projection of political neutrality. Equally problematic, however, is the traditional counter-position of rejecting 'theory' and returning to unalloyed practice or experience. Here too, there is a failure to consider the working of disciplinarity and thus what might appear appealing or even liberating actually serves only to mask the workings of power and regulation more effectively.

To appreciate this fully we need to draw upon conceptual resources outside those provided by the mainstream adult education literature. Our drawing upon Foucault for this purpose has helped foreground the place of power. Foucault's subtle conception of power highlights its *relational* rather than hierarchical characteristic. For Foucault, power is a way of acting upon subjects by virtue of their being active subjects, i.e., by their being capable of action. Power does not stand over and against subjects, therefore, since it has no existence outside or above active subjects – where there are active subjects, there is power. Subjects are empowered and disempowered – simultaneously. Disciplinarity that combines discipline (knowledge) and discipline (social regulation) is a key feature of this process.

Consequently, the notion that theory and practice can be separated because each is located in its own separate domain can now be seen as unsustainable. We can now perhaps more readily see that disciplinary knowledge (theory) is not a disembodied form but is itself inseparable from particular practices such as the vocational and the confessional. Adult education as a field of study cannot therefore 'draw from' disciplines in any Hirstian sense, not because disciplines are inadequate or because no integrating theory can be found but because it is already 'in' disciplinarity, if not 'in' disciplines. Thus, what is involved here is not so much *application* but what might be more accurately termed *implication*. Psychology, for example, in all its varieties, is both implied by and implicated in educational 'theory' and educational practices. In relation to adult education, therefore, the question is not so much whether disciplines have or should have a place, because that question has already been answered once adult education understands itself as a field of study and once its regulatory potential becomes apparent.

As 'adult education' with its institutionalised connotations evolves into 'adult learning', as adult learning moves from the wings more to centre stage, so its content changes. As we have pointed out, it is no longer a matter of initiation into 'worthwhile', disciplinary knowledge. The Hirstian notion of disciplines, linked as it was to a valorisation of 'liberal' education and individualistic personal development, is just too problematic to be sustainable. We can no longer believe in canonistic texts, enlightened pedagogues, disembodied subjects and disembedded 'rational' enquiry.

As higher education moves slowly but perceptibly from an elite to a mass system of higher education, with increased emphasis on adult students as one of the vehicles of this change, the worthwhileness of the knowledge-centred curriculum, the curriculum based on the study and mastery of disciplines, is increasingly brought into question and gradually downgraded. Instead, as we have noted, we have the competence-based curriculum or the learner-centred curriculum, or a combination of the two.

All this makes it that much more urgent to rethink the place of disciplines. We have examined how disciplines can be oppressive through their implication in power/knowledge formations, systems of regulation and disciplinarity generally. But, as we have seen, there are also empowering elements in modern regulatory systems. The creation of active subjects cannot be dismissed as mere illusion or false consciousness. To put it very simply, the mastery of psychology, for example, means at the very least that one is not unquestioningly mastered by it, or at least that a space for resistance potentially exists. At a time when there is a move to extend educational opportunities to those hitherto excluded, it is noticeable that there is also a simultaneous move to downgrade disciplinary study. Whilst this is understandable, and indeed, in certain cases desirable, it is itself problematic since it could work to remove one of the means by which learners can be empowered. The emphasis on learner-centred curricula, on negotiation and even competence-based curricula is an attempt to counter the oppression of the knowledge- or discipline-based curriculum and to remove from teachers, as purveyors of this kind of curriculum, control over the learning process. Yet, there is a clear danger that the emphasis on experience and process leaves empowerment empty of the empowering content which disciplinary study can provide. In an earlier chapter we referred to Burbules' characterisation of the postmodern attitude as one of incredulity towards grand narratives and overarching beliefs, an incredulity which comprised not rejection but scepticism and lack of faith towards things which we none the less still recognise as desirable in certain respects and which, despite all our doubts, we can barely conceive of ourselves doing without. This may well be the only position we can appropriately adopt towards the place of disciplines.

It may well be that the problem lies not so much in disciplines *per se* but with disciplinarity, although it is obviously difficult to make such a separation. At the very least, it is important that certain distinctions are made. For one thing, it is possible to reject a foundationalist epistemological grounding in disciplines without at the same time rejecting disciplinary knowledge *tout court*. As we have noted, mastering disciplinary knowledge, knowing how the world is known, is an aspect of becoming a 'power-ful' subject with access to alternative and oppositional discourses. Precisely because disciplines are 'other' to personal experience, they can be the means for positioning oneself in an alternative discourse through which 'voice' is found and people are enabled to speak for themselves. As we have argued, there is nothing essentially 'authentic' about expertise or experience. This repositioning is a precondition for any resistance or interruption of the regulatory practices of contemporary discipline(s). Furthermore, there is no necessary reason why disciplinary knowledge should be learnt in a meaningless and didactic way, or by a process that does not value or respect the learner both cognitively and morally, or through a problem- and issue-centred curriculum. A critical attitude towards disciplines, a questioning of their absolutist and universalist claims is, we would argue, perfectly compatible with a stance that seeks to master those claims. The study and practice of adult education, adult education as 'theory', is unavoidably 'in' disciplines but not in an epistemological, foundational sense. As we have seen, this has both advantages and disadvantages.

The clear implication that emerges from 'deconstructing' the effects of disciplinary power is the need for a body of knowledge *relevant* to adult education. In other work (Usher and Bryant 1989; Usher 1991) we have argued that adult education should not be located in disciplines such as psychology but in its own critical field of practice. As noted earlier, it is the field, not the discipline, which should frame the issues. Doing this ensures that the field of study is 'in' but not 'of' disciplines, informed but not 'in-formed' by them. This implies a certain critical posture towards disciplinary knowledge. We need to question epistemological foundationalism, the naturalistic claims of the technical-rationality model and its instrumental consequences. By treating it as a *strategy* rather than a given, we can begin to recognise domains of knowledge other than the disciplinary. By questioning the universalising and transcendental claims of disciplinary knowledge we can subject it to the kind of power/knowledge critique outlined above. By adopting a critical posture, we can provide ourselves with the conceptual resources to develop our own discourse, a discourse which would ensure that disciplines have a place but one which is not that of mastery. This is the only way that adult education, both as a field of practice and as a critical study of that practice, can hope to build its own research agenda.

The acceptable place of disciplines is therefore as knowledge discourses rather than power/knowledge discourses. One way in which this can be ensured is by focusing very clearly on developing *adult learning* as a critical field of practice. This requires a performative awareness that the practice of adult education is not in the business of constituting adults as 'disciplined' subjects, adults who are adapted to certain kinds of social structures and economic arrangements – even if these are cloaked in humanistic and learner-centred language. But, perhaps more important, this involves resisting the normative pressure of what appears to be value-neutral knowledge. We need to argue that empowerment has to be open-ended and untotalisable and that where it is not it becomes control-through-empowerment.

Second, and arising from this, there is a need to be reflexive, to look at ourselves and our practices with a critical eye in order not to unwittingly become enmeshed in power/knowledge discourses. Once a segment of the life-world becomes delineated as a domain of study, it is 'knowledged' into being and becomes subject to 'discipline'. This has implications for the role and status of research into adult learning, as we shall see in a later chapter. If the knowledge outcomes of research are increasingly implicated with power, then there is a need to exercise care about the unspoken assumptions that inform the content and direction of research. Certainly, our preconception that research uncovers the 'truth' and by so doing always allows us to act more effectively and with empowering consequences needs to be seriously questioned.

This is not to suggest that all research will be 'tainted', shaky in conception and with suspect outcomes. But it is important to recognise that there is a *politics* of research which cannot be ignored. By 'politics', however, we are not referring to the possibility of an unscrupulous use of research to further narrow political ends. Such research is anyhow rarely 'powerful', since it so clearly fails the test of scientificity and disinterestedness and therefore fails to gain the accolade of truth. Recalling the point made earlier, it is not sufficiently distanced to be effective. Research is 'powerful' when it passes this test with flying colours, where it is, as it were, *strongest* as research – and in this sense, distanced from practice. The implication of research as a knowledge-generating process within a nexus of 'disciplinary' power is much more subtle and ambiguous (Woolgar 1988; Steier 1991). At the very least, we need to develop a critical awareness of the discourses by which we are traversed and a critical understanding of the effects and implications of research and knowledge-building.

In Usher and Bryant (1989) a case was argued for a knowledge practice with curricular implications which we termed *review*. This again is a term that deliberately trades on an ambiguity of meaning in suggesting a process both of looking back at ('re-view') and critically examining (review) practice-based knowledge with the aid of disciplinary knowledge. This process of 'review' involves recognising and valuing practice as a realm of knowledge in its own right but at the same time confronting and questioning it. Practice-based knowledge is local and contextual knowledge, an essential component of the judgement and understanding needed to act rightly and appropriately in the contexts of practice. Disciplinary knowledge, on the other hand, purports, as we have seen, to be a universal and decontextualised knowledge of the world 'as it really is'. The process of 'review' contains no assumption that formal theory is a standard of veracity. Rather, the emphasis is on contextualising it in order to bring out its constructed quality and its location in discursive paradigms which create 'worlds' to be discovered. In this way, it becomes possible to see that at one level disciplines are 'yet another story' (Rorty 1989), albeit a powerful story, which elevates the universal and the abstract by privileging certain kinds of theoretical practice and those sites where such practices are located. Disciplinary knowledge, therefore, needs to be seen not as a standard or a foundation but as a sounding-board, a resource for critiquing practice-based knowledge and for exposing its limitations. 'Review' provides resources that allow the 'terrain' of practice to be seen more critically and facilitates location in alternative discourses for 'seeing' and acting differently within that practice.

Of course, we want to encourage research, theory-building and the development of knowledge about adults. We want as many people as possible to be 'power-ful' subjects. But although it is vital that we should know more about adults as part of the practice of adult education, it is important to ensure that we do not end up 'disciplining' those whom we seek to empower in a totalising desire to know. Historically, adult education has made a contribution to replacing premodern coercion and subjugation. But adult education now finds itself increasingly enmeshed in governmentality – the rationalities and technologies for producing consent. Power has become enmeshed with surveillance (seeing without being seen) and regulation, either panoptically or through the interiorisation of the gaze. We have seen how this works in two contemporary social practices. Clearly, adult educators are faced with disturbing problems and dilemmas which neither radical gestures nor philosophical analysis will help in resolving. No matter how emancipatory or serious our intent, we are never outside power.

Chapter 5

Reconfiguring the 'other'
Self and experience in adult learning

THE SELF IN ADULT EDUCATION'S TRADITIONS OF LEARNING

What conception of the self does adult education operate with? Adult education involves processes in which particular kinds of learners (adults) engage in activities leading to desirable kinds of change. Thus, the very notion of adult learning as a process where desirable changes are brought about is itself dependent upon particular yet very often taken-for-granted conceptions of the self. There are, however, clear if largely implied assumptions about the nature of the self in the way in which adult learning is typically conceived. The best way of showing this is by considering the notion of autonomy. As Boud (1989) points out, 'autonomy' in the context of adult learning refers both to a goal of self-awareness, of empowerment in the sense of an ability to exercise choice in relation to needs, and to an approach to learning of active personal involvement and self-direction.

Autonomy is the government of the self by the self, a freedom from dependence, a situation where one is influenced and controlled only by a source from within oneself. What prevents autonomy is therefore that which is outside or "other" to the self. Amongst the many forms that otherness can take the most significant in the context of adult education are didactic teachers and transmitted bodies of formal knowledge. Perhaps the most significant characteristic of the adult learner has been that of autonomy. As Candy (1987: 161) points out, the notion of the learner as an autonomous self is 'so deeply entrenched in the ethos of adult education as to be thought "obvious" or "self-evident" and to thus be beyond question'. It is this autonomous self in the form of the adult learner who becomes the centre or source of experience and knowledge, including self-knowledge.

It is not too difficult to see why this notion of the autonomous self possessing agency provides a vital rationale and ground for an educational practice such as adult learning with its emphasis on personal change.

Autonomy defines both a goal for and an approach to the practice of adult education. The rationale is that adult education, by its approach to learning, can bring to the fore and realise the autonomy which is always potentially present in adult selves. This is why the common theme which unites the various and disparate strands or traditions in adult learning is that of empowerment – an empowerment implicated with a particular kind of self who has a natural potential for autonomy and who can be empowered through a particular kind of practice.

Boud (1989: 40–3) refers to four main traditions of learning in adult education: training and efficiency in learning, self-directed learning or andragogy, learner-centred or humanistic, critical pedagogy and social action. These traditions, although very different, all seek to *remove* something from the process of learning in order that they can attain their goal. Training and efficiency in learning seeks to remove *distractions* which make learning less efficient in the attainment of pre-defined learning goals. The andragogical tradition seeks to remove the *restrictions* of didactic teachers and formal bodies of knowledge from learning. The humanistic tradition seeks to remove all internal and self-imposed *distortions* on learning whilst the critical tradition seeks to remove the *oppressions* of history and social context from learning.

At this point, it is worth noting the negative imagery. The learning process is characterised as one full of blockages and barriers, things which impede or hold back the self-as-learner from attaining various ends, such as efficacy, autonomy, self-realisation or emancipation which each tradition posits as the goal of learning. For the self-as-learner the learning process is one beset by distractions, restrictions, barriers and oppressions – all varieties of negative and feared 'otherness' which have to be overcome.

The tradition of training and efficiency in learning depends on a body of pre-defined knowledge or skills, couched in terms of objectives (often behavioural in nature) and learnt in a planned and efficient way. Pedagogy becomes a technical matter, with the learner receiving pre-planned inputs and producing or enacting pre-defined outputs; learning becomes a neutral process or system removed from the influence of socio-cultural factors. The specificity of learners, differences attributable to biographical factors such as gender, ethnicity and class are either ignored or programmed out. The self that is operative here is the classical scientific self – individualised, undifferentiated, an essentially abstract entity, the 'monological self', the self-contained individual having no transactions with and unaffected by anything 'other' to itself – a kind of pure 'learning machine'.

That is why it is a matter of removing distractions from a learning process whose goal is the acquisition by the learner of new knowledge and skills. This is what autonomy means here. Learners appear to have control of the learning process – the goal is clear, measurable and relevant, the learning process straightforward and flexible; they can work at their own pace and according to their particular circumstances. But, at the same time, this control is largely illusory because the knowledge and skills to be acquired are pre-defined. The control actually rests with the pre-defined knowledge and skills, both of which are simply assumed to be neutral 'givens' rather than socio-culturally constructed and therefore problematic. Autonomy, therefore, becomes induction into 'givens', predetermined meanings over which the learner has little personal control.

The andragogical tradition has been perhaps the most influential in institutional adult education. As Boud (ibid.: 41) points out, it is a tradition which emphasises 'the unique goals and interests of individual learners and places these as central in the teaching and learning process'. The focus of the andragogical tradition is the adult learner's experience, considered to be the foundation and most important resource for learning. It is what essentially characterises adults, that which uniquely defines their being as adults (Knowles 1978, 1985). Thus, in the andragogical tradition, experience is at the centre of knowledge production and acquisition. Using experience becomes not simply a pedagogical device but more significantly an affirmation of the ontological and ethical status of adults, in particular, the mark of their radical difference from children. This tradition is very anti-schooling, seeing as an important part of its mission that of 'liberating' adult learners from its unhappy consequences.

This emphasis assumes that experience provides a different knowledge, a knowledge of the 'real' world drawn from 'life', that is either an alternative or an enriching complement to formal knowledge. Learners are thus not to be seen as empty vessels to be filled with formal knowledge through didactic teaching, but rather as coming to learning situations with valuable resources for learning and with the attributes of self-direction, i.e., knowing their own learning needs, a knowledge not possessed by children.

The emphasis on experience constructs the adult as an active learner who comes to learning situations with personal resources in the form of experience. On the other hand, because of the way in which the self is constructed, this experience is taken as an unproblematic 'given'. Experience is unquestioningly seen as 'present', as an authentic source of knowledge once learners are left free to control their own learning and to realise their inherent self-directing tendencies; once, in other words, they position themselves correctly by freeing themselves from the 'otherness' of knowledge not based on their own experience.

Correspondingly, children's experience is denied a status because it is supposedly less 'authentic' than adults' experience, the assumption being that the child cannot have a self free from otherness. If adult learners are subjected to didactic teaching and a curriculum based on formal knowledge rather than their experience, if, in other words, the conditions of schooling are reproduced, then they revert to being children with a self still dependent on otherness. That the learner's own experience may not come indelibly stamped with the mark of authenticity is not considered.

The rejection of otherness means that andragogy cannot have a conception of experience as culturally constructed, pre-interpreted, complex and multi-stranded. The self is therefore conceived as a meaning-*giver*, the originary source of experience and knowledge in relation to experience, with a corresponding failure to recognise that selves, because they are linguistically and socio-culturally embedded, are also meaning-*takers*. The meaning of experience comes from 'outside' selves, although at the same time this outside is so much a part of us that we experience it as 'inside'.

The self of andragogy is the transcendental self of the Enlightenment. Persons are seen as individualistic and unitary with a core rationality enabling them to systematically reflect on and know their experience. They are pre-given and decontextualised and, although they are accorded a biography since without it they would have no experience, the assumption is both that they can distance themselves from it and that it is a linear record of the unfolding of the life of an essential self which can be, in principle, always decoded. In general, history, sociality and human practices apart from schooling are considered formative but not essential. It is precisely the quality of remaining 'inside', untouched by an 'outside', of being fully present to oneself, which enables the self-as-learner to exercise its own agency and realise its autonomy. This, then, becomes the justification and potential for the educational interventions by which autonomy can be realised through the removal of restrictions. The emphasis on the 'inside' also makes the andragogical tradition psychologistic (since the 'inside' is always associated with mind and mental activities) and ironically this has opened the door for the colonisation of its practice by psychology. Learners are thrown back on their personal resources which determine the path of their learning – a seeming control by the learner which, in practice, turns out to be illusory.

The humanistic tradition has its theoretical base in humanistic psychology, particularly the work of Carl Rogers (1967, 1983), one of its most significant exponents. Rogers emphasised the importance, first, of 'here and now' experiencing of ourselves and the world, of subjective consciousness and awareness in knowing and acting; second, the process of 'becoming', of choosing ways of living that realise an innate, authentic self, and third, the need to think holistically, in terms of the 'whole' person, the integrated biologically based organism, a unity of thinking, feeling and acting.

Rogers' authentic self, as we have just noted, although it is in many respects different from the rational self, is none the less similarly a transcendental non-contingent self, a unitary, self-knowing consciousness, disembodied and disembedded. So long as persons can remain in touch with their authentic core selves, their 'organismic' being, and can be fully themselves, then they will act rationally and responsibly. For Rogers, people become trapped in inauthenticity through oppressive social relations. We have an innate powerful need for external positive regard – for the love and respect of significant others – a need which can only be met by accepting the conditions which they impose for giving us what we desire. This causes us to act inauthentically, against our true selves. As a consequence, we become "blocked", unhappy and fail to develop our full potential, both generally as persons and particularly as learners.

Social relationships, therefore, exert an oppressive authority – 'anything taken in from others is by definition inimical to authenticity and spontaneity' (Richards 1989: 109) – and one of the most significant forms this authority can take is the pedagogic relationship. It is the pedagogic relationship which is the main enemy. Unless teachers are 'facilitators', giving up their traditionally didactic role, then this relationship will always be oppressive and will block rather than enable learning. As in the andragogical tradition, schooling and indeed any institutional form of education is seen as doing nothing but harm, and the need, therefore, is to ensure that the learning situation does not replicate this in any way. It must be learner-centred, controlled by the felt needs of learners and geared to optimising their development as whole persons. As Boud (1989: 42) puts it: 'Learners may be constrained by their own early negative experiences of learning and they need the context of a highly supportive and respectful environment to be able to recognise their needs and begin to explore them.'

Here, then, the self is essentially individualistic with an internal organismic rather than a social essence. The social is always 'outside' and oppressively 'other'. There is no recognition that selves might be socially located and no recognition that self and others are mutually constitutive within relationships. All social relationships are seen as inherently manipulative, functioning to distort the autonomy and agency of persons. A person's authentic self is inherently 'good', i.e., it is already socialised and eminently sociable. Social change, therefore, becomes a matter of the individual action of authentic selves; social harmony a product of persons being truly themselves. In learning, the learning of specific subject-matter becomes less important than learning about oneself, getting 'in touch' with one's authentic self and acting in accordance with its voice. Learning becomes a means of eliminating self-distortions and inauthenticity in the service of attaining a state of self-knowledge, self-presence and autonomy.

Both the andragogical and humanistic traditions have an individual–society binary opposition at their very heart. The social becomes cast in the role of the oppressive and feared other. As the point of origin, the authentic self is independent of the social realm. Individual autonomy and empowerment lies in liberating oneself from the social and its oppressive effects. In Rogers, for example, the social is something from the outside that gets inside and, like an alien growth, stifles authenticity and potentiality. To be truly autonomous we must therefore expunge the social that is inside us.

These traditions may make much of empowering the individual learner, yet they have shown themselves to be wide open to hijacking by an individualistic and instrumental ethic. The psychologism and individualism of humanistic discourse presented as a concern for the 'person' can lead ultimately and paradoxically to a dehumanisation through the substitution of covert for overt regulation under the guise of 'being human', enabling learners to 'open up', and provide access to their 'inner' world. This is an infiltration of power by subjectivity and a complementary infiltration of subjectivity by power (Rose 1994). We have highlighted this in the previous chapter when discussing confessional practices, disciplinarity and governmentality, and we will discuss it further later in this chapter.

In the critical pedagogy tradition, the emphasis is on attaining social change rather than personal autonomy, learning in the service of group or collective empowerment rather than individual empowerment. In the critical tradition, there is a rejection of individualism and psychologism, challenging a conception of the self which fails to recognise the effects of social structures and forces. For example, Brah and Hoy (1989) argue that although each of us does have a quality of individual uniqueness, we are socially positioned along power hierarchies constructed through class, race and gender.

Critical pedagogy's self is the exploited self of 'false consciousness' whose experience is rendered inauthentic by distorting ideology and oppressive social structures. Persons are first and foremost socially formed rather than socially isolated individuals. Their experience and knowledge arises from their social formation and positioning, but equally through these is it distorted by false consciousness. Learning in critical pedagogy, therefore, is centred on 'ideology critique', a stripping away of false consciousness. Learners, in dialogue with other learners who are similarly positioned, can understand the nature of their position, develop a 'true' consciousness and take action in conjunction with others to change their situation. Learning becomes, therefore, the acquisition of knowledge of an oppressive world, an awareness and understanding of one's social positioning and, through this knowledge, an ability to change the world and remove oppression.

However, a strong argument can also be made that this tradition is not actually so different from the others. Certainly, there is an emphasis here on the social, but all are as one in seeing the social as negative and distorting. All share a common conception of the relationship of experience to sociality. Critical pedagogy talks, for example, of experience being 'shaped by concrete social conditions' (Brah and Hoy 1989: 71) but, as in the humanistic tradition, this shaping is conceived as generally negative in its effects. The common feature here is that experiencing in a meaningful and authentic way is seen as the outcome of a freeing from oppressive social relations.

The social is seen in this way by the critical tradition because it is equated with social *forces* which are always portrayed as oppressive and crushing. The dimension of the social is theorised as a solid, reified 'thing', with the inevitable conclusion that the social can do no other than oppress and crush. Of course, this is not to deny that there is oppression or crushing of persons in the lived world, or that this can be explained in social terms. What we want to point to rather is that if sociality is seen purely as social *forces* that crush and oppress, then something very important is being forgotten, namely, that sociality is the *condition* of being a person. This implies, therefore, that it is our social practices that both create us as selves and enable us to be creative, indeed that learning rather than being something located "inside" is itself a social practice.

Implicit, then, in all the conceptions of the self we have studied so far are two structuring binary opposites; individual/social and voluntarism/determinism. Three of the traditions emphasise or privilege the 'individual' and 'voluntarism' poles whilst critical pedagogy reverses this and privileges the 'social' and 'determinism' poles. The danger with both these positions is that one constructs a totally 'free-wheeling' individualistic self, owing nothing to the social (constructed as oppressive) and where everything important is located 'inside' the person, whilst the other constructs a determined self which owes everything to the social and where conversely everything important (and oppressive) is located 'outside' the person.

There is a tendency in the critical tradition to end up with a conception of the self which is, on the one hand, oversocialised and overdetermined and on the other, patronising in so far as selves have to be seen as normally in a state of false consciousness. In stressing the negative and overwhelming effects of social relations and social structures, persons are made into social 'victims', dupes and puppets, manipulated by ideology and deprived of agency.

The dominant tendency in educational theory and practice has been to privilege the agency of the autonomous self and exclude any notion of determination on the grounds that to admit determination would be to render educational work impossible. However, in rejecting determination a self has to be posited as standing apart from any situatedness, outside of history, sociality and human practices. It is the power of the autonomous self to bestow meanings and shape experience which makes the self the condition and agent of knowledge. There is no situatedness other than the constraints and distortions from which the self can, exercising its agency, free itself by its own willing. In critical pedagogy, the self is shaped by its experiences, meanings are bestowed on them through ideology which becomes the source of (false) knowledge. The self is socially situated but frees itself and is able to experience truly through collective dialogue and action.

In the end, both these conceptions assume a self that is a unified consciousness with the power of self-presence and the capacity to act rationally. Critical pedagogy, although locating the self in social structures, still assumes a self capable of moving from false to true consciousness – both a unified self, self-knowing and self-present and a rational self capable of knowing its 'true' position and of acting on that knowledge. The critical tradition, in positing a socially embedded self, challenges the dominant conception of the self but the challenge is only partial and ultimately fails because it must also posit a fully rational, self-present self. In effect, then, the self that is operative in all the traditions of adult learning is the monological self of our dominant Western culture.

THE PLACE OF EXPERIENCE

In all the traditions of adult learning, experience has been accorded a privileged place as the source of learning in a learner-centred pedagogy and at the very centre of knowledge production and knowledge acquisition. One consequent danger is that experience comes to be taken as foundational and authoritative and hence we stop asking questions about it. It has become, in effect, an unquestioned 'given'. The questions that are asked are to do with the knowledge or learning which is the outcome of experience. Adult educators tend to explain learning in terms of foundational experience, since it seems incontrovertible that nothing could be more basic and hence more 'truthful' than someone's experience. Experience seems to be the incontestable evidence, the secure originary point, with the clear implication that explanation must be focused on what is learnt from experience rather than experience itself. Yet, it could be argued, and indeed we shall argue, that experience is not unproblematic that, in fact, rather than the origin of explanation, it is precisely that which is in need of explanation.

This conception of experience – that 'experience is the foundation of, and the stimulus for, learning' (Boud et al. 1993: 8) – is at the heart of pedagogies of experiential learning. The problem is that to see experience as originary in relation to learning fails to recognise that any approach to using experience will generate its own representations of experience and will itself be influenced by the way experience is conceived or represented, by the framework or interpretive grid which will influence how experience is theorised and how it is worked with in practice. In other words, the very *use* of experience presupposes a prior *theory* or epistemology of experience. The discourse and practice of experiential learning presupposes and practises something quite different – a theory of prior experience with experience as the foundational source of knowledge. We would argue that this leads to a failure to consider first, how experience *itself* represents (has meanings) and second, is itself represented (within theories and epistemologies).

Let us explore this second point first, since it links closely with the discussion we have had about the self. We have seen that the dominant conception of the monological self has rationalistic, humanistic and critical variants which, despite the variations, also have important things in common. Similarly, there is a dominant conception of 'monological' experience where the latter is constructed as a 'natural' attribute of selves. This conception is rooted in a rational/empiricist epistemology. Experience is constructed as transparent, giving unmediated access to the world. Language, symbolic systems and discourses are seen simply as neutral vehicles for describing what all rational selves can experience. Knowledge of the world is possible because there is a one-to-one correspondence between the world and the way it is represented through experience. Rational procedures such as reflection can be used by all and enable experience to be sorted, validated and transformed into knowledge. This monological conception of experience, certainly in its rationalistic and humanistic variants, is essentially individualistic and psychologistic. Consciousness is a key attribute with knowledge of the world a function of the autonomous, reflective self – the self as an ideal-knower, independent of contingency and specificity, disembodied and disembedded.

As Michelson (1996) points out, adult education has, throughout its history, tended to construct learning as a process where knowledge is created through the transformation of experience. Experience is *raw material* to be acted upon by the mind through the controlled and self-conscious use of the senses (observation) and the application of reason (reflection). Even the critical tradition in adult education, whilst it seeks to distance itself from the individualism and psychologism by emphasising the constitution of experience within social structures, still retains the notion of 'raw material' and of 'transformation'.

Let us consider these similarities in more detail. First, there is a common emphasis on the potential of selves to experience authentically. Experience provides a privileged access to the truth of reality where reality is itself understood as a given. Second, experiencing authentically and knowing truly is a matter of positioning which, whether socially structured or individually originated, is always ultimately a matter of methodical will – in other words, positioning is open to change by eliminating distortion through methodical techniques such as objectivity, reflection, introspection, dialogue and consciousness-raising. Third, there is an elimination of difference. The critical tradition appears to accept difference when it foregrounds the significance of different social positioning but, because it tends to reify and naturalise categories such as gender, race and class, it actually works to eliminate differences within categories. The very notion of 'positioning' is, therefore, rendered unproblematic to the extent that a potentially liberating practice can become totalising and oppressive. Fourth, all the variants fail to recognise that they are theorising or representing experience. What they think they are doing is simply describing or explaining in a neutral way the essential nature of experience or the nature of the pre-existing self. In effect, however, they are representing or discursively producing experience in a very particular way and with a very particular set of significations. There is nothing neutral about this – on the contrary, it is eminently political and contestable.

We can examine this question of representation more closely by going back to conceptions of the self and looking at their significatory force rather than their content. In other words, the way the self is represented does not merely describe and illuminate a pre-existing self but actually influences people's self-awareness and sense of individuality, the way their subjectivities are constituted.

Representations of the self can be seen as narratives or stories about the self, cultural texts which define subjectivity – Benhabib (1992), for example, refers to the *narrative structure of personal identity*. Our sense of ourselves as self-enclosed, independent, inner-directed, "sovereign" individuals is produced and maintained by narratives and ways of speaking (Shotter 1993). These provide meanings through which we define ourselves, meanings which function both as possibilities and constraints in relation to the forming of subjectivity – on the one hand, a set of enabling resources through which selves can be created; on the other, a set of limitations beyond which selves cannot be easily made and remade (Shotter 1989). Different cultural texts present different sets of possibilities and constraints.

As we have already seen, the dominant narrative projects the self as a natural, existent and universal category. The alternative narrative is one where the self is rather a culturally and historically variable category. Indeed, the very idea that this category of self is definitive of subjectivity is a specifically Western cultural phenomenon. In other cultures and in Western culture at different historical periods, subjectivity, or the sense of self, has been seen as relationally constituted – for example, in relation to family and kinship, to community, to the natural world. Modern subjectivity, however, is rooted in a logic of identity rather than difference and thus bound to a predominantly individualistic or monological conception of human beings as unique selves where subjectivity is inseparably linked to an essentialised and non-relational self.

Feminism, in critiquing this dominant representation of the self, argues that there is no essential pre-existing subjectivity and no universal category of the self. Rather, the self is located in concrete social relations and cultural texts with subjectivity defined by powerful gendered narratives where gender itself is storied into being as a 'natural' or biological attribute of the self (Flax 1990). Given its central position in the structure of oppressive patriarchy, feminism has sought, therefore, to displace modern Western culture's transcendental, universal and monological self.

The postmodern critique is also directed towards the notion of an essential human nature or true self. Postmodernists would argue that this 'true self' needs to be seen as a character in a narrative, a culturally produced 'fiction' presented in a naturalistic guise so that the narrative is concealed and the self appears as pre-existing and 'natural'. For postmodernists, the self is not a fact, a transcendental being, but an artefact socially, historically and linguistically produced. All social practices, including practices where meaning is attributed to the notion of a 'self', are not just mediated but constituted through language. As Weedon points out, language is the means by which:

> we learn to give voice – meaning – to our experience and to understand it according to particular ways of thinking, particular discourses which pre-date our entry into language. These ways of thinking constitute our consciousness, and the positions with which we identify and structure our sense of ourselves, our subjectivity.
>
> (Weedon 1987: 33)

The postmodern story of the self is that of a decentred self, subjectivity without a centre or origin, caught in meanings, positioned in language and the narratives of culture. The self cannot know itself independently of the significations in which it is enmeshed. There is no self-present subjectivity, hence no ultimate transcendental meaning of the self. Meanings are always 'in play' and the self, caught up in this play, is an ever-changing self, caught up in the narratives and meanings through which it leads its life (Lovlie 1992). As de Lauretis puts it:

> the process is continuous, unending or daily renewed. For each person therefore subjectivity is an ongoing construction, not a fixed point of departure or arrival, from which one then interacts with the world.
>
> (de Lauretis quoted in Gunew 1990: 28)

Thus, there is no non-linguistic or non-historical position, no originary point, where persons can gain a privileged access to the world or to themselves. As Flax (1993) argues, subjectivity is a discursive effect, a character in a story as much as the 'author' of the story. Representations of the self, instead of being seen as 'truth', need to be seen more usefully as stories, often very powerful stories, which perform a variety of social functions, including the construction of selves with appropriate characteristics. We shall discuss these issues further and with specific emphasis on research in Chapter 10.

In being positioned through narratives we get a sense of ourselves, but this sense is always changing. When we tell stories about our experience, these are not stories simply about ourselves as entities that exist independently of the story, although they may appear to be. They are not stories about or emanating from essential selves, but stories which help in the construction of selves. Subjectivity is never a once-and-for-all construction, and the experience which meaning can have is never permanently fixed. Human beings have many stories to tell and many different ways in which they can be recognised and give meaning to themselves through them. Subjectivity is therefore always shifting and uncertain and has to be continually 're-formed'. At any one point in time, experience can take on a specific meaning but there is no guarantee that the question of its meaning is thereby forever settled. Meanings are not the playthings of the essential self.

The place of language or signifying systems is a key issue in considering both the self and experience. If signifying systems are conceived as prior to experience then individual subjectivity cannot be the source of meaning. What experience represents cannot be divided into inside and outside sources. It is impossible, in other words, to work within this binary opposition. Certainly, what experience represents comes from 'outside'. Signifying systems, historically located cultures and discourses shape what is to count as meaningful experience and that experience itself counts. Here, therefore, experience is never fully 'present' because whatever presence it has is also constituted by an 'absence' – culture and language in the widest sense which form the 'unconscious' background of pre-understandings, meanings and interpretive schemes. Without these, it would not be possible to make sense of experience, to even conceive of experience as having any significance, let alone to analyse and reflect on it. But what comes from the 'outside' is also 'inside', experienced in a taken-for-granted way as part of self. As de Lauretis argues, experience is being placed in a social reality which is always perceived and comprehended as subjective, i.e., personal or 'inside'. Experience, then, becomes the effect of an interaction between the world (social reality) and the ongoing construction of subjectivity. The subjective engagement with discourses, practices and institutions lends significance, i.e., value, meaning and affect, to the events of the world.

It is difficult to see how selves could isolate their experience from its implication in historicality, sociality and discursivity. Here, the metaphor of experience as a 'text' has its use. To see experience in this way implies that experience is something to be 'read' or interpreted, possibly with great effort, and certainly with no final, definitive meaning. This must itself presuppose an interpretive, meaning-conferring structure of which selves (subjects) are part. This also highlights the implication of experience's representations and the representation of experience with power. How experience is made sense of (experience's representations) can be empowering or disempowering. The representation of experience influences the way we produce ourselves discursively and can make us into 'active' subjects or 'objects' of power (or, as we have seen, both at the same time in situations of contemporary governmentality).

Although experience is discursively articulated, since there is a multiplicity of discursive articulations experience can have many meanings, some of them conflicting and contradictory. Experience can be invested with a multiplicity of meanings, identity conducted through many possible stories. Even within any one articulation, the meaning of experience is never permanently fixed; thus, the text of experience is always open to reinterpretation. As O'Reilly (1989) points out, experience always has a quality of incoherence – it may come with predetermined meanings but this is never the last word, since experience can always be 'reread'. One could put it this way – experience always says less than it wishes to say, there is always more that can be read into it, it never reaches the destination of total clarity and definitiveness. As 'readers' we can never make it completely present. There is a sense in which experience is always out of control, always brimming over from the social contexts within which it is represented. This is perhaps why mechanisms that seek to accredit or recognise prior learning in totalising experience, to make it decidable and to bring it under control, always end up being oppressive.

EXPERIENCE, PEDAGOGY AND SOCIAL PRACTICES

As we have seen, experience in adult education discourse has mainly signified freedom from regulation in the service of personal autonomy and/or social empowerment. *Autonomy*, empowerment, *self-expression*, self-realisation are key signifiers. Other hitherto more submerged signifiers such as '*application*' and '*adaptation*' now also have a key significance. The meaning of experience will vary according to different discursive practices, as too will the particular significance given to learning deriving from experience. Although experiential learning has become central to the theory and practice of education in the postmodern moment, as a pedagogy it is inherently ambivalent and capable of many significations. There is a need to stop seeing experiential learning in purely logocentric terms, as a natural characteristic of the individual learner or as a pedagogical technique, and more in terms of the contexts, socio-cultural and institutional, in which it functions and from which it derives its significations. In itself, therefore, it has no unequivocal or 'given' meaning – it is inherently neither emancipatory nor oppressive, neither domesticating nor transformative. Rather, its meaning is constantly shifting between and across these polarities. It is perhaps most usefully seen as having a potential for emancipation *and* oppression, domestication *and* transformation, where at any one time and according to context both tendencies can be present and in conflict with one another. Accordingly, it offers a contestable and ambiguous terrain where different socio-economic and cultural assumptions and strategies can be differentially articulated. As a field of tension, it can be exploited by different groups, each emphasising certain dimensions over others.

Experiential learning can, for example, be deployed as a pedagogical strategy both in a disciplines-based curriculum and within a competences-based curriculum. Equally, it can be deployed as part of a continued questioning of and resistance to the forms of power that situate us as subjects. But at the same time, even here, experiential learning can function as both a more effective means of disciplining the 'whole' subject rather than simply the reasoning part and as a strategy to subvert the dominance of an oppressive universalistic reason by giving 'voice' to difference. What this implies, then, is that experience is always a site of struggle, a terrain where the meaning and significance of the experience to be cultivated in learning contexts is fought over. Central to this struggle is the reconfiguration of emancipation and oppression in the postmodern moment.

The schema or 'map' of experiential learning shown in Figure 5.1 attempts to depict the various possibilities. It is structured around in terms of two continua: *Autonomy–Adaptation* and *Expression–Application*. The resulting four quadrants represent four discursive/material practices, here referred to as Lifestyle, Confessional, Vocational, Critical. In effect, what is being depicted here is that application/expression/autonomy/ adaptation are the continua around which the pedagogy of experiential learning is differentially structured within different discursive/material practices. What these signify will differ relatively to the different discursive practices and the pedagogic and epistemological relationships within each practice. The schema enables an exploration of the contexts and meanings of experience, and hence the location of learning from experience, both between and within the quadrants.

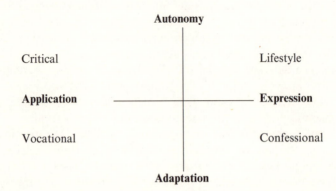

Figure 5.1 A 'map' of experiential learning in the social practices of postmodernity

LIFESTYLE PRACTICES

In Chapter 1 we highlighted the contemporary significance of lifestyle practices and touched upon their implications for a re-configuring of the theory and practice of adult education. In the postmodern, the educational is recast as the cultivation of desire through experience, both conditional upon and responsive to contemporary socio-economic and cultural fragmentation. Learning does not simplistically derive from experience; rather, experience and learning are mutually positioned in an interactive dynamic. Learning becomes the experience gained through consumption and novelty, which then produces new experience. Consequently, the boundaries defining 'acceptable' learning break down – in lifestyle practices learning can be found anywhere in a multiplicity of sites of learning. The predominant concern is with an ever-changing identity through the consumption of experience and of a learning stance towards life as a means of expressing identity. Pedagogically, experiential learning, sitting comfortably within the postmodern, gains an increasingly privileged place as the means by which desire is cultivated and identity formed.

Lifestyle practices centre on the achievement of autonomy through individuality and self-expression, particularly in taste and sense of style. Within a general stylisation of life, the mark of autonomy is a stylistic self-consciousness inscribed in the body, in clothes, in ways of speaking, leisure pursuits, holidays and the like. A lifestyle is adopted and cultivated but in a reflexive and self-referential way – lifestyle is never practised 'blindly' and un-self-consciously.

Lifestyle practices are firmly located within the play of difference that is characteristic of consumer culture. Unlike the mass consumption of modernity, consumption in the postmodern is based on choice as difference and difference as choice. In the postmodern, a lifestyle revolves around difference, the acquisition of the distinctive and the different within a signifying culture (Featherstone 1991) that summons up dreams, desires and fantasies in developing a life-project of self and where there is a continual construction (and reconstruction) of identity and a trying-on of relationships.

Empowerment through autonomy and self-actualisation (self-expression) becomes important but assumes a range of very different meanings, from the crumbling of hierarchy in new post-Fordist management to social and cultural empowerment in new social movements, e.g., the women's movement, and movements for ethnic and sexual awareness. One effect of this is that intellectuals, and indeed educators, are forced to assume the role of commentators and interpreters rather than legislators and 'enlightened' pedagogues. Educational practitioners rather than being the source/ producers of knowledge/taste become facilitators helping to interpret everybody's knowledge and helping to open up possibilities for further experience. They become part of the 'culture' industry, vendors in the educational hypermarket. In a reversal of modernist education, the consumer (the learner) rather than the producer (educator) is articulated as having greater significance and power.

On the other hand, consumerism knows no boundaries nor does it respect existing markers. Image, style and design take over from modernist metanarratives in conferring meaning. The 'culture' industry, advertising and the media, both 'educate' the consumer and, through the bombardment of images with which people must experientially identify and interpret, also make consumption necessary and compulsive.

It is the promotion of lifestyle practices, the obligation to shape a life through choices in a world of self-referenced objects and images, that influences the self in postmodernernity. Autonomy becomes a matter of expressing identity through the consumption of signifying choices. The project of self, rather than being unidirectional and governed by instrumental rationality, becomes one of the possession of desired goods and the pursuit of a lifestyle governed by the incitement of desire. Pleasure, once the enemy, is now considered indispensable. Rather than life being seen as a search for coherent and lasting meaning, it is construed as the pleasure of experiencing – from the immersion in images, from the flow of images in consumption and leisure and their combination in postmodern pursuits such as shopping. Here, experiences are valued *as* experiences – for example, one does not shop for the sake of satisfying 'real' needs (since needs are defined by the demands of lifestyle practices, there are no 'real' or 'underlying' needs), let alone for the utility of the goods purchased. As we have noted, when consumption is a matter of consuming signs, it is the experience itself that *counts*, i.e., that signifies and defines.

Selves become constructed through 'media-ted' experience. Consumption requires each individual to choose from a variety of products in response to a repertoire of wants that may be shaped and legitimised by advertising but must be experienced and justified as personal desires. However constrained by external or internal factors, economic or psychological, the postmodern self is required to construct a life through the exercise of choice amongst alternatives. Every aspect of life, like every commodity, is imbued with a self-referential meaning; every choice we make is an emblem of our identity, a mark of our individuality; each is a message to ourselves and others as to the sort of person we are; each casts a glow back illuminating the self who consumes.

Lifestyle is not confined to any one particular social or age group, nor is it purely a matter of economic determination. Economic capital is important but so too is cultural capital – both play a part in influencing the capacity of individuals to be more or less active in their exercise of lifestyle choices. The social group that is most readily associated with lifestyle practices, the so-called new middle class, demonstrates this. Their involvement in lifestyle practices cannot be explained simply as a function of income or ideology. We will argue rather that the key to their postmodern sensibility is the adoption of a learning mode towards life. Their habitus – their unconscious dispositions, classificatory schemes, taken-for-granted preferences – is evident in their sense of the appropriateness and validity of their taste for cultural goods and practices. They are the bearers of explicit notions of lifelong learning which are integral to their sensibility, values, assumptions and the aspirations of their cultural stance. They adopt a learning mode towards life – the conscious and reflexive education of self in the field of taste and style. They express their opposition to the established order by giving priority to experience as the mediator through which meaning is constructed, and to the demand for new experiences and new meanings. Thus, an emphasis is given to experiential learning which, for them, is invested with the significance of autonomy and self-expression in the pursuit of lifestyle practices. Coupled with this is a general tendency towards the relativisation of knowledge with knowledges generated from a number of local sources including everyday life. Here, experience is not pre-given but constantly reconstructed. Meaning is constructed through experience rather than simply being conveyed by it. Experiential learning is established as a legitimate ground for education but with contestation over its meaning and significance.

Within lifestyle practices, the relationship between experience, knowledge and pedagogy is articulated in a particular way. Experience is something to get immersed in, valued as a means of defining a lifestyle rather than something whose value lies in its potential for knowledge. It is consumed because it signifies in relation to a lifestyle. Knowledge is multiple, based on multiple realities and the multiplicity of experience. It is neither canonical nor hierarchical. There is no notion of intrinsically 'worthwhile' knowledge other than in terms of taste and style. Pedagogy does not seek to transmit a canon of knowledge or a single ordered view of the world. It is not concerned with Enlightenment 'messages'. Given this, therefore, the learner is positioned within a multiplicity of experience whose meanings are located within a consumerist market-led culture. Experience is the means by which a lifestyle is created and 're-created'.

In one sense, therefore, learners are positioned by lifestyle practices as active subjects, creating themselves, free from constraining traditions and ideologies. But they are also positioned as passive subjects, since lifestyle is socially defined, culturally legitimised, economically influenced and prey to consumerism and media-generated images. Flexible accumulation and the techno-scientific revolution have changed processes of production and reduced the need for manual work (hence creating active 'power-ful' subjects) but at the same time have invaded people's lives with a flood of commodities, seductive images and signifying rivalries. All of this can be seen as liberating but also as a seduction that constitutes a new form of social control and which in the process creates 'subjectified' power-less subjects. Furthermore, seduction goes hand-in-hand with repression (Bauman 1992), as those who are excluded from the realms of choice yet who are none the less affected by the global reach of consumer society find themselves increasingly subjected to the repression of poverty and marginalisation.

VOCATIONAL PRACTICES

As we have noted earlier, postmodernity is a global condition where both dispersal and fragmentation coexist. Flexible accumulation and post-Fordism bring more volatile labour markets, faster switches from one product to another, niche marketing and a greater consumer orientation. Post-Fordism involves changes in production and consumption – from mass-production, mass-market, machine-paced systems to the production of specialist, niche and luxury goods, and to production systems based on the application of IT. These fundamental changes in production – 'flexible specialisation' – have reduced the need for manual work and led to the development of a new form of social labour. At the same time, contemporary education is characterised by its increasing transformation into a market form, a transformation which is best understood as a postmodern phenomenon. Education appears to gain increasing autonomy from central and local government control but also loses autonomy through the emphasis on privatisation, marketisation and vocationalism. As non-market relations are redefined according to the logic of the market, education, unable to insulate itself from these developments, assumes a market/consumer orientation.

Vocational practices are constructed through the market form where multi-skilling and personal motivation are privileged. Here, learning signifies 'application', with pedagogy structured around problem-solving and project-based activities. The learner is required to be highly motivated in the direction of a personal change linked to 'reading' the market and continually adapting to the needs of the socio-economic environment. This reflects the post-Fordist organisation of work, marked by informal and networked social relations and flat/lateral hierarchies. Vocationalist discourse, therefore, personalises economic competitiveness by stressing the need for motivation and for becoming skilled. At the same time, it offers a formula for economic recovery, based on a reconfiguration of human capital theory, and a metonymics of blame ('If only you were trained and motivated, we wouldn't be where we are today!' – Ball 1993: 74). Education is cast as turning out the product which industry consumes. Changes in industry and changes in the processes of schooling go hand in hand, with educational institutions being expected to produce enterprising, consumption-oriented individuals with the attitudes and competencies, the flexibility and predisposition to change appropriate to the post-Fordist economy and ready to take their place in the market.

Vocationalism then is designed to produce flexible competencies and a predisposition to change. This is allied to a critique of the dominant liberal-humanist academic curriculum and draws upon some aspects of progressivist theories of motivation and learning (process-orientation, co-operation, problem-solving, open-ended investigation). It argues, first, that the 'real' world (by which is meant the world of post-Fordism and flexible specialisation) is not subsumable under academic subject divisions, and hence the academic curriculum provides an 'irrelevant' education and preparation for this world, and second, that the didacticism and teacher-centredness of this curriculum does not provide the appropriate attitudes and capabilities. These curricular changes, intended to enhance learning experiences and increase motivation, are implicated with the technological changes affecting the labour process and modes of production. New attitudes and competences are required from employees, and hence the relationship between the pedagogy, knowledge and the labour process changes. What is foregrounded is the need for flexibility and continuous learning, social skills and flexible competences, rather than subject-based knowledge.

As a pedagogy, experiential learning has the capacity to unsettle the established order and hence has a transformative potential. In vocational practices, experiential learning holds out the promise of breaking the stranglehold of a selective and elitist higher education. It challenges the notion that knowledge is only to be found within educational institutions and through a subject-based curriculum. It challenges also the prerogative of self-selecting and unaccountable academic professionals in controlling and defining what is to count as knowledge. Experiential learning, therefore, becomes the key to broadening access to higher education and to 'democratising' the curriculum.

At the same time, however, vocationalist pedagogy (as we have seen earlier when discussing the training and efficiency tradition in adult learning) creates a context where learning means proceeding to the correct answer in the most efficient way. Here, adaptation and application have no room for experimentation, open-endedness or unforeseen outcomes. Hence, the experience and knowledge of learners and knowledge arising from it becomes a mere device, a means for best achieving a pre-defined end. Learners are manipulated pedagogically to access already existing forms of knowledge either in the form of disciplines or, more usually, in the form of sets of behavioural objectives. Learner experience appears to be valued but its use is instrumental, selective and at best illustrative. It is only accorded significance if it contributes to the learning of the pre-defined knowledge or skills, if not it is discounted. This is then a 'techni-cised' pedagogy, where experience has no inherent value but functions merely as a tool for enhancing motivation. Experience becomes assimilated to behavioural competences.

Experiential learning is itself a pedagogy constructed through vocational practices; thus, it is both socially constructed and contested. Different social groups give it their own meanings, represent it in different ways. Thus, as we have seen, the new middle class invest it with a signification of autonomy and expression. For those groups associated with the New Right, it means adaptation to a pre-defined world and learning applicable and relevant to that world. Experience represents relevance, usefulness, self-discipline and market effectiveness. Paradoxically, however, and this is where there are resonances with contemporary lifestyle practices, experiential learning is the means by which the cultural and educational establishment can be resisted and subverted – for example, through challenging the power of the academy to define 'worthwhile' knowledge and by presenting alternatives to curricula based on disciplinary knowledge. Of course, this challenge has to be related to rapid economic and social change – flexible capital accumulation, specialisation, the rise of core and periphery work-forces coupled with the growth of an underclass, fear of inflation and the loss of confidence in government's ability to manage the economy. The resulting uncertainty and breakdown of established patterns of work and life lead to the possibility of deviance, delinquency and disorder.

For government, instability must be managed either directly through the law and order system or indirectly through education. One way of managing instability through education is by normalising discipline and, more importantly, self-discipline. In the post-compulsory sector this poses some difficulty since students are there by choice. Yet the need for self-discipline is not diminished nor is self-discipline easily attained. Rather than taking control of what happens in the post-school arena, government divests itself of control – directly by giving more power to employers, indirectly by encouraging opportunities for people to learn outside educational institutions and to have it accredited outside of the educational system. Hence, young adults are 'educated' into and by the self-discipline of labour. The focus is on an employability that somehow reinvents and captures the work ethic yet does not necessarily lead to paid work. Here then, we see experiential learning circumscribed by employers' needs for particular kinds of labour and particular kinds of consumers, and government's need for a means of social control through self-discipline.

Thus, a pedagogy of experiential learning can also have a domesticating potential. In vocational practices, experiential learning can be the means to control change – at the same time that it unsettles the established order it also functions to ensure that the unsettling remains within established parameters of social order. Thus, for example, assessment and accreditation procedures ensure that only certain forms of experience are valued.

Furthermore, the regulation of experience is taken out of the control of educational practitioners and placed instead in centrally formulated anticipated outcomes. Within vocational practices, what we see happening is the commodification of experiences – experience becomes a commodity to be exchanged in the marketplace of educational credit.

In vocational practices the relationship between experience, knowledge and pedagogy is articulated in such a way that experience functions to provide a personal motivation and a feet-on-the-ground pragmatism. Learning becomes a matter of applying knowledge where knowledge itself is narrowly defined, a heuristic, 'factual' knowledge which enables the learner to adapt to a taken-for-granted, pre-defined 'real world'. Pedagogy is the link between personal motivation and the learning of pre-defined outcomes in the form of adaptive skills. In this context, the learner is positioned as a subject in need of skills in the post-Fordist marketplace. Skills are empowering – through them one becomes more competent and 'employable'. Learning is a matter of applying what is learnt so that one can become better adapted and adaptable to the perceived needs of the economy. Experiential learning is open and closed in the same moment.

CONFESSIONAL PRACTICES

We have argued earlier that 'selves' are not natural givens in the world and that to have knowledge of them is not simply a matter of discovering or uncovering their reality. In discussing the significatory power of conceptions of the self, we noted how selves were constructed through these conceptions and their associated discursive practices.

In Chapter 4 in the discussion on disciplinarity, there was a highlighting of the contemporary significance of a pastoral power which works by enabling people to actively and committedly participate in disciplinary regimes. In effect, people are educated to govern themselves through bringing their inner lives into the domain of power. Pastoral power works, not through imposition or coercion but through people investing their identity, subjectivity and desires with those ascribed to them through certain 'knowledgeable' or expert discourses.

In this process, people's self-regulating capacities become allied with social and economic objectives. To know one's inner self is for that inner self to be known, and being known becomes the condition for a more effective regulation in the service of contemporary political rationalities which foreground the individual and the market. The private, in effect, becomes public and becomes a support for enterprise culture and the market. In other words, to realise oneself, to find out the truth about oneself, to accept responsibility for oneself, becomes both personally desirable and economically functional.

Contemporary governmentality works in terms of the affective and effective governing of persons where positioning and investment in a subject position is a crucial factor. What is involved here is a 'bringing forth of one's self' as an object of knowledge through a pedagogy which functions to open up for intervention those aspects of a person which have hitherto remained unspoken. As we saw in Chapter 4 when discussing Foucault's notion of confession, the self is constituted as an object of knowledge through discovering the 'truth' about itself. However, in confessing, subjects have *already* accepted the legitimacy and truth of confessional practices and the particular meanings and investments that these invoke. Adults, for example, accept themselves as 'learners' in need of 'learning' provided by professional adult educators for their future development. In doing so, they align their subjectivities with these educational discourses and meanings they invoke. They become enfolded within a discursive matrix of practices which constitute their felt needs and paths of self-development.

In contemporary society externally imposed discipline gives way to the self-discipline of an autonomous subjectivity. With confession, the emphasis is on self-improvement, self-development and self-regulation. It displaces canonical knowledge by valorising individual experience but, at the same time, rather than displacing power as such it extends the range of pastoral power embedded in the confessional regime of truth and self-knowledge. Confessional practices therefore create productive and empowered subjects who are, however, *already governed* (by themselves). Thus, externally imposed discipline and regulation is not required. There is regulation through self-regulation, discipline through self-discipline, a process which is pleasurable and even empowering, but only within a matrix from which power is never absent (Usher and Edwards 1995).

In confessional practices, psychotherapeutic expertise in a variety of forms from the academic to the 'popular' plays a key role in presenting a morality of freedom, fulfilment and empowerment. It offers the means by which the regulation of selves by others and by the self is made consonant with the current situation. Thus, in confessional practices, autonomy becomes adaptation, an autonomy enhanced through the application of expertise. Empowerment is psychological and individualistic. Political, social and institutional goals are realigned with individual pleasures and desires, with self-expression, the happiness and fulfilment of the self. Pedagogic practices, such as assertiveness training and educational guidance, illustrate this very clearly. They emphasise the 'liberation' of the self but only within the confines and limitations of understood and unchallenged contexts and systems.

Knowledge/expertise of the self stimulates subjectivity, promotes self-knowledge and seeks to maximise capacities. Persons are cast as active citizens, ardent consumers, enthusiastic employees and loving parents – and all of this as if they were seeking to realise their own most fundamental desires and innermost needs. At the same, however, by enhancing subjectivity (creating active subjects), subjectivity is connected to power by means of new languages (psychotherapeutic expertise) for speaking about subjectivity. However, confessional practices are not recognised as powerful because they are cloaked in an esoteric yet seemingly objective expertise and a humanistic discourse of helping and empowerment. Thus, an active, autonomous and productive subjectivity is brought forth in confessional practices even as it remains subject to the power/knowledge formations which bring forth this form of subjectivity and invest it with significance.

In confessional practices, the relationship between experience, knowledge and pedagogy is articulated in terms of a representation of experience as enabling access to knowledge and the innermost truths of self. Pedagogy involves the deployment of psychodynamic expertise to facilitate this process. Given this relationship, the learner is positioned to discover the meaning of his/her experience by becoming an active subject within a network of confession. The meaning of experience is bound up with finding the truth about self in order to enhance capacities and become adapted and well-adjusted, but this active subject in control of self is at the same time subjectified within a network of pastoral power. Experiential learning becomes a matter of self-expression in the interests of adaptation.

CRITICAL PRACTICES

Critical practices work through particular meanings given to autonomy and application. Autonomy in critical practices has a different signification to the autonomy of lifestyle practices. In the latter, it is oriented towards expression through the cultivation of desire and the display of difference through consumption. In the former, it is oriented towards application, which again is not the same as the 'application' of vocational practices. It is not the application of learning in the service of adaptation to the existing techno-social order but rather an application of learning in the cause of self and social transformation. It is in changing particular contexts rather than adapting to them that autonomy is ultimately to be found.

In critical practices, there is more of a recognition that meaning is discursively produced and that experience, therefore, is never simply an 'innocent' or basic given. Experience and the way it is represented are the stakes in the struggle to find 'voice', to exercise control and power. The key question, then, becomes how representations of experience are discursively produced and how subjects both position themselves and are positioned discursively. This opens up issues of power, given that discourses serve the interests of particular groups. Thus a pedagogy that assumes experience is innocent is challenged because it must inevitably be uncritically supportive of the *status quo*. The refusal to accept that the representation of experience is political means that the power relations embedded in discourses and the interests of particular groups served by particular discourses remain unseen and unquestioned.

In critical practices, therefore, pedagogy becomes a political practice. Allied to this is an emphasis on the cultural, a recognition that culture is a lived ongoing process as important as the material and the economic, and as much a terrain of struggle. Pedagogy is not seen as a technical matter directed to imparting a canon of knowledge but as vitally implicated in a politics of representation (how people present and understand or are presented and understood) in the cultural processes that shape the meanings and understanding of experience and the formation of identity.

The relationship between experience, knowledge and pedagogy is articulated in terms of a self-conscious questioning of the representation(s) of experience. There is an explicit recognition that experience 'signifies' and that the significations of experience are imbued with power and are influential in the shaping of identity. The relationship between experience and knowledge is not taken as either given or unproblematic, nor is it seen as purely a matter of deploying methodical will or eradicating false consciousness. There is an acknowledging of the place of desire in how people are positioning *vis-à-vis* their experience, the investments that tie people to particular positions and identities and the multiple and ambiguous positioning that people find themselves in.

Critical practices have a clear and explicit transformative potential, but this resides in localised contexts and operates through the deployment of specific knowledge. In their pedagogical aspects (and in a sense they are almost exclusively pedagogic), they reject the conventional domesticating effects of pedagogy. Experiential learning becomes a strategy designed to privilege 'voice' in the service of self and social empowerment and transformation. At the same time, however, it is this very emphasis which can give critical practices a regulatory dimension. The 'critical' easily becomes a norm, a final truth which is just as heavy in its regulation as any openly oppressive discourse – as, for example, in the worst excesses of political correctness. Indeed, in some ways this regulation may be even more difficult to resist, speaking as it does in the name of empowerment and transformation. As Gore (1993) argues, critical pedagogy, whilst rhetorically opposing 'regimes of truth', can itself easily become one. She refers to this as the difference between the pedagogy argued for and the pedagogy of the argument – in the case of critical pedagogy, the former liberatory and transformative, the latter totalising and regulative.

In Chapter 1 we discussed the significance of critical practices *vis-à-vis* consumption in the contemporary conjuncture. We highlighted new forms of critical practice associated with what some commentators have referred to as 'postmodern' social movements. They are characterised by a cultural activism and an emphasis on experience as an intense 'here and now'. Whilst seeking personal and social transformation they do in a non-totalising and non-teleological way and outside the comforting rationales of the grand narratives of modernity. Although pedagogic, they deploy a pedagogy of performance, often transgressive and sometimes 'outrageous' to bourgeois sensibilities. In critical practices, experience is not regarded as something that *leads* to knowledge but *as* knowledge. Knowledge however is in the service of action, an activity, a practice which does things.

RETHINKING EXPERIENCE IN THE CONTEXT OF CONTEMPORARY ADULT LEARNING

At this point it might be useful to relate these quadrants and the practices they represent to the well-known 'villages' of experiential learning as identified originally by Weil and McGill (1989a). To some extent they are representative of the mainstream discourse of experiential learning within adult education. These 'villages' have served a useful purpose as a heuristic device for conceptualising and categorising the various forms of experiential learning and for examining the assumptions, influences and purposes within and between these forms. Indeed, the very concept of 'village' was formulated in order to avoid creating exclusive distinctions and divisions between various forms and practices of experiential learning, and as a means of encouraging dialogue between them.

The exploration and development of the quadrants may help to complement and expand upon the impact of the villages. Indeed, meaningful distinctions and connections can be made between these categorisations in terms of their emphases, their dynamics and complexity. Within the quadrants as we have formulated them, the emphasis is as much on problematising and understanding experience in relation to different contexts and discourses as it is on focusing on the learning process contingent on experience. This wider empahasis may serve to avoid the danger of 'locking onto' a particular village because of its association with a specific ideological tradition or institutionalised educational practice. Equally, it may make it less likely that existing social relations are left unquestioned within a preoccupation with experiential techniques and methods.

The significance of the interrelationship of application/expression/ autonomy/adaptation within and between the different quadrants is that it allows greater fluidity in representing the dynamic interconnections between experience, knowledge and pedagogy in relation to different and changing discursive practices. By this means, it is possible to move away from the tendency of the villages concept to be overdescriptive and over-schematic and to counter the very real possibility of reifying the different villages. It also allows a more complex and flexible understanding of experience and experiential learning, which can take account of context, theory and practice enabling a move from what Wildemeersch (1992a: 25) calls an essentially 'narrative type of conversation' to a more challenging 'discursive type of conversation' about education and learning. This can help show the way towards the paradigm shift aspired to by Weil and McGill which looks to 'push the boundaries of our visions and our villages to acknowledge the inter-connectedness of the whole' (Weil and McGill 1989b: 269). In this wider context we can better understand the potential within the various discursive practices for experiential learning to be both domesticating and transformative.

We have argued that experience is not unproblematic, that it needs to be understood and interpreted in relation to differing contexts and the influence of a variety of discourses. It can function both to empower and control, to create both powerful and powerless selves. What, then, are the implications for educational practice?

In focusing on student experience, we suggest that educators need to help students to problematise and interrrogate experience as much as to access and validate it. Complementary to the acknowledgement that experiential learning is a holistic process, that it is socially and culturally constructed and that it is influenced by the socio-emotional context in which it occurs (Boud *et al.* 1993), must be a similar understanding about the nature, construction and context of experience itself. First, educators need to be wary of basing their practice on the proposition that experiential learning involves a 'direct encounter' with experience (Weil and McGill 1989b: 248). Whereas experience can provide new and useful insights into a wide range of issues and problems and can clearly be used to access, supplement, complement, critique and challenge understandings of the world derived from disciplinary knowledge, we agree with Wildemeersch (1992a: 22) that the creation of a specific 'opposition between experiential and theoretical knowledge is unfruitful and even false'.

A learning focus on experience certainly has the potential to be 'liberating' in its concern for the 'neglected learner' and its opposition to 'banking' education, in that it highlights and confers meaning on knowledge, skills and attitudes previously undervalued and motivates students to extend their learning and pursuit of knowledge. Yet it can also be domesticating, in that learners can become unreflexive prisoners of their experience or have their experiences colonised and reduced, on the one hand, by oppressive educational institutions and, on the other, by totalising 'radical' discourses. Such approaches run the risk of selling learners short on culturally valued knowledge and, at worst, lock them into second-best knowledge and, through uncritical and unrigorous approaches to recognising and accrediting prior learning from experience, even into second-best qualifications. At the same time, by continuing to see experience as the 'raw material' of knowledge, we are unable to create situations where we can examine how, as selves, we move back and forth between our own particular stories through we which we construct our identities and the social production that is knowledge. In the process, we fail to challenge dominant knowledge taxonomies and the relations of power in which they are implicated.

Educators need to move beyond practice based on oversimplistic observations that 'you can always learn from experience' etc. and look more carefully at the necessary preconditions for experiential learning. Part of this might involve, rather than an unsophisticated, untheorised and potentially threatening delve into student experience, working towards building the necessary psychological climate and infrastructure from which experience can both be explored and problematised. This might mean creating sufficient student security and self-confidence, 'the right emotional tone under which authentic discourse can occur' (Brookfield 1993a: 27) and at least an outline theoretical framework from which to examine and understand student experience. It might mean acknowledging more explicitly, honestly and sensitively the possibility of limiting or oppressive experience – for example, the experience of personal unemployment, bereavement or loss – as well as the difficulties involved in transferring learning from one experiential and cultural context to another – for example, the problematic connection between domestic management skills and knowledge and those in a more regulated, hierarchical and gendered workplace (Butler 1993).

A more productive approach to knowledge might be to engage in the process of 're-view' (Usher 1992; Brookfield 1993a), exploring how and why we theorise experience and critically examining the influence on experience of contexts, cultures and discourses in the past and for the future. Such a procedure avoids the pitfalls of a naive and even potentially manipulative pedagogical approach to learner experience where educator theories are present but unacknowledged and learner experience is foregrounded but inadequately framed or contextualised.

Equally, it may be necessary to reformulate Weil and McGill's location of experience in individuals who give personal meaning to different ways of knowing so that more account can be taken of selves as meaning-takers as well as meaning-givers. With this in mind, in reconfiguring a pedagogy of experiential learning, it may be insufficient to rely exclusively either on psychologistic models to uncover, diagnose, categorise or sequence individual experience or on the artificial creation of shared experience through gaming, role-play and simulations. An alternative approach to experiential learning might be, rather, to attempt to triangulate experience through an investigation of personal meanings alongside the meanings of engaged others and the presence and influence of different contexts and different discourses. Here, the quadrants we have presented could themselves function as a useful heuristic device. This might help learners to see their experience more as 'text' than as 'raw material', thus leaving open the possibility of a variety of interpretations and assessments of experience, including the possibility that experiential learning might be both 'liberating' and 'domesticating', according to its contextual and discursive location.

RECONFIGURING THE SELF AND EXPERIENCE WITHIN THE POSTMODERN

It could be argued that education in general has always taken itself very seriously and its Enlightenment inheritance impels it to construct learning as something purposeful, goal-directed and empowering. Adult education, in spite of repeated attempts to distance itself from schooling, still understands itself primarily in terms of Enlightenment values and purposes that schooling also shares. The story adult education tells itself, the story which provides the narrative structure of its identity and thus gives meaning to what is done in its name, is still very much the Enlightenment story of progress, objective knowledge and certain truth – all underpinned by the humanism of the pre-given self 'liberated' through structured curriculum-shaped learning.

As we have already noted, if we start thinking in terms of postmodern selves, a radical reappraisal of the theory and practice of adult learning cannot be avoided. The self which is at the heart of the traditions of adult learning we have examined is a necessary assumption for the educational project which motivates them. In this project, experience is linked to learning in a cause–effect relationship. Postmodern selves disrupt and reverse this link, with learning becoming experience – experience as the source rather than the raw material of knowledge, experiencing as pleasurable and valued for itself.

As Potter and Wetherell (1987) point out, a person's life has predominantly been seen as a quest for self-fulfilment, the search to establish a 'true' authentic self, either in an individualistic sense or within collectivist contexts. The educational project either in its liberal/rational, romantic/humanistic, or critical/radical forms has always been considered, despite the variation of emphases, a vital part of that process. Learning in this educational sense becomes a means of realising this self – hence the stress on 'autonomy'.

As we have seen in Chapter 1, learning in the postmodern has to be retheorised and autonomy recast. The self, because it has many realisations, does not realise itself in an essential way. Different and changing realisations, rather than being rejected for fear of incoherence, loss of mastery, discontinuity and inauthenticity, are rather embraced and celebrated. Correspondingly, autonomy is not some pre-defined end towards which a life must move. This means that the individualism, psychologism and essentialism which, as we have seen, constitute in varying degrees the dominant conception of the self, are not the only possibility. The self's formation in intersubjectivity and language, its reflexivity and its practical involvement in the world, including the process of learning, is a condition for the achievement of autonomy rather than a barrier to its discovery.

Donald (1992) has argued that education has historically been allotted two tasks, both of which it has been unable to fulfil properly. As we have seen in Chapter 2, one is a socialisation task, the other an individuation task. Adult education has been mainly involved with the latter, although its 'hidden agenda' has often involved the former. Both of these tasks require for their fulfilment a certain conception of the self and a certain conception of the nature and place of experience. If both conceptions, in the polarised way in which they are normally formulated, are questionable, then it is perhaps hardly surprising that adult education has consistently failed to fulfil either task. Different conceptions might better fulfil the realisation of these tasks; equally, however, it might also lead to their reappraisal and re-configuration. We shall consider this further in Chapter 6.

Reconceptualising theory and practice

THEORISTS AND PRACTITIONERS

A useful starting-point in considering the theory–practice problem is that any professional or semi-professional practice has a body of theory to which it relates. Historically, it has been the development of a body of theoretical knowledge with a clear relationship to either the natural or the human/social sciences, which has marked out a practice as a 'profession'. However, at the same time, it has been precisely the possession of a body of theoretical knowledge and what the relationship of this knowledge is to practice that has been the source of problems.

Certainly, for the practitioner, the relationship is very often problematic and, as such, is often experienced as threatening. Practitioners are never sure what their attitude should be towards theory. On the one hand, they tend to be suspicious of theory, which they associate with the unworldliness of the academy. However, theory signifies rigour, a rigour which is supposedly achieved either prospectively, through application, or retrospectively, through reflection. Rigour, the relationship to a scientifically validated body of knowledge, appears therefore to *warrant* practice. Yet, it is precisely this 'rigour' which often makes theory seem remote, irrelevant and unworldly.

The theorist, on the other hand, tends to regard the practitioner as someone too ready to be influenced by 'common sense' and custom and practice, too eager to work with anecdotal or trial-and-error knowledge. Theorists would not deny that practitioners possess expertise, but they would argue that this expertise is unsystematic and of questionable validity. Theorists claim the mantle of a different kind of knowledgeable expertise about practice. They would accept that they are not field practitioners but would argue that this gives them an advantage in enabling them to stand back or distance themselves from the day-to-day action imperatives of practice. Consequently, they are better able to investigate and uncover a 'real' world of practice which is hidden to the practitioner.

In effect, the theorist claims an expertise with the power to override the power that practitioners feel they have through their practice-based experience and knowledge. For the theorist, this seems self-evident, because theorists see their expertise as based on systematic and scientifically tested knowledge and therefore as naturally superior. On the other hand, the implication of the theorist's self-understandings is that practitioner knowledge – the knowledge practitioners have through practice – is a 'superficial' and inferior knowledge. Hence, the theorist is claiming a power to define the limits of knowledge and using that power to define the practitioner's knowledge as outside the limit.

From the practitioner's standpoint, it is rare for theory to be a settled, definitive and uncontentious body of knowledge. In many cases, therefore, practitioners are unsure which theory or which aspect of theory is relevant to the circumstances of their practice. This uncertainty is particularly endemic in those practices with a relationship to theoretical knowledge in the social and human sciences. Beyond this, however, practitioners, although claiming to integrate theory into their work, are often (although not always) unsure what it means to 'apply' theory in any concrete sense or to use theory to reflect on practice. To many practitioners, therefore, theory appears both remote and useless yet at the same time powerful and threatening. Elliott (1991) gives an example of this in relation to teachers and the notion of the hidden curriculum. He argues that the problem they face is that educational theory appears irrelevant to their practice but, at the same time, the theory of the hidden curriculum makes them feel that they are responsible for things over which they have no control.

It is certainly noticeable that the social division of labour between theorists and practitioners is not simply functional but serves to place the practitioner in a subordinate position. This is partly a historical development. Practices which understand themselves as professions developed at a time when science's status was relatively unchallenged both epistemologically and culturally. 'Science' was not only the signifier of rigour but also of human progress and betterment. Practices as professions, particularly the caring professions, developed within a modernist discourse at a time when modernity was at its height. As Polkinghorne (1992) points out, applying the methods of science in the human realm was expected to produce knowledge which could serve society by providing the means whereby children could be most efficiently educated, prisoners reformed, workplaces organised and mental illness cured. In so far as scientific knowledge was generated by research, and given that research was located in the academy, then practices which understood themselves in this way developed with a division of labour and differentiation of roles between theorists in the academy and practitioners in the field.

Epistemological as well as historical factors have played a part. As we shall see, the positivist/empiricist view of knowledge cast the only legitimate form that theory could take as logically connected, context-independent generalisations. The practitioner's knowledge, on the other hand, is narratively connected, context-specific and particularised. On the face of it, this seems to be a matter of different kinds of knowledge, each with its own limits and each with its own worth. However, things are not quite so simple because here an epistemological difference is also and more importantly a socio-cultural hierarchy. Context-independent knowledge is ascribed a superior epistemological status to context-specific knowledge. This status also becomes a *normative* status, where context-specific practitioner knowledge is constructed as a limited and inferior form of knowledge, in effect, it is defined as not 'real' knowledge at all.

This is also why the division of labour between theorist and practitioner has social consequences. It is not just a functional difference but a difference of status and power. The response of practitioners is complex, and we shall explore this in more detail later. At this point, we will argue that, although practitioners tend to implicitly accept this hierarchy, it does serve to further reinforce the practitioner's feelings both of powerlessness in the face of theoretical knowledge and of its remoteness in relation to specific practice contexts.

Theoretical knowledge is normative in another sense: there is a gap between how theorists understand theoretical knowledge and how theoretical knowledge works in relation to practice. Theorists understand their work as simply describing or explaining the world, but theoretical knowledge also generates an implicit *ideal* of practice. The problem here is not so much the ideal but its consequences, in particular the fact that practitioners invariably feel, as we have noted earlier, that they do not have sufficient control over situations to be able to implement it. Hence, they find it difficult to live with. Yet, if they do not, they are blamed for somehow not being sufficiently rigorous. It is this which Schon (1983) is highlighting when he refers to the problem of rigour versus relevance which all practitioners face and which they all have to resolve in some way.

For practitioners, therefore, theory remains highly problematic. But, the other side of this coin and one which is not so often touched on, is that the problematic features of theory are also very convenient for practitioners. If theory is agreed to be remote from practice and divorced from its realities, then this really does let practitioners off a lot of hooks. Provided they can live with the feelings of powerlessness, their life is in many respects made a lot easier. Practitioner knowledge remains in the largely untouchable realm of the individual and the private. Feeling threatened by theory and dismissing it as remote and 'airy-fairy' allows practitioners to cocoon themselves in 'experience', their craft knowledge and customary ways of doing things. Hence, a private world that is safe but unchallenged can be created. Practitioners may therefore have an *investment* in their subordinate positioning through the division of labour between theorists and practitioners. Professional 'autonomy' is, in practice, largely based on experience and craft knowledge rather than appeals to a base of scientifically validated knowledge. Keeping the nasty world of theory 'out' is a means by which practitioners keep their own world of practice 'in', immune to questioning and change – until, of course, theory is forced upon them and they find that they have no means of justifying their practice and hence no means of resistance to attacks on their professional 'autonomy'.

It was Schon, in his book *The Reflective Practitioner* (1983), who introduced the idea of 'reflection-in-action' as a means of overcoming the dilemma of rigour versus relevance. In the process, he also provided a means of seeing the theory–practice problem in a different way. He argued that practitioner knowledge, or knowing-in-action, was more than customary craft knowledge; indeed, that it was a realm of legitimate knowledge in its own right. He pointed to the difference between theoretical knowledge about practice and the practical knowledge which is inherent in practice. He argued that the former should not be privileged over the latter but that it is because this happens through the power of what he called the 'technical-rationality model' of practice. In short, he argues that there is a theory–practice problem.

LIMITATIONS OF TECHNICAL-RATIONALITY

The technical-rationality model assumes that theoretical knowledge must be the foundation of practice because it is research-generated, systematic and 'scientific' knowledge. In the technical-rationality model, theory is conceived as revealing the nature of the world – in other words, it is knowledge about what *is*. This knowledge takes the form of generalised propositions, the only knowledge considered worthwhile and secure. This privileging is taken to the point where every other kind of knowledge is demonised as mere belief, opinion and prejudice.

Furthermore, the 'worthwhileness' of theoretical knowledge is reinforced because of the apparent power of this kind of knowledge to make predictions about events in the world and hence to be able to control these events. It is this power of prediction and control that enables theory to be the means by which practice is justified or warranted – a warranted practice being based on predictive knowledge of the world. In this context, it is important to bear in mind that, historically, the human sciences were modelled on the natural sciences on the basis that, because the latter enabled prediction and control of the natural world, so too the former would enable prediction and control of the social world and of human behaviour.

We mentioned earlier that many professional practices developed within modernist discourses. Epistemologically, these discourses assumed that the world is orderly and knowable through the discovery of universal laws. The discovery of the laws which order the world leads to the accumulation of knowledge in the form of theory which enables the prediction of events and hence a control of the world for the benefit of all. Scientific knowledge and its application through practices as diverse as engineering and education were seen, therefore, as the condition of progress.

Seen in this context, practice becomes the solving of technical problems through rational decision-making procedures based on predictive knowledge. It is the means to achieve ends where the assumption is that the ends to which practice is directed can always be pre-defined and are always knowable. The condition of practice is the learning of a body of theoretical knowledge, and practice therefore becomes the application of this body of knowledge in repeated and predictable ways to achieve pre-defined ends. A certain kind of rationality, an essentially technical and instrumental rationality, is presupposed here. It is hardly surprising then, that practice comes to be seen as mere technique, the efficient matching of means to ends in predictable and routine ways. The practitioner is consequently reduced to the role of 'technician', the applier of techniques. It is also not surprising that practitioner knowledge becomes downgraded; its problematic nature is not so much a problem of its truth or utility but that when it becomes the basis of practice, outcomes can no longer be predicted and controlled.

The way that technical-rationality constitutes the relationship between theory and practice is now strongly contested. There is a much greater readiness to reject the notion that theoretical knowledge can simply be applied or 'mapped' on to practice. The argument is that the nature of practice is such that it must always be *underdetermined* by theory. The performative question 'What is to be done?' which is at the centre of practice, is not one which can be answered simply by reference to theory's propositional 'What is?' The kind of acting-in-the-world that practice requires is not a matter of repetitive routines in the securing of pre-defined ends.

Schon argued that practitioner knowledge is *performative* rather than propositional, in other words, that practice is centred on action. This, however, is a particular kind of action, it is neither random behaviour nor behaviour predictable from a body of theoretical knowledge. Rather, it is appropriate or right action – and what is appropriate or right depends on the context or situation. Every context of practice has its own distinctive features which provide possibilities and impose constraints on what can be done. Here, then, action is conceived as being inseparably linked with, indeed constituted by, contextual knowledge.

The critics of technical-rationality point out that, unlike this practical knowledge, theoretical knowledge is neither situational nor action-oriented. The 'What is?' of theoretical knowledge strives for a universality which cannot 'speak' to particular contexts. It therefore cannot tell practitioners what is the right action in relation to a concrete problem in a specific context; it is simply impossible to translate it into rules and techniques which can be applied by practitioners in concrete situations. For them, what is always at stake is the very relevance of theoretical generalisations. The problem is compounded because theoretical knowledge is not monolithic. Thus, there could be many generalisations which might be relevant in any practice situation, and some of them might be in conflict with others. In other words, there is always a question about the criteria for deciding relevance, and these criteria are not themselves to be found in theoretical knowledge. Rather, they are a matter of deliberation, interpretation and interaction – the 'action reasoning' of practice.

THEORY AND PRACTICE IN TEACHING

If practice is seen as being a matter of technique, this obscures the possibility of practice having its own realm of knowledge, in other words that of there being a knowledge *in* practice rather than simply knowledge *for* practice. If the possibility of the former is dismissed, then it is easy to fall into the position of seeing practice purely as a realm of techniques. Of course, any practice does involve particular skills for which practitioners can be trained. Furthermore, there is always a tendency for practice to become routine and predictable. But, at the same time, and this is a point that Schon strongly emphasises, practice situations are not only unique, they are also characterised by a complexity and uncertainty which resist routinisation.

Teaching is a familiar example – there have been continual efforts to routinise teaching by reducing it to a set of behavioural skills, but despite all these it continues to resist routinisation. To be a teacher is not to apply a set of skills derived from theoretically based knowledge, for example, that of behaviourist psychology. It is certainly not a matter of acting in repeated and predictable ways learnt from a body of theoretical knowledge. The skilful knowledge of teachers is manifested in their actions and cannot be derived from a theoretical framework or from the application of a single type of rationality.

Thus, the tendency towards the routine and the predictable would be now regarded as a 'pathological' rather than a 'normal' characteristic of practice. This is probably a function of changing discourses and theorisations of practice. Modernist discourses of practice are increasingly being challenged by postmodern discourses. These are sceptical of the attempts by modernist epistemology to gate-keep knowledge, to define anything other than scientific knowledge and generalised theory as non-legitimate and to privilege predictability and control. In postmodern discourse, there is an emphasis on diversity, on different forms of knowledge and the significance of contextualised knowledge, and on the possibility of multiple rationalities.

Elliott (1991) talks about teachers' 'practical wisdom', by which he means their capacity to discern the right course of action when confronted with particular, complex and problematic states of affairs. This practitioner knowledge is not stored in the mind as sets of theoretical propositions but as a reflectively processed repertoire of cases. Within these there is theoretical knowledge, but understanding and acting in practice situations does not depend exclusively on this knowledge. It does not provide the practitioner with a prior knowledge of the right means to realise particular ends in particular contexts.

The possession of practical wisdom or knowledge, therefore, is knowing how to act appropriately in relation to the circumstances of a particular situation or context. This may involve general or universal knowledge (theoretical knowledge) but by being contextually mediated it becomes particularised. It is knowledge of the world mediated by the need in practice for action. This mediation is not 'accomplished by any appeal to technical rules or method (in the Cartesian sense), or by the subsumption of a pre-given determinate to a particular case' (Bernstein 1986: 99).

Practical knowledge cannot be universal because it cannot 'look away' from its context. Contexts are not particular instances of a universal characteristic because they have too many unique and indeterminate features. A context cannot be acted upon through the application of rules invariant across all contexts. Furthermore, practical knowledge is not knowledge of what is right 'in principle' or 'in theory', since it is not contemplative but performative knowledge – it is the enacted answer to the question 'How ought I to act?' It cannot, therefore, be knowledge which is external or 'objective' to the knower, rather it is knowledge 'with prejudice', where the knower is constituted through a set of pre-understandings through which to know the world and act within it.

These characteristics of practical knowledge show why it is inappropriate to see it as a matter of skills. Whilst it is 'know-how', it is not the know-how of techniques. A technique is learnt and therefore can become 'rusty' with disuse. Practical knowledge, because it is knowledge embodied in acting-in-the-world, is not subject to this possibility. As situated beings we always find ourselves in the position of having to answer the question 'How ought I to act?' with right and appropriate action. We can take up a skill and put it down again as the need arises, and if it falls into disuse then this will only be significant in the event that we wish to achieve the predetermined goal to which the skill is directed as a means. But we cannot do the same with practical knowledge because it is always present in the life of a situated being, although it can be ignored. It is always there and ongoing because we always find ourselves in situations where we have to make choices about how to act and then put those choices into effect, even if the choice is not to act. We might act inappropriately but that is not due to rusty or inadequate skills but because we have not 'read' the situation properly, we have, as it were, not confronted the 'text' with the right questions.

The second thing is that a technique is a means to achieve a pre-given and determinate end. When we use a technique we know in advance what the end-result will be. The technique is the most efficient and effective way to achieve the end and usually it is itself fixed within fairly narrow parameters and hence admits only a certain limited degree of variation. Practical knowledge, on the other hand, involves neither fixed ends nor fixed means known in advance. Within situatedness, ends may tentatively be known in advance but will change as the action unfolds and as the situation itself changes as the result of the action taken. So ends are always in a process of dynamic change. The same is the case with means – one cannot know in advance what the best means will be. Means have to be right and appropriate in the light of the situation, not in the light of achieving known and fixed ends. Thus, practical knowledge can be said to be characterised by a co-implication where the distinction between means and ends cannot be sustained. As the practitioner thinks about the end she or he wishes to achieve, the way it might be achieved is altered and, equally in acting, the end can itself change. Techniques, then, cannot be equated with practical knowledge since they are to do with instrumentality, where a sharp distinction between means and ends has to be maintained.

An action is always directed towards an end and in any practice the end is always constituted as a value. Think, for example, of what it means to act in any practice. What is the end to which action is directed? Nurses might say it is 'patient care'; teachers might say it is 'student learning'. The actions one takes as a practitioner are directed towards realising that end. But in both examples the ends are actually *values*. Thus, ends are constituted as desirable or valuable things to attain.

As the technical-rationality model indicates, practitioners are in the business of matching means to ends. However, means are chosen on the basis of whether they will realise the values that constitute the ends of practice. In the technical-rationality model, ends are always given or pre-defined, and the practitioner's task is simply one of choosing the most technically effective way of achieving the given end. What is most technically effective is decided by predictive theoretical knowledge. The counter-argument to this highlights what is most fundamentally wrong with the technical-rationality model in the eyes of its critics. In teaching, for example, it would be possible to say that student learning as an end having been pre-specified in terms of certain observable outcomes could then be achieved by selecting the most technically efficient means. What these were would be decided by, for example, behaviourist psychology. This might be some form of conditioning or shaping. At this point, it would be quite acceptable to question whether this would be appropriate or, indeed, acceptable.

The fact that such a debate is conceivable and proper shows that more is involved than the criterion of technical efficiency. Conditioning legitimately could be rejected on the grounds that teaching is a practice where student learning as an end cannot be separated from the means by which it is achieved. The end, student learning, is not neutral or value-free but is constituted as a value. As such, it cannot be realised simply by achieving a certain pre-specified outcome but rather in the quality of the means chosen. In other words, the value is realised through desirable, i.e., 'value-able' means. That is why conditioning might be considered unacceptable. It could be argued that conditioning is doing something but that whatever it is, it is not teaching – in other words, that conditioning is not appropriately part of an *educational* practice. The very idea of student learning does not make sense other than through the way it is brought about. Student learning as an end to be achieved does not have a meaning independent of the means used to achieve it. Conditioning as a means will certainly realise some end and, indeed, might be appropriate in certain practices, but the end will not be 'student learning' in an educational practice.

What this seems to indicate is that in a practice such as teaching it is never a matter of the most efficient achievement of neutral pre-defined ends nor of deciding what those means are purely in terms of predictive theory. Those who seek to foreground practical knowledge argue, therefore, that it is knowledge that enables practitioners to realise, in concrete and 'right' action, the values that define the ends of any practice. But 'right' actions must also be appropriate actions or means. The appropriate means of realising the values that are the ends of practice are context-specific. Practitioners are always in the business of having to make judgements in relation to the particular circumstances in which they find themselves. The question which always faces the practitioner – 'How ought I to act?' – does not have an invariant answer; rather, there are different answers for different contexts and different values.

Values are themselves not invariant but always open to interpretation. They do not as it were 'fall from heaven' ready made. What they precisely mean and what they precisely imply has to be figured out in the light of particular concrete situations. Practitioners always have to ask themselves the questions 'What do the values that define the ends of my practice mean in this particular context in which I am working?' 'How can they be properly realised in this particular context?' 'Can I act in the same way as I acted in the context in which I found myself yesterday?' The value 'student learning' can be interpreted differently and is capable of being realised differently according to context. In certain contexts, for instance in a training context, conditioning might well be considered appropriate. Thus, practitioners act in relation to an understanding of the context in which the values of their practice are to be realised and in which action is taken. It follows, therefore, that the way they interpret values and the way they understand the actions needed to realise values will be contested and changing. What always remains the same is the co-implication of means and ends.

The weakness of the technical-rationality model is perhaps revealed most clearly in educational practice. In practices such as engineering and medicine it is possible to argue that ends might well be determinate and knowable in advance. Here technical-rationality probably is a dominant meaning in defining practice. Thus, whilst ends are still constituted as values, they are perhaps not subject to the same value-conflicts. But it has been argued that, in education, means and ends are inseparable – the relationship is intrinsic rather than extrinsic or instrumental. As we have seen, means are never simply technical matters; indeed, in education they hardly ever are. As Carr and Kemmis (1986) point out, means are about what it is permissible to do to other people and what it is not.

A practice such as education has ends, but these are not given and are only temporarily determinate. Value-conflicts about the nature of education, what goals it should be directed towards and what purposes it should serve are endemic and intrinsic to the educational project. It also follows from this that, since there is always conflict over ends, in other words, since ends cannot be pre-defined, there is also conflict over the choice of means, a conflict which cannot be resolved by means of a set of technical rules or procedures.

These are the problematics which many practitioners, and not just in education, always have to face and work through. For them, practice presents itself through dilemmas and choices. The situations within which they work are often ambiguous and uncertain. The application of invariant rules or the following of algorithmic procedures is therefore highly inappropriate. This perhaps makes it very clear why the point discussed earlier about the practitioner's stance towards theory is so apposite in relation to educational practice. In a dilemmatic world of uncertainty, where ends and means are co-implicated and where practice is so closely bound up with the realisation of values, it is hardly surprising that theory appears remote, irrelevant and threatening.

A third aspect is to do with the instrumentality of techniques. This emphasis on instrumentality means that technical-rationality cannot take account of the ethical and social dimensions of practice. Practical knowledge, on the other hand, in so far as it is implicated with values, always has an ethical dimension which, as we have seen, is an intrinsic and integral feature of practice. But again, it is important to recognise that practical knowledge is not just a matter of applying universal ethical rules or standards of behaviour. In the same way that theoretical knowledge in the form of generalised propositions is mediated and particularised, so too are universal ethical rules.

There is, however, another aspect of this ethical dimension which foregrounds the *social* nature of practical knowledge. Practical knowledge is not something that exists solely in the minds of individuals, because it is rooted in sociality and intersubjectivity. The situatedness of practical knowledge involves the socio-cultural biography of individuals, their immersion in historically located and culturally derived meanings. Situations or contexts also involve the intersubjectivity of self–other relations, and practical knowledge is about acting in relation to others.

The Schonian dilemma of rigour versus relevance is a characteristic of practice which is also found in the education and training of practitioners or in continuing professional development (Usher and Bryant 1989). Here, the dilemma arises because continuing professional development has a rationale which is invariably 'practical', in the sense of helping practitioners to develop the skills and capabilities that will enhance the quality of their practice. Yet, because continuing professional education curricula emphasise theoretical knowledge, the practical aim is invariably not realised.

In the same way as this dilemma is resolved in practice by emphasising rigour, so too in continuing professional development the dilemma is invariably resolved in the same way. This indicates that the same technical-rationality model found in practice functions as a dominant and oppressive paradigm in the practice of continuing professional education. Again, for practice to be relevant, there is a need for practice be addressed as it 'really' is. This means that practitioners invariably have to abandon the rigour postulated by the technical-rationality model.

Equally, the privileging of theoretical studies in professional education and training appears to inculcate rigour yet so often leaves practitioners feeling that they have not learnt anything relevant to their world of everyday practice. Of course, this dilemma is well known in professional schools and is usually thought to be the outcome of a gap between theory and practice, a gap that can be bridged by communicating theory more effectively. Yet, doubt has been expressed about this resolution, since it is unclear that theory can be made more accessible and relevant in the terms asked for. Another solution, one informally adopted by many practitioners, is to abandon theory altogether and concentrate instead on improving techniques. This is an attractive and to some extent powerful resolution but again doubts have been expressed on the grounds that this is likely to deprive practitioners of the means by which they can confront their practice critically. In removing the possibility of change, it would seem to be ultimately a conservative position. It is also the source of endless dispute because the 'practical' as understood by practitioners does not have the same signification as the 'practical' defined by the essentially philosophical (or theoretical) arguments we have been deploying so far.

If we return for a moment to educational practice, then it is clear that the nature of this practice has implications for the education of practitioners. It would seem sensible to have a curriculum based on practice rather than on, for example, theoretical knowledge organised in disciplines. The dilemmatic nature of practice, the co-implication of means/ ends and the constitution of ends as values would need to be properly reflected in such a curriculum. One could go further than this and argue that since 'educational' practice is no longer confined to those who practise in formal educational institutions but embraces all 'enablers of learning', then the question of what is an appropriate curriculum, a curriculum which does not simply transmit or which is not based on the technical-rationality model, is likely to be a relevant one for any continuing professional education.

RECONSIDERING THE NATURE OF PRACTICE

One of the paradoxical outcomes of the privileging of theory is a failure to problematise practice. It also arises when the dilemma of rigour versus relevance is resolved purely in terms of relevance. What results is 'practicism' – a position based on a privileging of the practitioner's understanding of the 'practical' which we mentioned earlier and which is still caught within a technical-rational discourse.

One possible way forward, therefore, is to begin by clarifying the nature of 'theory'. In Usher and Bryant (1989) it is argued that there is another and more productive way of understanding theory, a way which relates it to the actions and intentionality of practitioners. Since action always involves intentionality, the intentions of the practitioner are a crucial feature of practice. Intentions are embedded in conceptual frameworks which are referred to as 'informal theory'. The argument is that practice presupposes that the practitioner has an informal theory. If 'theory' is interpreted in this sense, then the relationship between theory and practice is not contingent but conceptual, i.e., necessary. Informal theory becomes a condition of practice.

Of course, this assumes a distinction between 'theory' in the conventionally accepted sense of the term as against theory which is 'of' and 'for' practice, located in and directed towards a particular field of activity. At the same time, if practice always involves theory, then it follows that theorising, the process of theory-generation, is itself a practice. A useful initial distinction might be that there is 'theorising-in-practice' which prac-titioners do, 'theorising-for-practice' which theorists do, and 'theorising-of-practice' which practitioners can but often do not do. What this highlights is that every practitioner is involved in both theory and practice in some form. In other words, theorising is a practice; theorists as conventionally understood are also involved in practice just as practitioners are involved in theory.

What distinguishes practitioners of whatever kind is their contexts of work, their discursive traditions and their 'raw materials'. These differ-ences mean that concerns, meanings and 'objects' are framed differently. Theorising which is an outcome of a theoretical practice is therefore differ-ent from the theorising which is a condition of a 'field' practice. As field practitioners, teachers, for example, do not work with abstract universal categories such as 'students' or 'learning', or if they do then these categories are mediated by the nature of specific contexts where there are specific students with specific learning needs and problems and where there is a need to act within these contexts. As we have seen earlier, theor-ists, as conventionally understood, do work with abstract universal categories.

One of the advantages of seeing things this way is that it allows the theorist to be located. The conventional picture we have is of the theorist as disembodied and disembedded. However, if theorising is seen as a prac-tice, then theorists are brought back 'down to earth' from the transcen-dental realm. We can ask the same kinds of questions that we would of the field practitioner – 'What is the theorist's context of practice and what is the theorist's "informal" theory?' We shall return later to these questions and the issues they raise.

The more conventional way of reversing the 'theory–practice' dualism by privileging 'practice' simply creates another radical separation. The reconfiguration of theory, however, enables the theory–practice relation-ship to be itself reconfigured in such a way as to subvert the dualism with-out putting another one in its place. It affords an understanding of theory as interwoven with and inseparable from practice. It can be seen as the means by which practice is made meaningful. Theory, in this sense, cannot be mechanically applied to practice since it is always *already* in practice. Furthermore, practice cannot any longer be seen as routine and predictable behaviour because it is always imbued with the practical knowledge of informal theory.

The argument, therefore, is that informal theory enables practitioners to work within the contexts of practice which they find themselves in. As we saw earlier, Elliott's practical wisdom consisted of situational repertoires, a notion which Schon also uses. He refers to the practitioner as building up a situational repertoire by means of which the new and unfamiliar is related to similar but different situations previously encountered. Every practice situation can therefore potentially both extend and reconstruct the repertoire. Although he does not use the term 'informal theory', his notion of the situational repertoire comes close to it. For Schon, every practitioner has a 'theory-in-action', a theory which is neither generalisable, predictive nor rigorous in a positivistic-empiricist sense.

This informal theory can be seen as part of the experiential world of practitioners. It is a kind of knowledge which is not abstract and decontextualised, yet equally is not merely intuitive and unsystematic. It is situated theory both entering into and emerging from practice. With this notion of informal theory, it is the inseparability rather than the separability of theory and practice which is emphasised. Practitioners are not confined simply to applying theory developed elsewhere by theorists but are themselves engaged in theoretical and practical resolution of the dilemmas presented by their day-to-day practice.

This means that there is no longer any need to accept the troubling theory–practice dualism and the confusing metaphor of 'gaps'. In Usher and Bryant (1989) the conclusion is that practice needs to be conceived as action informed by theory. The implication of this is the rejection of any notion of practice, particularly educational practice, as founded on a bedrock of formal theory or being about technical control. Instead, a notion of practitioner expertise and judgement was argued for with the practitioner as sense-maker and action-taker where, in true Schonian fashion, action, situational knowledge and judgement are mutually interactive.

Of course, we were also aware that the status of informal theory was problematic. Informal theory must be largely implicit, certainly not always present to the consciousness of the practitioner. Also, it is assumed that informal theory is practical knowledge, but not in the practitioner's sense of 'practical'. The very notion of practical knowledge is contentious. Viewed from the standpoint of technical-rationality and even of critical theory, practical knowledge can be and often has been characterised (usually dismissively) as mere anecdotal or common-sense knowledge – the unquestioned assumptions held in common by practitioners and supposedly derived from personal experience. In essence, practical knowledge tends to be thought of as knowledge derived from *personal* experience. For technical-rationality, such knowledge is unsystematic and untrustworthy. For the critical theorist, both formal and informal theory are problematic. The practitioner knowledge of informal theory is not just a product of personal experience but also of professional socialisation, but whatever its source it has an inherently oppressive and conservative tendency. Formal theory is not just an 'objective' way of deciding how to practice but is also implicated with powerful interests.

Craft knowledge and practical knowledge are very often thought of as identical, a position which is frequently due to an unproblematic acceptance of the practitioner understanding of the 'practical'. Elliott (1991) describes craft knowledge as know-how encapsulated in behavioural repertoires, fine-tuned in trial-and-error experience and transmitted as common-sense tips within the professional peer group. Craft knowledge and common-sense knowledge seem to be barely distinguishable, and certainly they have a common characteristic in being a taken-for-granted form of knowledge. As Elliott puts it, a practice that works on craft knowledge alone cannot be a reflexive practice. In being oriented towards what works, it cannot easily reflect upon and change itself.

This immediately points to certain problematic elements in informal theory. First, given that it is practitioner-based, it will be private and unique to the individual practitioner. To what extent, therefore, it can be 'public', shared and hence open to change is problematic. Second, informal theory may be limited in scope and depth. In a sense, the problem with informal theory is that its very strength – its rootedness in practice – is also its weakness. Although we referred to it earlier as a necessary condition of practice, it is not a *sufficient* condition. In the same way that practice is more than the application of theory, so practice is more than the use of informal theory. Practical knowledge is not the same as 'practicist' knowledge.

On the one hand, informal theory need not simply be a set of taken-for-granted assumptions based on habit, routine and disabling prejudices. In dilemmatic situations, situational repertoires function only as a starting-point for understanding and action. New situations need not necessarily be seen in routine and habitualised ways as identical copies of past situations, since the job of situational repertoires is to differentiate between the same and the different. Here, informal theory can go beyond the routine and habitual and become the ground of creativity without becoming detached from its situational roots.

Even here, however, informal theory has its limitations. As Schon himself admits, practitioners may engage in reflection-in-action but do not always do so. Part of the problem is that since reflection-in-action is about experimenting in unique and uncertain situations, risk and unpredictability are inherently present. It is the very characteristics which give reflection-in-action its own particular rigour which may also lead to perceived threats of unpredictability, uncertainty and loss of control on the part of the practitioner. Practitioners may, therefore, remain enclosed in what Schon calls 'knowing-in-practice'. Even when they do engage in reflection-in-action, they may not be able to articulate what they are doing or may be unable to find an authority for what they do. Working reflectively may often appear to have no external justification – it may feel right for oneself but at the same time may seem to have no generalisable value.

If the theory–practice dualism is rejected on the grounds that it is impossible to conceive of practice without informal theory, this implies that the term 'theory' refers to practitioners' informal theory and not to the formal theory located outside practice. It could be argued that the failure to recognise this and to distinguish between formal and informal theory is the origin of the notion that a 'gap' exists between theory and practice, where formal theory is the theory being referred to. The implication of this position is that the 'gaps' are really situations where informal theory and practice are not 'meshing'. Here, the source of the problem lies in the practitioner's informal theory. This suggests that improving practice is a matter not of making practice more rigorous through the application of formal theory but through changing informal theory. The changes may be small or they may be of such a magnitude as to involve a fundamental change in practice – a paradigm shift in informal theory.

If we say that practice is located in informal theory (equally, one could put it the other way and say that informal theory is located in practice), theorising is seen as an inevitable feature of practising. It would be possible to argue, therefore, that the theory–practice hierarchy has been 'deconstructed' rather than simply reversed by privileging the normally subordinated pole of the theory–practice dualism. The dualism is dissolved through showing how theory and practice are always co-implicated.

One consequence which seems to follow from this is that practitioners need to be aware of the place of theory in their work. On the other hand, this raises the question of what the place of formal theory might be. Ideally, those whose practice is the generation of formal theory need to have the concerns of practitioners as their starting-point. Although it is impossible to conceive of practice without informal theory, the latter, as we have seen, may be limited in terms of its degree of articulation, coherence and consistency. Formal theory, it might be argued, can play an important part in making explicit what is largely implicit and, beyond that, as a means of critically appraising informal theory.

Becoming aware of informal theory can make practitioners more conscious of routine and habitual modes of working. In Usher and Bryant (1989) we referred to the need for practice to become praxis – a form of practice which is both reflective and reflexive. Reflexivity requires that theory and practice are mutually interactive and recognised as such. Here, informal theory, by being brought to consciousness, becomes open to change in the light of practice, which itself changes with changes in informal theory.

The argument is that the tools needed for critical appraisal can be at least partially provided by formal theory. At this point, we introduced the notion of 'review', deliberately trading on the multiple meaning of the term in order to suggest both a process of looking back at ('re-view') and of critical examination (review). Whilst formal theory seeks to represent and explain the world, informal theory is concerned with judgement, interpretation and understanding. Practice needs to be re-presented and it is here that formal theory can be a useful tool for 'reviewing' practice in a different way. Here, therefore, formal theory is not *applied* to practice but is one means by which practice is re-viewed and reviewed.

The process we had in mind involves recognising and valuing practice as a realm of knowledge in its own right but also confronting and questioning it. This is not a smuggling-in of formal theory through the back door, since its function is not to serve as a standard of veracity or as an indubitable foundation. In a sense, its purpose is to present 'yet another story' (Rorty 1989) – a story which elevates the abstract and the universal – and by being presented as another *story*, its implication in certain kinds of modernist discourse is more obviously revealed. The role of formal theory is to be a sounding-board, a resource for critiquing informal theory and exposing its limitations. As one component in a mutually interactive process, it can itself become more easily subject to critique.

The existence of practice problems indicates a failure of informal theory; their resolution requires an engagement of informal theory with something outside itself (an other). This engagement has to be a two-way traffic, otherwise one will submerge the other and the resolution will only be apparent. If formal theory submerges informal theory, any resolution would not involve action sufficiently situated to be appropriate to practice. If formal theory were submerged by informal theory, the apparent resolution would only be a restatement rather than a resolution of the problem.

Formal theories are bodies of knowledge which are themselves socially located and implicated in discursive practices. They help to normatively regulate practices. The power of formal theory is not always immediately apparent. Part of the problem the practitioner faces is to become aware of formal theory's place and power. The development of this kind of critical consciousness is the other side of the 'review' process. We have mentioned the role of formal theory in bringing a critical and positive dimension to bear on informal theory and practice, but it is clear that the problem becomes one of becoming critically aware of the existence, power and potential oppressiveness of formal theory within informal theory and practice. This issue is dealt with more extensively in Chapter 4.

So far, we have been discussing the relationship between theory and practice in very general terms, in effect, in terms of different theorisations of the theory–practice relationship. The fact is, that to speak of this relationship beyond feelings of uneasiness and threat is itself to speak theoretically and through the conceptual critical resources provided by a theoretical discourse.

METAPRACTICE

The theorisations we have been discussing tend to revolve around the relationship of thought or ideas and action. This is not surprising, since theory or theorising is generally considered a cognitive product or process and practice a matter of action. Thought or ideas has been conceptualised as taking the form either of formal or informal theory. Since it is the former which is invariably privileged, we have concentrated on those positions which highlight the key role of the latter. Yet, whichever is highlighted, the framework is always the same, i.e., one which privileges thought or ideas. In other words, the theorisations we have been discussing and working with have a strong psychologistic and rationalistic tendency. Our description, for example, of informal theory in terms of situational repertoires, makes it easy enough to assimilate this notion into a cognitive psychology where repertoires are understood as cognitive templates. To argue that every practitioner is guided by informal theory can easily become a more sophisticated way of saying that the practitioner has a set of ideas which guide what he or she does.

We can see that, to an important extent, this is what Schon is saying, and here perhaps is the major weakness in the Schonian 'paradigm'. Schon's primary concern is with the relationship between thought and action and the key role of a particular mode of thought, reflection-in-practice – reflection both after the event of practice (reflection-*on*-action) and during the event (reflection-*in*-action). What he wants to do is reconfigure the relationship and he therefore does not argue for a simple unidirectionality of thought causing action. He portrays the process as much more complex than that, a relationship of mutual interaction with thought informing action and vice versa.

None the less, the Schonian paradigm is essentially rationalistic in its emphasis on the significance of thought. It is also individualistic and psychologistic in the sense that reflection is cast as a psychological act carried out by individual practitioners. In Schon, we find no awareness of the socio-cultural location of practitioners and acts of reflection. Thus, Schon's resolution of the theory–practice problem, although highly illuminating, is in the end problematic. Schon's individualism and psychologism casts reflection and the notion of informal theory adrift in a cognitive limbo. He has tried to replace one set of ideas – formal theory – with another – informal theory – but the replacement does not work because ideas (thought) are still at centre stage and it is the very assumption of the centrality of thought which is problematic.

Kemmis (1989) has suggested that we should understand the relationship of theory and practice as embedded in social processes. He argues, rightly in our view, that the theory–practice relationship is not simply a matter of philosophical analysis but is itself a discursive and material social practice whose purpose is to secure agreements about the nature and conduct of a practice. He refers to this as a *metapractice*, i.e., a practice about a practice. Thus, for example, there is educational practice and a metapractice about educational practice, the metapractice being about what education is, its aims and purposes, how it relates to the economy and society, the nature of the curriculum and of its transmission through teaching. It is within the metapractice of education that the meaning of the theory–practice relationship in educational practice is forged.

A metapractice, by virtue of itself being a social practice, is both a material and a public process. Being in the public domain, it is transindividual and not simply a set of ideas. It is through a metapractice that a particular practice is constituted and, by being constituted in a particular way, shapes the consciousness of practitioners about the nature and significance of their work – in other words, it is through the metapractice and the meanings it provides that practitioners understand the work that they do. It is the metapractice which constitutes a practitioner's informal theory. So a metapractice does not provide the practitioner with a set of ideas but it does *locate* the practitioner within its dominant meanings. Conversely, informal theory is not just a practitioner's intentions. Discourses are transindividual and informal theory is formed through discourses and the meanings they provide. To what extent individual practitioners make these meanings 'their own', or make a personal investment in them, and to what extent they resist dominant meanings, will depend on a variety of complex factors which will discussed more fully in the chapter on reflective practice.

It is within a metapractice that the theory–practice relationship assumes a particular meaning within a particular practice. This meaning will define the place of theory, both formal and informal, within that practice. So, for example, the emphasis may be on formal theory and the need for its application in practice. In this metapractice, modernist discourses of foundational knowledge and instrumental rationality will provide the dominant meanings. Alternatively, the emphasis may be on informal theory and practical knowledge where hermeneutic discourses and notions of judgement and practitioner expertise provide dominant meanings. There may be an emphasis on reflection, either of the instrumental variety or of critical reflection for emancipatory action. Another possibility, as we have seen, is a more postmodern emphasis on multiple rationalities, diversity and fragmentation in practices.

Thus, in some metapractices, the meaning of theory and its relationship to practice may be settled and uncontentious. In others, such as, for example, education, it may be multiple and contested. Metapractices will themselves change over time, unsettling or radically changing dominant meanings. But, at any one point in time, the relationships between theory, practice and policy will be constituted through a metapractice, in a concrete way and with a set of dominant meanings.

Kemmis's emphasis on metapractices as social, public and material has the advantage of bringing the theory–practice relationship 'down to earth' from the philosophical plane of discussion where it is normally situated to the 'real world' of argument and conflict, competing discourses, interests and dominant meanings. The theory–practice problem is not a purely philosophical problem which can be resolved by deploying logic and systematic reasoning. Of course, it takes that form in becoming part of the metapractice of a practice. But, once we start conceiving of it in terms of notions such as 'metapractice', we realise that there is no superordinate resolution or 'truth' of the theory–practice problem.

The relationship between theory and practice is one which can only be understood in terms of particular socio-cultural contexts. If there is a problem, and there invariably is, it is a problem within the terms of a metapractice and this is always parasitic upon the particular practice. Here, the notion of a 'problem' does not refer to a universal or transcendental problem of theory and practice but is the signifier of the contest between different meanings of what a particular practice is about, what its ends are and how those ends are best achieved. Because it is also a contest which involves power, particularly the power to impose certain meanings rather than others, the stakes are high. It is also a contest which goes beyond a particular practice in the sense that defining the relationship between that practice, the economy, the state, etc. may be part of the stakes in the conflict. This is the case in education, for example. The metapractice of education involves not only educational practitioners but also politicians, bureaucrats and businessmen as well as educational theorists and researchers. Here, the 'resolution' of the theory–practice problem, for example, by emphasising either a return to a curriculum based on disciplinary knowledge or a vocationalist curriculum based on the needs of the country's economic standing is a stake in the conflict over how education is to be defined and who is to do the defining.

Thus the theory–practice 'problem' is implicated with what groups of people (practitioners but not just practitioners) say and do (their discursive and material practices), with the meanings generated through this and the investments and interests which groups and their members have in sustaining or challenging these meanings. To conceptualise the matter this way allows us to get away from the individualism, psychologism and rationalism presented by disembodied and disembedded philosophical accounts. Theorising does not take place in a vacuum. This is equally the case for the formal theorising of the theorist, the informal theorising of the practitioner and the theorising which constitutes the theory–practice relationship in particular ways.

Chapter 7

The reflective practitioner revisited

In this chapter, we return to the idea of critical practice as reflection-in-action and revisit the influential ideas of Donald Schon as set out in his widely-used texts *The Reflective Practitioner* (1983) and *Educating the Reflective Practitioner* (1987). In the present authors' own work *Adult Education as Theory, Practice and Research: The Captive Triangle* (1989), we incorporated some of Schon's ideas into an examination of adult education practice and action research as an associated mode of enquiry. In the light of our re-examination of the relationship between theory and practice, and our own experiences in exploring educational practice with graduate students and fellow adult educators, we now believe that there are some problems with Schon's analysis of reflective practice. It is not our intention to belittle the contribution that he has undoubtedly made to furthering an understanding of practitioner development but rather to build on his understanding by reviewing the claims that Schon himself makes on behalf of 'reflective practice'.

In revisiting Schon, we first set out his propositions about the nature of reflection-in-action, asking the question 'To what extent can these be considered to constitute a *theory* of (adult) education practice?' Second, Schon's *methodology* in discovering the nature of reflective practice and in reaching certain conclusions about how it can be enhanced is examined. This is an issue neglected by Schon's commentators, one which we believe to be important since it raises questions about the relationship between 'reflection' and 'reflexivity'. By treating Schon's own major works as examples of *textual practice*, we can ask 'To what extent do they exemplify the qualities that he commends?' In the context of these questions, the rest of the chapter is devoted to a consideration of how some adult educators known to us go about their own practice as 'reflective practitioners'. We have collected evidence in the form of interview material, transcript extracts of which we try to analyse reflexively as textual accounts of our own (i.e., the interviewers') and others (i.e., the interviewees') practices.

THE ARGUMENT FOR REFLECTION-IN-ACTION

The opening chapters of *The Reflective Practitioner* tell a story of the crisis of the professions and propose the route to a possible solution. It is a compelling account, inviting readers who are concerned about the quality and grounding of their practices to question the status of professional knowledge claims. The 'crisis' is interpreted by Schon not just as that of the professions' self-interest, misconduct or failure to solve society's problems (though this is presented as its context), but more fundamentally as one of the grounding of professional knowledge. Technical-rationality is a positivist epistemology of practice, the dominant paradigm which has failed to resolve the dilemma of rigour versus relevance confronting professionals. A new epistemology of practice is proposed, in which the knowledge inherent in practice is to be understood as artful doing. In setting out his case for reflection-in-action, Schon argues that its distinctive structure as the key ingredient of reflective practice can be theorised and illustrated by means of 'a sample of vignettes of practice, concentrating on episodes in which a senior practitioner tries to help a junior one learn to do something' (Schon 1983: viii). He is therefore proposing a theory of the process of reflection-in-action, substantiated by case examples, which is explicitly intended to encourage the practitioner as researcher and researcher as practitioner to improve the quality of their thinking in action and thereby become 'reflective practitioners'.

In view of the dominance of the technical-rationality model and its understanding of theory as something separate from and applied to practice (which is effectively critiqued), this is nevertheless an ambitious and somewhat paradoxical project. For, if Schon himself is indeed proposing a *theory* of reflective practice by unpacking and explaining the process of reflection-in-action, as we believe to be the case, then what is there to discourage would-be reflective practitioners from simply attempting to 'apply' Schon's analysis, i.e., treating it instrumentally, in the belief that they could thereby reach this state? Schon would doubtless argue that this is not what he intends. We would want to argue, however, that this is irrelevant and that it is frequently how Schon is read. The canonical nature of Schon's works, their prominence in postgraduate education curricula and the paucity of critiques of Schon all support this view. Certainly, Schon's own view is that the theory of reflective practice is not one to be 'applied' but enacted. But the problem seems to us to lie with Schon's own failure to address the lessons of reflection-in-action to his own practice as a producer of text. This is a problem of the *absence of reflexivity* in his works. To understand the nature of the relationship between reflection and reflexivity, to explore the relationship more self-consciously than Schon himself demonstrates, we need to consider how practices themselves are inscribed – including the situated practice of academic writing. This is a dimension of practice which Schon does not attend to when setting out his understanding of reflection-in-action.

Professionals are increasingly coming to realise that practice is not just about 'problem solving' or selecting technical means to achieve given ends, but concerns 'problem setting', defined by Schon as a non-technical process, one 'in which, interactively, we *name* the things to which we will attend and *frame* the context in which we will attend to them' (ibid.: 40; emphasis in original). This often happens in contexts where something previously thought to be settled turns out to be surprising. Reflection, as the process of turning 'thought back on action and on the knowing which is implicit in action' (ibid.: 50), is stimulated by surprise, an invitation to renaming and reframing. Naming and framing are parts of process by which we come to understand what is going on in practice situations. Through renaming and reframing we revise our views of practice and discover new action possibilities. The knowing which is implicit in action, or 'knowing-in-action' is defined as 'the characteristic mode of ordinary practical knowledge' (ibid.: 54). Schon appeals to our common-sense appreciation of know-how and cites examples of the improvised performances of peasant craftspeople, musicians, baseball players, children learning to balance blocks, that readers can readily identify with, as well as referring to Polanyi's (1958) concept of tacit knowing and Ryle's (1949) performative knowing, to illustrate this process. Formal or propositional knowledge (i.e., the state rather than the process) is often something that we do not have of our own knowing. One way of putting this is to say that knowledge may be the result of a knowing which is theorised *for* us rather than *by* us. Adults, for example, theorise the knowledge that children have; children just get on with knowing. Passive knowledge, though our own, may be the result of a *post hoc* reflection-*on*-action. Reflection-*in*-action, by contrast, focuses 'interactively on the outcomes of action, the action itself, and the intuitive knowing implicit in the action' (ibid.: 56). The promise of reflection-in-action is that it can cause us to rethink and possibly abandon previously-held tacit knowledge or theories-in-action, and actively to build new theories suggestive of new courses of action. The new theories may themselves be either informal or couched in more formal and explicit propositions of an 'if–then' kind. In principle then, reflection-in-action may produce performative and/or propositional knowledge. In either event, the test of reflection-in-action is successful action, not knowledge as such. Reflection-in-*practice* is bounded by what Schon calls an 'action-present' and is more or less immediate, depending on the exigencies of the situation in which practitioners are required to act. It is recognised that, as a practical matter, reflective practitioners cannot engage in reflection-in-action all the time.

These are powerful ideas, posing serious theoretical challenges to the technical-rationality model of practice and the positivist paradigm. If we are to play Schon off against himself, and reflect as educators on the value of his own construction of the process of reflection-in-action and recommendations for practice, an important practical question arises. Given that we are interested in helping professionals become reflective practitioners and that we believe Schon has a place in the curriculum, how are we to teach him: a) as a formal theorist of reflective practice, b) as an exemplar of how in particular cases to tease out, challenge and change our knowing-in-action or c) some combination of both? Certainly, Schon is challenging the theory–practice dualism and the presumed dependence of the latter on the former; in a sense we can say that he reverses the relationship. Reflection-in-action is a practice of generating theory which speaks back to and revises action. Theory is to be seen, therefore, as something which is practised or enacted and not merely the result of disembodied contemplation. In offering his understanding of reflection-in-action as a new epistemology of practice, Schon is 'doing theory'. The result, we contend, is certainly theory , but what kind of 'theory' is it and how is it produced through his own textual practice? From our practical interests as adult educators, the first of these questions can be approached by looking at some of the criteria for formal theory in adult education to see if Schon's own understandings of reflective practice fit them.

SCHON AS A THEORIST

Brookfield (1992) reports that recent explanations of teaching and learning in adult education have been characterised by an emphasis on the development of informal theory and situationally specific knowledge. The experiential learning and reflective practice movements have encouraged this trend. We have shown how formal theorising has been disfavoured by practitioners in the belief that it is overly abstract, inherently disputatious and does not speak immediately to practice. Yet, there are a number of reasons why, according to Brookfield, the attempt to build formal theory should not be abandoned. First, adult education as an academic practice has to address the contexts of that practice and its location within a discourse which has elevated formal theory; if it is to be a critical and reflective practice then there will be occasions when it needs to engage with formal theory and address its own concerns at that level. Second, formal theory can help 'to convert situationally specific, informal hunches into well framed theories of practice' (ibid.: 80). It is part of the armoury of reflective practice and can help to reframe that practice. In contrast, informal theory is grounded in the particular and local. Without testing and review through the perspective of formal theory, its horizons are limited to the anecdotal (Usher 1985). Third, as generic practitioners, adult educators are engaged in a common pursuit of helping adults to learn and need to examine those aspects of their practice which transcend any particular distinctions. Formal theory is potentially an aid to com-munication between researchers, teachers, administrators and policy-makers, all of whom may have a common interest in adult education but operate in different practice contexts with different informal understandings.

Brookfield maintains that formal theories have to be a) appropriately grounded in practitioners' experiences, b) accessible to practitioners in terms of language and c) critically sensitive to the contexts of practice. These criteria are central to Schon's project, since he is explicitly trying to develop a new epistemology of practice to counter the positivist para-digm. He is theorising a process of reflection-in-action which is extremely difficult to pin down, rather than a set of bounded activities. It is necessary to make inferences from observations of practice in order to decide what is to count as an instance of reflection-in-action and what is not to count. The grounding of Schon's theory is, therefore, of particular significance. As we shall see in a discussion of Schon's methodology later in this chapter, his analyses are limited to short strips of practice and, in key cases, to records generated by others. Given that the process of reflection-in-action can be rather prolonged, both the identification and research ability of reflective practice can be practically problematic. Even though Schon regards 'practitioners of the unique case [to be] of special interest from the point of view of the study of reflection-in-action' (Schon 1983: 108) he sees many practices as exhibiting a 'generic design process' (ibid.: 77). His domain, therefore, is the effective design of practice, as an ongoing activity, generalisable to professions beyond those concerned explicitly with design *per se*.

Schon's project in *Educating the Reflective Practitioner* is directly con-cerned with communicating the new paradigm when he asks at the outset 'what kind of professional education [is] appropriate for an epistemology of practice based on reflection-in-action?' (Schon 1987: xi–xii), thus directly addressing the practical question of teaching for reflective practice. In this work, Schon extends his analysis of reflection-in-action to show how practitioners can use their past experiences by drawing on a repertoire of practice examples and understandings in order to make sense of new and problematic situations. Unique cases are reviewed in terms of how similar or different they appear to be to those encountered in the past, an exercise in reframing which then needs to be tested in action by conducting local experiments to discover their practical consequences. 'Move-testing' experiments can be conducted in which 'the test of the affirmation of a move is not only Do you get what you intend? but Do you like what you get?' (ibid.: 71). The successful teacher of reflective practice is one who exemplifies in her/his own practice the possibilities for reframing practice through move-testing, gaming, and 'as–if' reconstructions of problematic situations. This is why Schon emphasises the value of considering *practice as design*, whereby virtual worlds can be constructed and modified at will, and why the design studio is for him a prototypical site for researching the process of reflection-in-action. Teaching for reflective practice 'makes use of actions as well as words; and it depends upon reciprocal reflection-in-action' (ibid.: 101). He presents a model of teaching based on coaching principles, learning by doing and commentary on doing. Coaching is a transactional and reconstructive process, incorporating demonstration and commentary, imitation and review, in which the student adds to her/his own repertoire of actions. From the perspective of the coach, 'every attempt to produce an instruction is an experiment that tests both the coach's reflection on his own knowing-in-action and his understanding of the student's difficulty' (ibid.: 104). From that of the student, 'imitative reconstruction of an observed action is a kind of problem solving. . . . Its constructive process is none the less a form of reflection-in-action – an on-the-spot enquiry in which the imitator constructs and tests, in its own action, the essential features of the action it has observed' (ibid.: 109). Coach and student are each adjusting to perceived errors in performance, and these adjustments are chained in a reflective sequence which Schon describes as a 'ladder of reflection'. 'Climbing up the ladder, one makes what has happened at the rung below into an object of reflection . . . climbing down the ladder, one acts on the basis of a previous reflection' (ibid.: 114).

The result of successful reciprocal moves up and down the ladder of reflection is a 'convergence of meaning' (ibid.: 116), or what we have also described as a hermeneutic 'fusion of horizons'. In any learning transaction, however, the parties will bring their own theories-in-use or 'stances' to bear. These can be exemplified by the use of what Rorty refers to as 'final vocabularies' (Rorty 1989: 73 ff.) which foreclose reflection and create what Schon calls 'learning binds'. Drawing on his earlier work with Argyris (Argyris and Schon 1974), Schon demonstrates how learning binds are the result of single-loop learning and Model 1 theories-in-use, in which participants seek, through win–lose strategies, only knowledge that would confirm their own stance. This creates a problem for the teacher of reflective practice who needs to get learners to interrogate such theories and associated actions as a condition for removing a learning bind. In practice, the responsibility is placed on teachers to open their own theories-in-use to reflection and scrutiny by students – acting as exemplars of a process that they are commending to others.

It is in relation to the contextual sensitivity of his notion of reflection-in-action that we would wish to argue that Schon's theory of reflective practice is less 'critical' than it appears to be, since it is not directed to its own situated practice of doing theory. It does not examine its own context nor the contexts of practitioners whose exchanges are offered as evidence of the process of reflection-in-action. According to Brookfield, 'to satisfy the criterion of contextual sensitivity the theory would . . . have to make explicit the context specific aspects of the case studies from which formal theoretical propositions were derived' (Brookfield 1992: 89). Schon's cases are one-to-one encounters and reconstructed examples of practice as coaching and design, and it is on these cases that he builds a theory of (and recommendations for) practice. His two major works also demonstrate, as one would expect, that the theory of reflective practice has developed over time, through extended commentary on new cases. But, as we hope to demonstrate, this does not amount to a reformulation since it misses an important critical dimension of practice.

What Schon does develop in his 1987 work is the idea of the 'reflective practicum' to institute his recommendations for enacting this new epistemology of practice. Here, he is concerned with the problematics of the practicum, both in terms of its internal arrangements and how it sits within the context of wider institutional concerns. He reaffirms the nature of practice as design-like, something that is learnable and coachable but not teachable. The practicum is concerned with 'building a relationship conducive to learning [which] begins with the explicit or implicit establishment of a contract that sets expectations for the dialogue' (Schon 1987: 167). Developing the reflective abilities of practitioners places the emphasis on the holistic, creative and quality dimensions of action. Learning outcomes cannot be prescribed and are difficult to describe. Consequently, 'in order to be credible and legitimate, a practicum must become a world with its own culture, including its own language, norms, and rituals. Otherwise it may be overwhelmed by the academic and professional cultures that surround it' (ibid.: 170). Establishing a reflective practicum is itself a problem of design (ibid.: 305 ff.), one which has to take account of the dual orientation of schools of professional development to academic disciplines on the one hand and the world of practice on the other. It is here that Schon returns to the rigour/relevance problematic and proposes that the design problem for the practicum is one of 'bridging'. The practicum 'must cultivate activities that connect the knowing- and reflection-in-action of competent practitioners to the theories and techniques taught as professional knowledge in academic courses' (ibid.: 312). There are many factors acknowledged by Schon and with which we can readily identify which discourage the development of sites for promoting his epistemology of practice. These include conventional academic demarcations, conceptions of normal science research, the reward structure, loss of professional autonomy, pressures for quick-fix technical solutions and clearly identifiable vocational competencies. The practice of teaching for reflection-in-action can easily be marginalised by such powerful forces. Schon's proposal is therefore to 'revitalise a phenomenology of practice [which] . . . must be substantively connected to traditional disciplines' (ibid.: 321). He suggests that the connection can be made by the tacit theories of practitioners engaging with the formal theories of traditional academic disciplines. Any exploration of the possibilities for reflection-in-action also needs to take account of theorisations of the organisational life of practitioners, 'and here a constructionist perspective is critically important' (ibid.: 322). Likewise, the disciplines need to be taught so that their methods of enquiry – as actual practices rather than abstract procedural logics – can be examined.

In the latter part of his text, Schon is clearly engaged in meta-reflection, i.e., reflecting on the conditions of possibility for reflection-in-action. The invitation to adopt a constructionist perspective, coupled with the demand to make method more visible, is paradoxical and highly significant. We have already argued that by stringent criteria Schon is indeed producing formal theory, embodied in a traditional academic product – textbooks. What we do *not* find in Schon is a reflection by him on his own textual practice in giving the kind of account that he does of reflection-in-action and the reflective practicum via presentations and interpretations of cases. He does not interrogate his own method. These are texts about reflection, but they are not reflexive texts. This we believe to be the root of the problem of teaching Schon's ideas by the unreflective use of his texts. They seem to be important and are quoted everywhere. It is not surprising, therefore, since these are well-regarded conventional academic products, that students think that in reading them they can learn how to become reflective practitioners. On the basis of our own experience in teaching graduate students in education, we have come to realise that there is a critical dimension of practice that Schon ignores; it is one which we need to consider in relation to any and all practices – our own, our students, and Schon's – namely, that practices are *inscribed*. We now turn to consider the implications of this in relation to aspects of Schon's methodology, especially the way in which he makes use of evidence in developing the case for his new epistemology of practice.

SCHON'S METHODOLOGY

It is our experience that educators who as graduate students are interested in professional development have an ambivalent attitude towards Schon. As practitioners they have misgivings about formal academic theory for reasons which Schon himself (ironically, in his role as an academic author and theorist) explains so well. At the same time, Schon's books appear to be directly addressing practitioners in offering suggestions in the form of case examples demonstrating the value of reflection-in-action in dealing with practice problems. As such, they are practitioner texts. But as Usher has noted, 'one of the most significant characteristics of the "practitioner" text is that *it does not draw attention to itself as a text*' (Usher 1993: 100; emphasis added). Schon does not 'read' his own text as a practice that, consistent with his own propositions, itself needs to be reflected upon. The few who have been fortunate in being able to engage directly with Schon in his seminars can participate in an enactment of his ideas. For most of us, however, an understanding of reflective practice is mediated through his writing.

> Theorising is a practice of writing. One writes about the meanings in practice and through writing creates the meanings of practice. Practice is itself always changing hence there are always new meanings to be written about. At the same time, through writing, the meaning of practice is re-created, always cast anew.
>
> (Usher 1993: 100)

This comment is as appropriate for Schon as it is for any other theorist. Schon produces (as we are also doing right now as academics writing this book) a 'conventional' text in generating a theory of reflection-in-action, and these conventions are not questioned as practices of inscription in their own right. This is an important dimension of practice that is missing from Schon, who wants to theorise the process and conditions for reflection-in-action in offering 'practical solutions' to practice problems, and who hints at metapractice, but who doesn't take the reflexive step required. Mutual reflection-in-action is scripted as an inherent problem for self and other, dramatically constructed through characters and their lines (Quist and Petra, Supervisor and Resident, Judith and Northover, etc.), tension and plot ('Will they/won't they solve the problem?'). This is engaging stuff, but it is limited. The problematic of reflection-in-action is individualised. To take the message of reflexivity is to question the scripting of practice as social convention in such a way as to produce writing which questions both the conventions and itself in the very act of its production – i.e., to demonstrate reflection-in-action as a critical practice, one which is open to a questioning of its own situatedness. Given the conventions of academic writing, this is difficult and perhaps ultimately impossible, but as Woolgar and others have shown (Mulkay 1985; Woolgar 1988; Steier 1991), the attempt is worthwhile. Woolgar and his collaborators produce 'self-conscious' text which is a mixture of informal commentary and conventionally structured and referenced 'academic' accounts, in the course of which they show how reflexivity turns on questions of representation: 'we need continually to interrogate and find strange the process of representation as we engage in it' (Woolgar 1988: 29). Reflexivity becomes a methodological issue concerning the narrative construction of objects and processes.

Schon does not discover reflection-in-action as something 'found' within experienced practitioners, but in his case examples he assembles evidence in the form of transcripts, many of which are admittedly not first-hand gatherings, and crafts an analysis of problem-solving exchanges between more and less experienced practitioners. The evidence is treated in an apparently straightforward (i.e., conventional) way, e.g.:

Example 1

The design studio (transcript evidence in italics, originally indented and non-italicised)

At the beginning of the review, Petra is stuck:

I've tried to butt the shape of the building into the contours of the land there – but the shape doesn't fit into the slope.

Quist criticises her framing of the problem, pointing out that she has tried to fit the shapes of the buildings into the contours of a "screwy" slope which offers no basis for coherence. Instead, he resets her problem:

You should begin with a discipline, even if it is arbitrary . . . you can always break it open later.

Petra should make . . . [etc.]

(Schon 1983: 93)

Example 2

The artistry of psychoanalytic practice (transcript evidence in italics, originally indented and non-italicised)

The supervisor's questioning suggests a repertoire of psychodynamic patterns accessible to him (but apparently not to the resident). He uses these to flesh out the resident's stories until they seem ready for interpretation, at which point he shifts abruptly to a search for explanations:

Well, that's your understanding of why it's this way. Do you have some sense of what the conflicts are?

With this, he indicates a direction of search: the patient's stalemated relationship with her boyfriend suggests a dilemma rooted in inner conflicts. When the resident goes on to tell more stories, the supervisor pulls him back to the search for interpretation:

You know, I don't get a sense of what you feel from seeing her. How would you characterise her problems in your own mind, psychodynamically ?

The resident attempts an account of her difficulty . . . [etc.]

(Schon 1987: 236)

In these examples, we have Schon's commentary on what is going on interspersed with illustrative extracts of practitioner talk. They are just two of many occurring throughout his works. But how did the evidence get to this point, and how is it 'worked' to make the case? If we are to take reflexivity seriously (and one might think this to be especially important in relation to research about reflective practice), these questions need to be addressed, since they will also be pertinent to the transcript evidence of our own research on reflective practice, reported below.

Adult education researchers often favour the use of interviews and qualitative methods of analysis, but have paid little attention to the nature of transcript evidence or to the procedures for its generation and use. This is surprising in view of the theoretical and practical importance attached to documenting and authenticating the experience of adult learners, and the value assigned to the process of generating text (e.g., in the form of a personal journal or portfolio) as a vehicle for reflection. A transcript is both more and less than the experience it reports. There's many a slip 'twixt talk and text, and no simple rules for the construction and use of transcripts. To get to the stage of making a case in writing by drawing on recorded interview or observation data, one needs:

- some kind of practice,
- talk about that practice,
- recording of that talk,
- textual rendition of the recording according to transcription conventions,
- reading of the transcript,
- marginal commentaries on what seems to be happening at different points in the text,
- the selection of strips of transcribed talk as evidence for some proposition, and
- their incorporation in the researcher's own exposition.

Since this whole process is a practical accomplishment, how one is transcribing, reading, writing and rewriting is itself a question about reflective practice. Paraphrasing Stubbs (1983), Potter and Wetherell note that 'transcription is a constructive and conventional activity. The transcriber is struggling to make clear decisions about what exactly is said, and then to represent those words in a conventional orthographic system' (Potter and Wetherell 1987: 165). Edwards and Potter (1992) suggest ways of exploring reflective practice by examining how people talk about their practice, where the issue of reflexivity arises in writing one's own account of other people's accounts. Schon is engaged in dissecting reflection-in-action through an accounting strategy which is not itself questioned.

In a lengthy commentary on the textual construction of ethnography, Atkinson comments that:

> In principle, the notion of reflexivity recognises that texts do not simply and transparently report an independent order of reality. Rather, the

texts themselves are implicated in the work of reality-construction. This principle applies not only to the spoken and written texts that are produced and interpreted by social actors, but to the texts of social analysts as well. From this point of view, therefore, there is no possibility of a neutral text.

(Atkinson 1990: 7)

In so far as Schon's accounts are ethnographies of reflective practice, then a further comment by Atkinson is apposite:

The typographical convention whereby the fieldwork excerpt or interview quote is cited as 'data' and set off from the main body of commentary – by means of indentation, italicization or similar marks of difference – is important in the production of the ethnographic account. . . . The text embodies and renders in graphic form an internal dynamic at the heart of the enterprise . . . 'dialogue' reflects a shifting temporal order, from the 'events' that occurred and were reported 'then', to the reflection and reportage that occurs 'now' . . . the text persuades in so far as the reader concurs or acquiesces in the dialogue between the exemplar and the commentary, and draws on the exemplar so as to find the commentary adequately plausible. . . . The exemplar gives us, as readers, fragments of recorded talk, reported talk and action, which we can take to 'stand for' the social world under scrutiny. . . . The exemplar is 'representative' in the sense that it signifies or 'stands for' cultural themes or social types.

(ibid.: 83)

PERCEPTIONS OF REFLECTIVE PRACTICE: FOUR CASES

The dialectics of reflection and action are encoded in textual arrangements, and we can get an additional handle on practice by treating it critically as the production of text. To be consistent with our analysis so far, we would need to interrogate our own methods in trying to understand what some university adult educators known to us perceive to be 'reflective practice'. Our approach is a conventional one to the extent that we invited teachers just to talk about their practice in one-to-one guided conversations. They are collegial encounters, but of course the 'just talk' that we recorded is an understated conceit. The text that we produced, initially in the form of complete transcripts, totalled some 50,000 words, and we are here trying to represent certain kinds of practice through selected and manageable extracts and commentary, a distillation and reconstruction at a distance from the practice itself. We then reflect on the interviews with practitioners via the reproduction of extracts from our own transcripts in which we talk about what has been generated. Readers are invited to review the following 'cases' illustrating various aspects of reflective practice in the light of this last interview, as well as the foregoing comments. Please note that, in each case, the interviewer is represented by 'I', the practitioner by 'A', 'B', etc.

Case 1

I: What I'm trying to do is to get some views about what people understand by reflective practice . . .

A: My first getting into it . . . we were all people who were in the business of working with groups of other people normally in some kind of professional development role in all sorts of complex situations, and I was led to think about notions of reflective practice through the kinds of things that we did when we looked at each others' practice as facilitators . . . then we discovered that Schon had been here before, had written on reflective practice . . . I've never quite sorted out all the differences between his perspective and what we adopted, but at the very least it has a very different flavour.

I: Has [Schon] subsequently become an influence in any way?

A: You can't sort of ignore the fact that he's made a contribution in that area. On the other hand, because my ideas were formed pre-Schon, I don't, his ideas don't sit easily.

Comment: A relates getting into teaching reflective practice via working with groups for professional development. A's practice as a professional developer led into thinking about 'reflection'. In an unsolicited comment, A claims not to have been influenced by Schon.

A: The touchstone for all we did, it was practice.

I: Yeah.

A: Was it work that, did it make sense, was it stuff we could do, was it the language that kind of respected the things that went on in the context we were involved in? That was what we judged it all by. So in that sense it was influenced by practice, but there were a whole lot of ideas that we pulled on – some consciously and some unconsciously . . .

I: OK, good. Turning to your students and the sort of things you do with them. Do you make it one of your conscious aims . . . that you want them at the end of the day to, as it were, become more reflective practitioners as a result of what you're doing with them?

A: Oh, yes.

I: That's a conscious aim?

A: Yes, yes, yes.

I: Right.

A: It's very upfront and it's probably a higher priority aim than any content objective I have. And what I try to do is to introduce them in my teaching to whole lots of devices . . . I use a learning portfolio. I ask people to keep a learning portfolio as part of their work . . . I introduce the idea of learning partners whereby they get together with another member of the group they choose to talk through what's going on for them in the class. The assessment practice I use is that a lot of the assessment is based on a self-assessment schedule that gets them to focus on and reflect on a whole range of their learning that is somehow connected to that particular subject and is a way of pulling together to create a document which is in a sense a summary of their learning.

I: Right.

A: So that in all sorts of different ways the idea of reflective practice is reinforced.

I: Right.

A: Although I don't make a big thing about theoretical input about reflective practice.

I: Right, this is what I was going to ask you. I mean does the term 'reflective practice' as such ever figure in your teaching? I mean do you kind of utter the words, or . . .

A: Not very much.

I: No, no no. Why is that?

A: Well, I mean in one sense it seems more important to do it than to kind of talk about it. [later] I always teach subjects that have their feet in the world of practice.

I: Hm, so you feel that for yourself you've happily resolved the theory–practice conflict?

A: In a kind of everyday way, yes, yes. In that I'm continually using strategies and techniques and things that I do in normal situations and I'm converting them into things that you can do in a class with students.

Comment: The idea of 'reflective practice' is conveyed and reinforced through the teaching practices that *A* describes. It is a self-exemplifying process, *being* reflective rather than talking about it. Because *A* teaches subjects that 'have their feet in the world of practice' there is a feeling that the theory–practice conflict has been resolved in an 'everyday way'.

I: From the way in which you've described your own teaching practices, is it possible in this way to have a pretty good idea at the end of it whether the students have actually developed as reflective practitioners?

A: To some extent, yes. I mean, you can tell to some extent in class. I think that's one way. But you can never be sure in that context.

I: Hm.

A: The most useful document that gives me a clue is the self-assessment schedule. Because in a sense it's there as the medium *par excellence* that demonstrates whether you're reflecting on the practice level. Some people just go through the motions . . . what you see in those assessment schedules is examples of how they've used what we've been doing in the class are now in practice.

Comment: Asked about knowing how students have developed as reflective practitioners, *A* is clearly aware of the problem of evaluating what people do in practice. In offering the self-assessment schedule, a distinction is drawn between 'true' or 'authentic' reflection and 'going through the motions'.

[*A* has written extensively on the use of experience in learning and is questioned about students using these texts as part of their learning]

A: . . . they think that just by reading what I've written they understand what it is like.

I: It's always different when you're actually doing it.

A: Because it's got a very strong kind of affective dimension that doesn't come across in the text.

I: Yes.

A: I mean, the anxiety and the tension and the uncertainty and all the stages you go through. It describes them all, but until you've been there . . .

I: Do you think that the concept of reflective practice has on the whole been a useful one, or do you think that it is one which perhaps is beginning to do more harm than good?

A: Ooh, that's a tricky one. It's definitely increasingly misused; there's a lot of going through the motions . . . people pay lip service to the idea, but it doesn't actually get in touch with their practice . . . I don't know what we can do about that. I know a lot of it comes from people reading about reflective practice without having engaged in the experience of grappling with it – I think unless you've grappled with it and got some personal meaning and it's related to what you do in your life or in work in some way then you've missed it.

Comment: *A* acknowledges that writing can never convey what reflective practice is like, particularly failing to capture the affective dimension, and reports that people pay lip service to the idea of reflective practice without really knowing what to do with it. Although a plausible discourse, it is not one which is readily adopted without understanding (which means internalising) it. *A* attributes the problem to the gap between talking about reflective practice and actually experiencing it.

I: Do you think that as a concept [reflective practice] is inherently personalistic, inherently individualistic . . . because it's very individualistic it points away from structural questions about practice which may often be invisible?

A: The answer is yes and no. There are examples of that. Schon is a good example of that. He's quite individualistic. My own notion of it is much more robust. It does encompass the group dimension, although I have to admit that in much of my writing it still comes across as an individualistic idea, but I think that my notion of it is broader than that . . . I think that the challenge for us at the moment is to shift it away from that part of the spectrum to other areas that recognise context. Some of the recent stuff I've done with — is trying to look away from the idea of reflection. Reflection is still very strong but it's very much more about people living in context.

Comment: Here, *A* equates 'structure' with the group, admitting that the notion of reflective practice could be interpreted as individualistic. In saying that we need to look at context, however, this is not equated with structure.

Case 2

B: I first of all became interested in reflection as part of the learning process through interest in experiential learning . . . so the thing that then took my attention was Schon's *Reflective Practitioner*, the book and the ideas. And I really liked his, particularly I mean the thing that characterised it for me was that metaphor about the hard high ground of technical-rationality and the swamp of practice. Because working with students who were already practitioners . . . looking for things that would help them with their practice . . . we didn't have a great deal of technical-rationality to offer them . . . that wasn't what they were going to get here, sort of research-based proven recipes for doing things . . . that metaphor of the swamp just really seemed to explain or, or to epitomise, the way that people had to work, and what they needed, which was the ability to think about what was going on and make decisions about it, um, from moment to moment, almost. And not just act on automatic, to actually be angled, to be aware of what was happening in different situations and draw on a repertoire of experience. And maybe what they would get from us was broadening their repertoire of skills.

Comment: B offers an unsolicited expression of the value of Schon as the provider of a metaphor for thinking about practice. The process of helping students with their practice involves broadening their repertoire of skills, but not just that. The course taught by B is an opportunity to look at what is actually done in the 'swamp' by reflecting on experience at different levels.

B: I don't know if Schon talks about it or where I came across, um, Van Mannen's idea about levels of reflection and that also seemed to explain some of the things that we should be doing. That being able to think about solutions to immediate classroom-type problems was important and we were trying to give them the skills to deal with teaching. And then being able to think about the implications of whatever decision they made, in terms of educational decisions – how it was going to effect the sort of long term, things like students' attitudes and so on . . . reflecting on the underlying effects of what they might do. The third level that he talks about which is more about having a broader social appreciation of what was going on and asking questions about, particularly things like 'Who are my students?' and then 'Who are the people who are not here?' – looking at those sorts of issues.

Comment: B now illustrates three levels of reflection – immediate classroom problems, educational implications of practice, broader social appreciation – and argues that all three levels are required in the professional development of adult educators.

I: Are you looking for some kind of evidence that they've become reflective practitioners as a result of being on this course?

B: I usually use . . . the idea that consciously taking time to reflect on something, to look back on it and consider if it's something that's going to happen or something that has happened; to not just kind of leave it and move on but think about what it means and to think, to tell the story of what happened. And pay attention to how they feel about it – to validate the importance of that, and then think about what it might mean.

Comment: B answers indirectly by pointing to how students are encouraged to reflect by returning to and attending to experience, especially its affective dimensions.

I: This business of looking back . . . how do you focus this?

B: . . . I'm just thinking of examples. Um, I can remember a student . . . having difficulty with, um, behaviour in a group. . . . So we agreed that she would keep a journal of her week-by-week experiences and what, what she thought might be able to be done to interrupt or change this behaviour. So, she was really sitting down after each class and looking at what had happened, particularly in relation to that . . . her reflection was sort of quite rueful, but it had just got out of hand, and by the time she really faced the fact that there was a problem it was too late to do anything about it. And nothing that she tried to do really worked, so at the end the feeling, and she talked about feeling frustrated, um, but she also wrote down what she thought were possible strategies for the future. . . . [the story continues, some months later] . . . the question came up in the class, something about reflection. And she was really enthusiastic and then she had another story about saying, 'You remember that I did that contract around the journal and I had some ideas about what might happen next time, well it's just happened again. I started a new class and this kind of behaviour was going on.' And she said, 'I knew I'd written it down.' The thing that impressed me about what she said was, 'so I followed the strategy that I'd identified, that was that I had to speak to the students involved immediately', and so she said, 'I hauled them off to my office and spoke to them and my colleague said, "Goodness, I've never heard you be so definite with students."' And 'Look', she said, 'it was because I'd written it down and I knew you'd read it that I had to act.'

I: Right.

B: . . . it made a difference to her, the way she acted because she'd written it down.

I: She'd written it down. Yes, that's very interesting.

B: And she was excited about that. The power of that. And I suspect that there are quite a lot of people where it sort of sinks in later.

Comment: B tells a story about focusing, rather than analysing the process abstractly. The point of this example is that reflection didn't help the student in dealing with an immediate classroom problem, but it did provide a strategy which could be used on a subsequent occasion. The importance of writing is endorsed in subsequent remarks. The lesson that B draws is that there is a power in scripting practice possibilities, the value of which often doesn't sink in until later.

B: In the Master's programme . . . I ask them to keep a weekly journal relating to their experience as a learner in the course, and any interaction that's having with their practice because they're all working as educators . . . they're getting a lot of stuff that's coming to them from the outside. But what's, the also, the reflections on their own experience are legitimate information. . . . So, the experience they're having is absolutely relevant and I want them to kind of, kind of extract that by writing about it, and feed it back to me.

Comment: B argues for the importance of journalling in producing evidence for oneself and others of personal development, and of having experience valued.

I: You know, sometimes it's difficult for somebody who teaches a subject called 'reflective practice' or 'the reflective practitioner' to sort of actually know how to kind of exemplify this in themselves.

B: Mm.

I: For themselves to be a reflective practitioner. I mean, is this something that you feel? If it is, then is there anything you can do about it? Obviously, in terms of your own classroom practice I can see from what you say that you yourself try to be a reflective practitioner. Is that a fair analysis?

B: I hope so.

I: Yeah, but do you feel that? Do you feel there's a problem – something that you always have to be kind of aware of?

B: I mean, it's taken me a while for me to understand how difficult it is to understand what I'm talking about. So in the Master's, which I've only been doing for two years, I would write my journal, I mean I would write in the time we were writing, so I'd be writing my thoughts about what was going on.

I: Right.

B: Um, then at the beginning of the next week, we, I'd ask people to comment on, or talk about it . . . so there's that kind of modelling by talking about what's going on . . . and in the feedback on that, students spoke enormously favourably – when we did the feedback on the course, students said that was, I mean more than I realised, extremely useful to actually seeing what reflection looks like.

Comment: I probes B quite hard here, as there seems to be a degree of uncertainty about the self-exemplification of reflective practice. Student feedback suggests that this has been achieved, however. The exchange reinforces the importance of giving students 'voice', a key concept in experiential learning classes.

Case 3

I: Does the notion of reflective practice play any part in your teaching?

C: Yes. Erm, it's been an important part of me trying to come to terms with, trying to make sense of what's all this adult education stuff about. I was a student here myself, on this same course, on the one that I teach, the one that I've been running . . . there's this body of knowledge or this sort of thing called the theory, theories of adult education, principles of adult education . . . it's a kind of reification, I suppose . . . a lot of this theory of adult learning side didn't seem to make a lot of sense in adult basic ed. Because of that, a lot of us looked to Friere as making more sense . . . I've found the notion of reflective practice and the reflective practitioner helpful. And I know I came across the idea through the writings of Donald Schon . . . I think it was because the way Schon writes actually helps one make, it does help you make sense of being in a job, being in a position, I think he just helps. He relates to the actual practice. Er, so that was partly what I think was the most important influence – making me think about the notion of being a reflective practitioner . . . I suppose there's just that personality thing too, of the notion of being a reflective practitioner – it seemed quite an appealing label.

Comment: C does not work in the mainstream adult education tradition, had an uncomfortable experience in relating to theories and models in the field and is pointing to the existence of a dominant and 'oppressive' discourse. Schon is foregrounded as helping to make sense of 'being in a job'. But C doesn't equate reflective practice with experiential learning.

C: I suppose I'm trying to teach about the role of, or the place of reflection in adult learning. I went to a couple of experiential learning conferences and I loathe, I hate that, I loathe it with a loathing, you've no idea. I cannot, I would never impose a role-play on my students.

I: (chuckle)

C: And that's the thin end of the experiential. . . . I think that what that experiential learning experience made me realise was that, the significance about debriefing . . . so that was my next bit of reading, if you like, to do with the notion of group dynamics and debriefing, and trying, and applying that to sort of workshops, day-long workshops that the students themselves organised. And a lot of our adult basic education students are drawn to the kind of counselling erm, er, stress management, those sorts of aspects of working with disadvantaged adults . . . the appeal of the term 'reflective practitioner' was very much, was sort of an emotional one. It made sense to me because of the way, the kind of person that I am. . . . But interestingly enough, I could never remember whenever I looked at the models of reflective practice and so on, I could never remember them . . .

I: Hm.

C: So I, I've never really taken it on . . .

I: Yeah, that's interesting. So . . . in a sense you kind of see yourself as a reflective practitioner, or at least trying to be one?

C: Well, I think I am . . .

I: Right.

C: . . . in the sense that a reflective practitioner is somebody who thinks about what they're doing . . .

I: Yeah, yeah.

C: . . . yes, I'm a reflective practitioner and trying to, I'm very open to the notion of change . . . [and] thinking about whether something's working or not.

Comment: For *C*, being a reflective practitioner relates to the kind of person one is. Formal models of reflective practice don't make much sense to *C*, who interprets reflective practice as not treating things at face value, being open to change and examining the working of practice.

C: Er, it's very common sense, the thing about the notion of a reflective practice it's a very common-sense kind of notion. Er, and it may be an irony to an extent that the literature is mystifying what is really a very common-sense notion.

I: Donald Schon, what he wrote. Would you consider that to be a statement of the obvious, common sense?

C: To some extent, yes. I mean I haven't read all of his stuff . . .

I: Have you got some kind of ideal or model in your mind as to where you hope the students will get to?

C: . . . in terms of wanting to teach my students to become reflective practitioners . . .

I: Hm.

C: Yes, that's what I'm after. But I don't want to teach them about what other people have written about reflective practice any more.

Comment: *C* makes the point that reflective practice is a common-sense notion that has been mystified. How reflective practice is written about and formally theorised contributes to that mystification. As a 'radical' literacy worker, *C* has a personal understanding of the job as in part that of demystification.

I: I mean do you have some kind of ideal model in your mind of what that [i.e. becoming a reflective practitioner] involves?

C: Yeah, competencies (laugh), the competencies of a reflective practitioner (laugh). 'A competent reflective practitioner will' – yeah, I do. I want students to be asking where things are coming from – where the things that are having an impact on their work and their students' lives. Most of all, actually most of all I want my students to be able to, yeah, ask different kinds of questions about what's happening in their working lives . . . you've got to have some understanding of the history of what it is you're doing to be able to make some sense of it.

Comment: C interprets the question of a 'model' as teaching about the 'competencies' of reflective practice, illustrating the way in which reflective practice as an idea can easily be hijacked in the service of technicist ends. The importance of questioning practice in its historical contexts is affirmed.

I: . . . in terms of what you do in the classroom, do you work with problems that students bring about their own practice? Do you encourage that or make that in any way a sort of focus for what goes on?

C: . . . to encourage some kind of reflective practice . . . I created a series of dilemmas I suppose, situations like er, consider we're working in a period of rapid change, er, think about something in your own teaching practice that you consider to be absolutely non-negotiable, there's no way you're gonna change it . . . together they have to work out what, what it is and why is it non-negotiable.

I: Yeah.

C: And what does that say about their values and . . .

I: Sure.

C: . . . their stance towards their teaching practice . . . a lot of the point is actually getting people to talk about their practice in a reflective kind of way . . . but the problem [is] what's the point of surfacing that sort of knowledge if you're not going to do anything about it . . . talking about being a reflective practitioner by talking about the writing. I mean it's interesting but it doesn't connect . . . for some of them to name their world . . . doesn't then empower them to change it. . . . But I think we need some other different strategies. So that's where I'm at at the moment.

Comment: C employs a way of investigating stance and values in order to encourage reflective practice. At the same time, the danger of passivity in reflective practice is underscored and doubts are raised about its efficacy.

Case 4

I: . . . in helping people to become reflective practitioners . . . the kinds of ways in which you work with students.

D: Er, I think one of the big problems that people face in reflecting on their practice . . . is often associated with where affect, where they've had an affective response. Something really pushed emotional buttons or something like that.

I: Does there have to be a trigger, for reflection of that kind, do you think?

D: Well, no . . . none of that in essence is about reflective practice as Schon would talk about it, although Argyris and Schon sort of invent the ideas of theories of action, looking at what you do, which is a form of reflection . . . it's the emotional trigger that gets my attention before the cognitive part and I need to go back and figure out what was I thinking in order to have felt that way . . . so that in some sense it's a very rational approach to dealing with feeling. It takes feeling as data, as legitimate data.

I: Do you have to resolve your emotional tangles as a precondition for reflection?

D: I'm not sure you have to resolve them as much as you have to understand them in order to work with somebody. Many of the cases we have . . . I don't describe the problem as their not being able to deal with their emotions, as much as I believe there are in the ways we deal with stuff, behave, ways of thinking and acting that are counter-productive and that we're unaware of them. So that I come in with a theoretical perspective which says two things: one is, there is some benefit if you want to increase your effectiveness, you need to look at your practice. I have a way that I want to propose would be effective in helping you look at your practice and this is what it is, I need to look at your theories in action, how do you design your behaviour, what do you do?

Comment: Invited to comment on the affective dimensions of practice, *D* reports that getting students to engage in reflective practice is primarily a cognitive matter. In effect, this means working the Argyris/Schon meta-theory of 'theories of action' in examining case presentations of their practice problems.

I: What kind of resources are you offering them [i.e. students]?

D: The methodology?

I: Yeah.

D: Of cases, of looking at cases. And the argument is . . . that you can't produce in a case study anything that's inconsistent with your theory. Your theory-in-use is what really drives your actions, so you can espouse all you want but what you write, it comes from your theory-in-use . . . I can map that onto their case studies and they, they accept the map. . . . The idea is that it would be critical theory as I understand it, which is you have a model to explain in some sense the mess we're in, the situation, as well as an alternative which you believe is better. So when I map Model 1 as a theory of use to describe what you were doing in this case, it both describes what you do and what is counter-productive about what you do . . . and provides an alternative . . . then I would offer you as one alternative, there may be others, I'm not saying that there aren't others, I'm just giving you an alternative which is Model 2. And there are, it's easy to imagine, although difficult to produce, behaviour which is consistent with this alternative. . . . Here's an alternative which, if you can produce it, will make it less likely that you will get stuck and more likely that you will uncover what it is that's getting you stuck if you're getting stuck and be able to correct it. . . . So really what I'm teaching is a way of reflecting on your practice consistent with a theory of action perspective. The theory of action perspective says 'You've got a theory of action; is it productive or counter-productive?' and map in to Model 1 or Model 2.

Comment: Case presentation and discussion surfaces and critiques theories-in-use which, *D* submits, students accept. *D*'s approach to teaching for reflective practice is quite specific, a model is 'applied to' cases. Reflection is not free-ranging or an unfocused trawl through experience. It is specifically linked to criticising Model 1 type behaviours and proposing Model 2 type alternatives, which are admittedly harder to reproduce in practice.

I: Let's talk about . . . the way in which you organise the group, the kind of requirements you place upon them in the groups and as individuals.

D: I start the course by saying 'What I want you to do is to become a researcher into your own practice, which requires that you look at your practice, you test it against the toughest standards, tough, test it against your highest standards for excellence'. That 'you need to become skilful at taking risks and becoming vulnerable in order to learn this'. And the fourth one is that 'you need a theory to connect it to'. . . . So my theory of teaching essentially is: act and reflect on your actions. And all along it, I'm going to be acting and looking at my actions. So the essence of the teaching for me to try as much as I can to behave consistent with this new set of values. . . . For me, one of the struggles is, the decisions about how often to intervene and what kinds of interventions to make. I'm trying to change the norms of this group dramatically . . . yeah, managing the group is a big issue.

Comment: D tries to exemplify the qualities of the reflective practitioner by the continual self-interrogation of practice and theories-in-use. Students 'need' theory at least in part to protect them when they are exposing practice problems and their own theories-in-use to critique and remodelling.

I: Several times you used the expression 'the theory says', as if in some way [you] are detached from this. Now [I've seen you operate and] I know different . . . I think you inhabit the theory. There is a sense I get that you are discounting what you are doing as merely being an agent.

D: Well . . . in looking for ideas worth committing one's professional energies to, this by far for a long time has been up there as a really good idea. It turns out it's a complicated idea because it's not enough to know the words. It's a theory of action so you've gotta get it into practice. So that makes it difficult, because it's not a theory that says, you know, 'Do you know how to differentiate er, quadratic equations or something?' This is a question that says 'Do you behave consistent with a set of values?' . . . to the extent that you can see a theory in action, a theory being used skilfully, I have in some sense that as a standard for my own practice . . . when I saw him [Argyris] in action I saw a level of skill that dazzled me. His ability to be there and attentive, and his insight, that kind of stuff, set for me a model that I would have for my own practice.

Comment: The exemplary modelling of reflective practice 'in action' is for D (who has had direct experience of this) the best way to appreciate the theory behind it, and to transmit it to students.

REFLECTIONS ON THE CASES

These four cases have been scripted as part of our own research practice. In presenting them to the reader, it was decided that they should be partially 'decontextualised' in order just to make the point that, as text, they do in fact also have a context. They are collegial exchanges based on certain shared assumptions between participants who 'inhabit' or practise within the same general domain of higher/adult education. But readers will note, for example, that we supply little specific information about our practitioners, other than that they are university teachers in various adult education programmes. This is deliberate. The case comments have also been 'de-gendered', and readers are invited to consider which cases represent female practitioners and which male (there are two of each). As with our case respondents, other practitioners will bring their own particular context to a reading of what theories of reflective practice mean for them.

Following the collection of our transcript 'evidence' of reflective practice, *IB* and *RU* reviewed what had been obtained as text and commentary in the form of a recorded conversation. An extract is reproduced below:

IB: I wonder whether we could look at what we've got as textual evidence about reflective practice and ask the question 'Who's text is it now?'

RU: Well, I personally don't think it's anybody's text . . . obviously it can be read, that's the important thing, but there are many texts at different levels . . . each of these has a context, a pretext and a subtext, and, er, reading text has to take that into account.

IB: Does that give us an additional handle on reflexivity?

RU: Yes, that's right . . . take the people that I interviewed, there's the text of their practice. Now I didn't get at that, because in order to have got at that I would have had to somehow record them in action . . . there's no doubt that the text we have is not simply a faithful reflection of the text of practice, it's the product of an interaction between me and them. So it's a text in its own right, which has some relationship with the text of practice . . . and again this can be read in terms of context, [etc.] . . . the third level is then the commentary on it . . . and this is in a sense what we are doing, we're reading the text and producing another text . . .

IB: And at each of these levels, you've got a playing back of one against the other . . .

RU: Yes.

IB: . . . as it were.

RU: That's right, there's a kind of . . .

IB: There's a multi-layered . . .

RU: Yes . . .

IB: . . . process of reflection going on.

RU: That's right . . .

IB: . . . to, through the different textual levels . . .

RU: Yeah.

IB: But one of the concerns I have in using his [Schon's] texts as providing exemplars about how to go about being reflective in one's practice and teaching about reflective practice is that he doesn't address these different textual levels. . . . I feel that he's missing out an important dimension of reflecting by not reflecting on the textuality of his own practice, as a writer about reflection-in-action.

RU: Yes, I think that's right, er, and I think the reason for that is that he's in a sense constructed a text which is supposed to be about practice. I mean, he presents these transcripts as if they were in a sense faithful reflections of what happened. . . . But of course it's very clear that Schon is constructing a text with a purpose in mind. And that purpose is to show the existence of reflection-in-action. And I think it goes beyond that, er, and here we start to get into questions about the pretext and so on, the subtext, and that, is I mean, that Schon is trying to construct a universal model of reflection-in-action. It's kind of a strange thing because at one level he tries to present this as very contextualised, but at the same time he's wanting to say that, you know, there's this phenomenon as it were. And not only that, but, er, we can analyse this phenomenon and that we can then sort of go away and use it.

IB: There's a certain irony there, isn't there, in that . . .

RU: Yeah.

IB: . . . er, if he's offering a model, then he's at least implicitly suggesting that in some sense this is foundational . . .

RU: Yes.

IB: . . . for reflective practice.

RU: That's right. Oh, yes . . .

IB: But he's building that on an anti-foundationalist argument.

RU: Yes, exactly right. And I mean there are all kinds of questions which one could ask about these texts which he presents as texts which, if you like, are not text (chuckle). Who are these characters which are sort of set up as Aunt Sallies, you know?

IB: And I mean, some of this applies to our own texts, of course, even though they are not set up in the same sort of way.

CONCLUSION

In reflecting upon the comments of our reflective practitioners, we want finally to draw attention to some dimensions of practice that are important to our interviewees, and which we also regard as being both theoretically and practically important, but which are not addressed by Schon. In decontextualising reflection-in-action, Schon neglects the situatedness of practitioner experience. Our reading of his cases, in the light of a reading of our own cases, is that they reveal Schon's failure to convey an understanding of reflection-in-action that is as radical or critical as he himself would wish. The consequence is that reflective practice can easily become accommodated to a technicist implementation of adult education, notwithstanding the powerful critique of technical-rationality that Schon himself offers. The problem is that this critique is delivered at the level of theory, and is not enacted in the way in which he reports his own case examples of reflection-in-action and teaching for reflective practice. In not being reflexive, Schon's methodology does not exemplify the critical promise of his theory.

1 As teachers, our practitioners are at home with the ideas of reflective practice in various ways. They have an ambivalent attitude to theory. Many adult educators emphasise the experiential basis of reflection-in-action. People may be more or less 'good' at reflection-in-action, depending on where they are coming from and not because of any defectiveness in their cognitive abilities or understanding of the underlying theory of reflective practice. In practical terms, it is just as important to establish a common experiential base in the classroom as it is to focus on specific individual practice problems or design issues.

2 The ability to be a reflective practitioner does not appear to depend on the possession and implementation of a specific 'theory' of reflective practice, but it does depend upon the willingness of practitioners to engage in, and maybe demonstrate to others, a critique of their own practice, in part through an examination of its situatedness. Such a critique may draw on both formal and informal theory which is not necessarily Schonian in character. Reflective practice can be self-exemplifying through reflexive critique.

3 Successful reflective practice entails engaging in a continual rescripting of one's own practice, not in merely having it rescripted and played back by others. In 'practical' terms, keeping a journal (and sharing its content with others) is the key to this. In the kinds of one-to-one exchanges reported by Schon, the impression is created that one does not necessarily have to take responsibility for the ownership and description of one's own practice problem, since a 'master practitioner' or coach is available to provide the necessary redescription. Implicitly, a dependency relationship is thereby created. This is part of a general problematic of a humanistic approach in which learners are constituted by sympathetic others – not by and for themselves.

4 Schon writes context and history out of practice. His texts are as significant for what is not there as for what is there. Practitioners are not just bounded by an 'action present', but are historical actors. Their theories-in-use are cultural as well as personal artefacts. 'Stance' is more than a personal matter. The 'convergence of meaning' that he seeks can only be partial in the absence of a reflexive critique of the situatedness of practice. For example, gendered practice does not figure as a dimension of his theory of reflection-in-action.

5 The affective dimensions of practice are rendered as cognitive problems, and (ironically) thereby as candidates for technical solutions, e.g., having an inappropriate view of situations (theories-in-use) which result in

counterproductive behaviour. This opens the door to allowing reflection-in-action to be seen as a set of corrective competences.

6 For the teacher, working a model of reflective practice is equally a matter of a) believing in the underlying theory for good reasons (theory can be foundational for practice in this sense) and b) demonstrating its potential and limitations in action as both an embodied and a situated practice.

7 The ability to critique mainstream practices appears in some instances at least to depend upon one's own situatedness as a 'marginal' practitioner, or the ability to locate oneself 'outside' practice. Reflection-*outside*-action may be as critically significant as reflection-in-action, whether being 'outside' is taken as a choice or is imposed. If one's actions always take place within a mainstreamed practice, then reflection-in-action is little more than accommodative and loses its critical edge.

Chapter 8

Changing paradigms and traditions of research

Historically, adult education has adopted a critical stance towards, almost a mistrust of, theory and has instead valorised practice and experience. It has been inexorably 'pulled to the practical'. At the same time, however, it wants to be taken seriously as a professional activity and therefore finds that it cannot remain entirely in the realm of the practical. It needs a publicly stated rationale which its practitioners can believe in and disseminate; it must justify its claims to be valuable and significant and seek to persuade those outside the field of practice of its 'truth' and desirability. It is forced, therefore, to move from the particularised discourses of practices to a more universal 'knowledgeable' discourse which can provide a justification for policy.

Research has a key role to play in this process. Adult education has now reached a stage where the involvement in research poses the need both to locate and problematise the activity of research. There has been a tendency to direct critical scrutiny, first, to the kinds of research that needs to be done and second, to the appropriateness of various methods of carrying it out. There has been an attempt to resolve the perceived tension between theory and practice by preferring practitioner-based enquiry and action research. There has been a privileging of 'lived experience' as a subject and field of research appropriate to adult education's critical concerns.

It could be argued that we now have an adult education research or knowledge-producing community. If we follow Kuhnian arguments, then any research-based knowledge always takes place within a community (in the sense that it is the community that validates it *as* knowledge). Communities display a great of variation in their cohesiveness, the strength of their 'disciplinary matrix' and the flexibility of the procedures by which they validate knowledge claims. Adult education, because it is not rooted in a particular strongly bounded disciplinary matrix, probably lies at the weak end of the spectrum, although this is not to be construed as a weakness in itself. Indeed, it could be argued that adult education is beginning to find the search for a strongly bounded disciplinary knowledge increasingly restrictive and incongruent with the way its practice is developing.

RIGOROUS RESEARCH

What is it we are doing when we do any kind of educational research and what is the relationship of this to educational practice? One possible answer, and the answer likely to be given in the majority of cases, would be that we are systematically attempting to address and investigate educational questions, issues or problems. Of course, in one sense, as practitioners we do this in our everyday practice all the time, and in a more or less systematic way. Is practice, then, 'research'? Are we, as educational practitioners, also always educational researchers? To some extent, the answer must be yes. Certainly, as practitioners, we are also researchers more often than we think and, undoubtedly, to be effective practitioners, we ought to try and be researchers of our practice. But can we in our everyday practice also be researchers in the way in which 'research' is conventionally understood?

Even to pose such a question assumes that there is a difference between 'research' as conventionally understood and the problem-solving, 'finding-out' and Schonian displays of 'artistry' which typify everyday practice. Look in any standard textbook on research methods and what one normally finds is a definition of research that stresses its 'systematic' nature. Of course, once research is characterised in this way, certain other related characteristics such as 'rigorous' and 'methodical' are also implied. In effect, all this is encapsulated in the emphasis placed on *method*, and it is this emphasis which is at the heart of the distinction between researchers and practitioners. We shall examine this in more detail. At its most basic, research is conventionally understood as a process where primary data is collected, analysed and presented in a rigorous, systematic and methodical way. Thus, although addressed to issues of practice, in particular to some problematic, it is not itself the same as practice.

There would be little disagreement that data, whatever the source, is not on its own of much use and that research, therefore, is not simply a matter of gathering data. This is because data has to be organised into descriptions, explanations and generalisations. Generalisations, or the answers to 'why' questions, utilise the notion of causation where explanation goes beyond a particular setting, e.g., not 'Why does X happen in this particular classroom?' but 'Does it happen in all classrooms and if so is there an underlying and common cause, Y?'

Generalisations have traditionally been seen as the highest level of research – the level to which all research should ideally aspire. This is largely because research in the natural sciences, particularly in physics, aims for generalisations, and such research has generally been considered the model for all other forms of research, including educational research. Generalisations become theory and theory is universal, unbounded by particular contexts.

In the natural sciences, generalisations are sought because they enable predictions to be made. Generalised explanation and prediction are two sides of the same coin. The ability to predict makes the ability to control possible. Thus, if you know that X causes Y, then you can predict that where X is present then Y will happen, and if you know that then you can control the presence of X in order to make Y happen. In this way, research becomes a vital tool in decision-making and policy. Causal knowledge of the world enables successful intervention in the world. In the research tradition shaped by the natural sciences, the main purpose of research is, through the use of appropriate methods, to construct a body of systematic knowledge comprising generalisations or statements of universal laws which have been empirically derived and tested.

The problem with generalising this conception of research is that there are few, if any, predictive generalisations that have emerged from educational research. There are two possible explanations of this – one is that educational research has not been systematic enough, the other that the natural science model of research is inappropriate. Furthermore, it is this conception of research that has shaped common understandings that there is a hard distinction to be made between researchers and practitioners. The former, it is argued, are concerned with the generation of theory, with generalisable knowledge that is not confined to any one particular context. The latter, on the other hand, given their concern with practice, must operate in the realm of particularised, context-bound knowledge.

POSITIVIST/EMPIRICIST EPISTEMOLOGY AND RESEARCH

Any research, whether in the natural or social sciences, makes knowledge claims and therefore raises epistemological issues. We would argue that all research is based on an epistemology, even though this is not always made explicit – in fact, most of the time the epistemology that underlies any particular piece of research is taken for granted and not regarded as worthy of consideration.

Epistemology, in its broadest sense, belongs to philosophical discourse, where traditionally it is seen as being concerned with what distinguishes different kinds of knowledge claims – specifically, with what are the criteria that allow distinctions between knowledge claims to be made. In effect, to ask epistemological questions is to ask questions about what is to count as knowledge. Ontology, on the other hand, is about what exists, what is the nature of the world, what is reality. Epistemological questions are about how what exists can be known. Epistemological and ontological questions are thus related, since claims about what exists in the world imply claims about how what exists may be known.

Epistemology is not simply a set of rules about what is to count as knowledge, although this is how it tends to be understood and certainly how it understands itself. It is itself historically and socially located, evolving as part of the struggle against the medieval Church with its monopoly over knowledge and its construction of truth in terms of the authority of divine texts. Epistemology provided a justification for a different way of grounding knowledge through the empirical rather than the divine, the emerging natural sciences and the notion of the 'democracy' of knowers. Experiment and observation replaced tradition; validation became a function of measurement and intersubjective testability; sense experience mediated by rationality the source of knowledge.

The question that epistemology asks, i.e., 'What is to count as knowledge or how is the status of knowledge claims to be decided?', is as old as antiquity. However, what was new was the notion that epistemology could itself provide the means of deciding, of adjudicating rival claims, of sorting knowledge from mere opinion or belief. Any claim to knowledge had be justified on the basis of how the claim was arrived at, hence the emphasis on method noted earlier. Thus, if the claim is based on systematic and methodical observation, then epistemologically, this constitutes good grounds for considering the knowledge claim to be valid or true. The 'best' or most strongly grounded knowledge was that which emerged from using scientific method, hence this came to be seen not as a set of methods that led to useful results in the natural sciences but as a set of universal rules and procedures for conducting research in all fields and the making of any publicly warrantable knowledge claim.

An important aspect of these epistemological 'good grounds' is that the researcher was 'objective' i.e., s/he was unbiased, value-neutral and took care to ensure that personal considerations did not intrude into the research process. When we do research we tend to take objectivity and the procedures for attaining it as a 'given', a taken-for-granted and necessary aspect of doing research. As a consequence, we find it difficult to recognise that, in accepting this definition of objectivity, we are at the same time implicitly accepting a particular epistemology and all the commitments and assumptions contained in that epistemology.

The most powerful epistemology, the one which is the basis for the conventional picture of research discussed so far, is usually referred to as *positivist/empiricist*. It makes the following assumptions:

1 The world exists independently of knowers, i.e., that it is 'objective'. This world consists of events or phenomena which are lawfully organised and orderly. Through systematic observation and correct scientific methods, i.e., by being 'objective', it is possible to discover this lawfulness and state it in the form of theory. It is then possible to explain, predict and control events and phenomena.

2 There is a clear distinction or separation between the 'subjective' knower and the 'objective' world. There is also a clear distinction between facts (which are 'objective' and belong to the world) and values (which are 'subjective' and belong to persons). The researcher's concern is only with the former. Consequently, the subjective (the concerns and values of the researcher as a person) must not interfere with the discovery of objective truth.

3 Research establishes knowledge about the world which is empirically validated. Only knowledge claims based on the experiential, on observation enhanced by experiment and measurement, can qualify as knowledge. Furthermore, knowledge claims are reliable when they are inter-subjectively validated, i.e., different observers with unimpaired senses and an equal capacity for reasoning when exposed to the same data should be able to come to the same conclusions.

4 There is order and reason in the social world, social life is patterned and this pattern has a cause–effect form – things don't just happen randomly and arbitrarily. The goal of research, therefore, is to develop general and universal laws that explain the social world.

5 The sciences or disciplines (systematic and verified bodies of knowledge about the world) are all based on the same method of finding out about the world. The natural and social sciences share a common logic and methodology of enquiry. Through this common logic and methodology, subjectivity and bias are minimised and the legitimacy of knowledge claims guaranteed.

6 Epistemological enquiry and critique (such as we are engaging in now, for example) is an unnecessary distraction.

In sum, therefore, the assumptions of a positivist/empiricist epistemology shape an approach to research where the emphasis is on *determinacy* (that there is a certain truth that can be known), *rationality* (no contradictory explanations, convergence on a single explanation, as there can only be one 'true' explanation), *impersonality* (the more objective and the less subjective the better), the *ideal knower* (anyone whose senses are not impaired and whose faculty of reasoning is fully functioning) and *prediction* (that research must aim for generalisable knowledge from which predictions can be made and events and phenomena controlled). In order to count, knowledge has to be dehistoricised, detached from its source in experience (since only experience mediated by reason can be a source of knowledge) and from the place where it was made. Furthermore, it defines an attitude and approach that rejects reflexivity. In other words, it is methodologically critical but not self-critical. It is precisely the exclusive focus on methods and outcomes which leads to a failure to ask any questions about the research process itself and which leads to research being seen as a purely technical process.

Understanding research in this way involves accepting the claim of positivist/empiricist epistemology that it provides a set of logical rules of explanation, independent of the world and its social practices, rules which can distinguish between and judge *all* knowledge claims. But this claim is itself problematic. When we make a claim to knowledge it is not simply a matter of appealing to these logical and universal rules because, since all knowledge claims involve justification, they all have a social dimension. Claims are justified because of prior and collectively held conceptions about the world, how to relate to it and how to know it. Positivist/empiricist epistemology is a good example of such a conception.

Of course, some conceptions have more credibility and therefore more power than others. The most powerful conception is positivist/empiricist epistemology itself, where the methods and procedures of the natural sciences (scientific method) are presented as the model for all 'proper' research. This implies that a positivist/empiricist epistemology is not so much a matter of abstract, universal logic but more a matter of politics or power. In other words, the rules are themselves neither neutral nor universal!

What we can conclude from this is that every research method is embedded in commitments to particular versions of the world (an ontology) and ways of knowing that world (an epistemology) implicitly held by the researcher. No method is self-validating, no method is separable from an epistemology and an ontology. Furthermore, every ontology and epistemology is itself culturally specific, historically located and value-laden. 'Scientific method' is not, therefore, an abstract set of logical rules 'made in heaven' and universal in their applicability but a way of working specific to particular research paradigms (for a fuller discussion of this see below) and to particular disciplinary pursuits. It has evolved historically with the growth of the natural sciences and of Western philosophy and is therefore unique to a particular socio-cultural configuration. We can see this illustrated very clearly when we consider how Eastern philosophy has a very different conception of what constitutes knowledge and the conditions that define what it is to be a knower.

If scientific method is understood as universal and 'made in heaven', then research is itself understood purely as a 'technology' or a technical process, a matter of applying an invariant procedure that can be carried out only by 'experts' with a mastery of method. This is another means by which the distinction between researchers and practitioners is maintained, since the latter, by definition, do not possess this mastery.

The dominance of positivist/empiricist epistemology has had two major consequences for social and educational research. The first is the pre-eminent place accorded to the production of knowledge based on the discovery of facts and the formulation of theory in terms of generalisations;

the second, the attempt to adopt the language, methods and quantification of the natural sciences into social and educational research.

The search for generalisations and the power of prediction, as we have seen earlier, have not been realised in educational and social research. The search is probably doomed to failure anyway, since it is questionable whether generalisable and predictive knowledge is possible in the social domain. The reason for this highlights a fundamental weakness of positivist/empiricist epistemology, namely, its ontological assumption that the world, although complex, is orderly, lawful and hence predictable.

If, however, we conceive of social events, processes and phenomena as indeterminate, then generating predictive generalisations requires a closure which itself assumes a determinate world. Hence, the closure that is necessary is not 'natural' but can only be *imposed*. But if it is imposed, then the very status of the knowledge generated (the predictive generalisations) itself becomes questionable. So it is not so much that closure is impossible, but rather that if it is done then the imposed closure must inevitably raise questions of *power*, which in turn raises questions about the 'objectivity' of the research process and the resulting knowledge claims.

Positivist/empiricist epistemology projects an image of research as the evolutionary, cumulative and linear construction of knowledge. This image of science has for some time now been the subject of a major critique. One of the leading figures in this critique has been Thomas Kuhn, whose most well-known work, *The Structure of Scientific Revolutions* (1970), provides a significant alternative way of understanding scientific method. Kuhn highlights the historical process of scientific discovery and of the way scientists actually work. By this means he has helped to show that the image of science and of 'scientific' research projected by positivist/empiricist epistemology is limited and unrealistic.

Positivist/empiricist epistemology projects an image of the natural science and of scientific research generally as essentially an *individual* enterprise – carried out by 'ideal knowers', individuals who can stand on an Archimedean point, detaching themselves from the world they are researching. This is another reason why practitioners have not be seen as researchers. These ideal knowers are like no persons recognisable in the real world. They have no history and are unaffected by the culture, values, discourses and social structures of which they are yet still a part and of which they can claim certain knowledge.

Kuhn (1970), on the other hand, attacks this individualistic picture and instead presents science as a socio-historical practice carried out in research *communities*. He presents scientists and scientific research as being shaped by factors such as socialisation, conformity, faith and processes very much akin to religious conversion – in other words, not as rationalistic 'ideal knowers'. Researchers are not isolated individuals disinterestedly pursuing the truth. Rather, they pursue a truth which is commensurate with a dominant paradigm's framework of understanding and within a context of expectations and values prescribed by that framework. Scientific research is a collectively sanctioned and controlled activity, carried out as routine, problem-solving 'normal' science but marked by occasional but significant ruptures and discontinuities (scientific revolutions).

Kuhn's key concept is the *paradigm*. A paradigm is first, 'the entire constellation of beliefs, values, techniques shared by members of a given scientific community' (1970: 75) and second, it is an exemplar or exemplary way of working that functions as a model for what and how to do research, what problems to focus and work on. A paradigm defines its own conception of the world and thus the range and kinds of problems which require investigation. Scientists carry out 'normal' science through a framework which enables the world to be understood and acted upon. A paradigm is a scientific community's map or guide, determining important problems or issues for its members to address and defining acceptable theories or explanations, methods and techniques, to solve defined problems.

When a paradigm becomes settled and dominant, Kuhn calls the research carried out 'normal science'. But from time to time paradigms shift, they are overthrown and new paradigms take their place. He calls this 'revolutionary science'. A paradigm shift is a process whereby a new way of looking at the world and hence new ways of working come to prevail. A shift comes about through, first, the awareness of anomalies by the scientific community – problems that cannot be solved which scientists become increasingly concerned about – and second, the existence of an alternative paradigm that apparently better accounts for the anomalies. At some point, this new paradigm comes to replace the old one and in its turn becomes the dominant paradigm. The new paradigm is accepted when a sufficient number of scientists in a community become convinced of the *efficacy*, rather than the truth, of the new paradigm (its 'truth' being promissory rather than actual).

During the course of a scientific revolution the struggle between rival paradigms is not conducted at the level of universal logic or reason. The choice between rival paradigms is not ultimately made by proving that one paradigm is logically superior to another or that it provides a more truthful explanation of the world. Rather, the choice is made on the basis of a belief, sufficiently widely held within the community, that one paradigm will provide a better way of working and clear up more anomalies than any other. In the end, this is always a matter of faith rather than logic, since it is impossible to know in advance how a new paradigm will work out.

Because of the powerful influence of positivist/empiricist epistemology and its abstracted model of the logic of scientific knowledge, we think of science as a linear, cumulative process whereby increasingly correct descriptions of the world are discovered – i.e., that scientific work is marked by an increasingly better 'fit' between scientific theories and an independent 'objective' world. Kuhn, however, by focusing on the practice rather than the logic of science, wants to critique this and argue instead that data and observations are theory-led. He challenges the emphasis of positivist/empiricist epistemology on rationality and neutral observation. Facts cannot be observed neutrally, they are not simply 'there' waiting to be discovered. To discover a fact requires a prior decision as to what is to count as a fact. Thus, facts are only facts and observation can only work in terms of some guiding framework. At the same time, Kuhn argues that theory is paradigm-led in the sense that it is not developed by how the world is, in other words, it is not externally generated, but is generated by the paradigm, i.e., it is internally generated. Finally, he argues that paradigms are themselves historically and culturally located.

Kuhn's work challenges a number of solidly entrenched orthodoxies:

1 Scientific research cannot be examined in the same way that other social processes can. Kuhn argues that doing scientific research is a social, communitarian practice. Thus, as he himself shows, it is itself researchable.
2 In doing research, any knowledge claims that emerge are relative to paradigms rather than 'independent' and universal knowledge of the world.
3 The assumption of a fixed absolute reality against which theories about this reality are tested. What is to count as 'objective' reality changes with the change in the paradigm. After a paradigm change, scientists work in a 'different world' because what they take to be the world is shaped by their paradigms.
4 The criteria which are used to decide between competing theories are not just those of a theory's predictive accuracy, reliability, scope, etc. Consensus based on shared values and communal judgement is equally important and determines how these criteria are evaluated and applied in particular pieces of research.
5 At the same time, paradigms and their associated research communities define boundaries which exclude and silence. In other words, research communities exercise power in having the world seen in a particular way and in having that way of seeing accepted both inside and outside the community. Equally, a community is able to exercise its power to silence or marginalise those who are considered 'deviant' or who do not adhere to the unspoken rules and norms.

Kuhn's work shows that there is a crucial hermeneutic/interpretive dimension to science (for a fuller discussion of this see below). In other words, the practice of science, the way in which scientific research is carried out is not itself positivist/empiricist. The 'truth' that the natural sciences' own epistemology seeks to convey is belied by its practice. This epistemology therefore provides an idealised yet powerful picture of scientific research which is made even more powerful because it is a picture which the natural sciences and other 'scientific' disciplines seek to project as the *only* possible way of doing research and of making valid knowledge claims.

However, it is interesting to note that Kuhn's arguments are supported by developments within natural science itself – for example, chaos theory, which undermines the notion of a deterministic, lawful world. Quantum physics showed Kuhn to be right when he argues that the physical world should not be seen as independent, mechanistic and orderly. A more apt way is to see it as holistic, indivisible and in flux. In quantum physics, events do not have well-defined causes, since they occur spontaneously, their occurrence depending on the dynamics of the system rather than on a single cause/effect, part/whole interconnectedness. Furthermore, phenomena, in order to be observed, require an observer – so decisions about *how* to observe will determine *what* is observed. Hence the subject–object separation and the assumption of a knowable, independently existing world become impossible to maintain.

Kuhn's view of science as it is actually practised – that theory or paradigm choice depends on normative consensus and commitment within scientific communities – means that the natural and social sciences are perhaps not that different. Certainly, they are not different in the sense that the former is 'objective' whilst the latter is 'subjective'. Since any process of research has a hermeneutic/interpretive dimension, the natural sciences are just as 'subjective' in this sense as the social sciences. In both, data are not detachable from theory – facts do not 'speak for themselves', they are not simply 'discovered' – phenomena of all kinds are interpreted by 'scientists' through their paradigmatic frameworks.

Furthermore, in both, there is no set of logical rules which are universally applied. Research is a social practice carried out by research communities, and what constitutes 'knowledge', 'truth', 'objectivity' and 'correct method' is defined by the community and the paradigm which shapes its work. This means that how the rules will be understood and applied will differ between communities. Research is therefore not simply a technical process involving the application of universal rules of 'scientific method'.

Above all, however, Kuhn shows that knowledge in both the natural and social sciences is an ongoing historical and social achievement characterised by disruption and discontinuity. In this sense, he forces us to rethink the strong belief we have in the cumulative 'progress' of knowledge and of research as a matter of getting closer and closer to a single, determinate truth.

HERMENEUTIC/INTERPRETIVE EPISTEMOLOGY

Despite the sustained critique to which it has been subjected, the positivist/ empiricist epistemology and its associated methodology still has a powerful position in social and educational research. There is, however, another influential, although not dominant, epistemology in social and educational research which is usually referred to as 'hermeneutic/interpretive'. This argues that the model for research and knowledge-generation should not be the idealised and universal logic of scientific research because this is an inappropriate model. In social and educational research, knowledge is concerned not with generalisation, prediction and control but with interpretation, meaning and illumination.

Hermeneutic/interpretive epistemology focuses on human action and assumes that all human action is meaningful and hence has to be interpreted and understood rather than methodically known in a natural science sense. There is a questioning of the wholesale application of methods appropriate to the natural sciences since such methods, it is argued, cannot elucidate the meanings of human actions. If the concern is with *meaning* within *social interactions*, then confining research to the observable or empirically 'given', as a positivist/empiricist epistemology does, is to miss out the most important dimension in social enquiry.

To explain the social world we need to understand it, make sense of it and hence we need to understand the meanings that construct and are constructed by interactive human behaviour. Human action is given meaning by interpretive schemes or frameworks. The critique of the positivist/ empiricist model is therefore that it fails to recognise the capacity of human beings not only to experience the world empirically but also to interpret it – indeed, that to experience the world is to interpret it. Interpretation is meaning-giving (or hermeneutic), a representing of the world through significatory systems such as language and culture. This has to assume the prior existence of a social order and social interaction which is a 'given' background to all human actions. We are 'immersed' in the historical and cultural contexts of this given world

As researchers engaged in the human action and social practice of research, we are also seeking to make sense of what we are researching and we do so through interpretive schemes or frameworks. It is this which constitutes the 'double hermeneutic'. In other words, unlike the situation in the natural sciences, in social research, both the subject and object (other people) of research have the same characteristic of being interpreters or sense-seekers and sense-makers. It follows, therefore, that it is impossible to make a strict subject–object separation between the researcher ('subject') and the researched ('object') on the grounds that they have radically different characteristics. Subjects and objects, people and world are co-constituted and mutually constituting.

It follows also that, since all sense-seeking is from an interpretive framework, then all interpretation is perspective-bound and partial, i.e., relative to that framework. Gadamer argues that it is impossible to separate oneself as a researcher from the historical and cultural context that defines one's interpretive framework. He argues that this framework (or what he calls pre-understandings) constitute 'the initial directedness of our whole ability to experience . . . it is the conditions whereby we experience something – whereby what we encounter says something to us' (Gadamer 1975: 173).

As well as being perspectival and partial, interpretations are always circular. The interpretation of part of something depends on interpreting the whole, but interpreting the whole depends on interpreting the parts. As an example, think of what happens when you read a book – the meaning of the book depends on the meaning of each of its chapters (the parts) yet each chapter's meaning depends on the meaning of the book as a whole. Furthermore, it would be impossible to even begin to make sense of the book without some pre-understandings of what the book might be about, and without a pre-given culture where 'books' are defined as things to be read and made sense of. This process is called the *hermeneutic circle* of interpretation and its existence means that knowledge formation always arises from what is already known, even if only as a tacit 'background', and is therefore circular, iterative, spiral rather than linear and cumulative as portrayed in positivist/empiricist epistemology.

An important characteristic, therefore, of the hermeneutic circularity of interpretation is that it always takes place against a background of assumptions and presuppositions, beliefs and practices, of which both the subjects and objects of research are never fully aware and which can never be fully specified. Gadamer calls this 'tradition'.

Let us take some examples to illustrate this. First, an example of an apparently simple action such as raising one's arm. How are we to interpret or make sense of this? Obviously, a mere physical description would not be enough, since it would tell us nothing about the meaning of this action and unless the action has a meaning it is impossible to explain it. A fuller interpretation would require an account of intentions, e.g., that one wished to leave the room. Yet this in itself would still not be enough. There would have to be some description of the context in which the action took place, since arm-raising might mean different things in different contexts, e.g., in a classroom or in an athletics contest. But we could go even further than this; for example, we might want to specify how arm-raising is culturally understood as a form of signalling, how it is associated with practices such as turn-taking, and so on. We could then go even further and compare the meaning of arm-raising in other societies.

The point is, therefore, that in order to understand the meaning of an apparently simple action such as arm-raising it is necessary to understand how it is immersed and inseparable from a network of culturally conditioned beliefs and practices, assumptions and presuppositions. It is clear also, that in raising one's arm it is possible to be conscious of an intention, but it is unlikely that one would be conscious of the cultural background or 'tradition' wherein this action has meaning. In other words, 'tradition' is not *empirically* present.

Another, more complex example, might be that of the act of negotiating. Again, this cannot be understood simply at a descriptive level, e.g., of exchanging offers, because this itself presupposes a whole set of background beliefs and practices such as the autonomy and distinct identity of human beings, cultural values such as conflict and self-interest, other practices such as the drawing up of contracts, and a number of different and related actions such as bargaining, making offers, etc. which are part of negotiating. It is clear that none of these individually can be understood in isolation from the whole practice of negotiating. Thus, again, the act of negotiation only has meaning in relation to a background or tradition of which those negotiating are unaware yet which in a very real sense is 'present'. This is a common enough situation in adult education. For example, in negotiating a curriculum, learners and teachers will come to the transaction with different 'backgrounds' of which they are largely unconscious yet which give meaning to and which play a vital role in their actions, perceptions and expectations.

One implication of this is that no matter how full our interpretations, the knowledge that we as researchers can have of arm-raising and negotiating will never be complete. Human actions are interpretable only within the hermeneutic circle, hence knowledge of them is indeterminate – that is why a positivist/empiricist methodology is inappropriate. As we have already noted, such a methodology requires a closure, and any understanding of human actions based on closure would necessarily be incomplete. To refer back to our example, closure would involve understanding the action of raising one's arm only in terms of the physical movements involved.

The existence of a background or 'tradition' means that there is no 'fact of the matter' or empirical 'given' which could be appealed to in deciding between different interpretations. Meaning is not a representation of an independent objective world. As we noted earlier, it is impossible to separate subjects and objects, the observer and the observed, the interpreter and the interpreted, researcher and researched, background and method, science and culture.

The kind of understanding required is not the algorithmic outcome of correct methods and procedures. It cannot be this, because all understanding is circular, always already an interpretation. Research involves interpreting the actions of those who are themselves interpreters, it involves interpretations of interpretations – the double hermeneutic at work. Rather than avoiding the circle, the aim should be to recognise its existence and get into it properly.

Several questions now arise for the researcher. As research is itself a human action, then are researchers not themselves part of a background or 'tradition' which gives meaning to their actions as researchers yet of which they are largely unaware? The answer is, of course, that they are and, as we saw when discussing Kuhn, this is the case even with researchers in the natural sciences (in a sense paradigms can be seen as a 'tradition'). Given this, therefore, the notion of the individual researcher standing outside the world in order to properly understand it seems highly questionable. Caught within the hermeneutic circle, it would seem impossible for researchers to take such a stance.

This immediately poses the problem of how we can, as researchers, as interpreters, as meaning-producers, be 'objective' about the meanings produced by those we are researching. One answer which is normally given to this problem is that, although we must recognise them, we must at the same time 'bracket' i.e., temporarily set aside, our meanings, suspend our subjectivity and assume the attitude of a disinterested observer. The philosopher Husserl, working in a purely phenomenological tradition, argued that it was necessary to suspend all preconceptions, in the sense not only of personal/emotional biases but also of scientific notions such as causation and lawfulness, and to focus only on 'things-in-themselves'.

A moment's thought shows that this position is not altogether satisfactory. An alternative suggested by Gadamer (1975) shows why. He argues that it is impossible to escape from our preconceptions or pre-understandings, even in terms of temporarily suspending them. Our pre-understandings are not something we can bracket because, to use a term from Heidegger, they are the mark of our '*Dasein*' or 'being in the world'. Equally, it could be argued that bracketing our pre-understandings is undesirable since it is precisely through the interplay between one's interpretive framework, or pre-understandings, and that which one seeks to understand that knowledge is developed. In other words, one's pre-understandings, far from being closed prejudices or 'biases' (as they are commonly thought of in positivist/empiricist epistemology), actually make one more open-minded because, in the process of interpreting and understanding, they are put at risk, tested and modified through the encounter with what one is trying to understand. So, rather than bracketing or suspending them, we should see them as the essential starting-point for acquiring knowledge. The condition of knowing, therefore, is not methodological but a matter of being aware of one's pre-understandings, recognising that they cannot be transcended but, at the same time, putting them to work.

Gadamer characterises research within the hermeneutic circle as a *fusion of horizons*. 'Horizon' here refers to one's standpoint or situatedness (in time, place, culture, gender, ethnicity, etc.). The fusion, or bringing together, results from seeking knowledge whilst grounded in a perspective arising from one's situatedness, a perspective which cannot be bracketed during the process of enquiry. Because it is situated, this horizon is inevitably limited but it is open to connecting with other horizons (perspectives, standpoints), in particular with the horizon of what one is trying to understand. What results from this is a fusion of horizons, a new horizon as well as an enlargement or broadening of one's own horizon.

The fusion of horizons defines a way of attaining an objectivity which functions as an alternative to the objectivity of the positivist/empiricist epistemology. The fusion of horizons is the outcome of intersubjective agreement whereby different and conflicting interpretations are harmonised. By comparing and contrasting various interpretations, a consensus can be achieved despite differences – indeed *because of* differences. This implies, on the one hand, that there is nothing which cannot potentially be understood and, on the other, that understanding is not simply a knowledge of events and phenomena but also an awareness that everything cannot be methodically known. Hermeneutic understanding is, therefore, a learning experience involving 'dialogue' between ourselves as researchers and that which we are trying to understand; the dialogue is always ongoing, never completed.

As we pointed out earlier, a case could be made that both the natural and the social sciences are based on hermeneutic understanding. Rorty (1980) has sought to show that scientific knowledge is not a reflection or 'mirror' of the world and science is not legitimised because it tells us what the world 'really' is. The sciences are an effective vocabulary for coping in the game of prediction and control, but this does not mean they are a privileged vocabulary, even less that they are a model for other forms of discourse and practice. To argue this way is not to attack the status of science or scientific knowledge; rather, it is an attempt to 'conventionalise' science, to see it as one social practice and one language game amongst many, to argue that it does not exist outside history and society.

The existence of the double hermeneutic means that 'social science cannot help but be engaged in a discourse with its own subject matter' (Hughes 1980: 126) – although this is not to say that it always does. When it does not, when it adopts a positivistic/empiricist model, social enquiry is severely limited. Theoretical knowledge is floated off into a situationless vacuum, the 'stuff' of enquiry is detached from its locating paradigms, researchers are cast as ideal knowers who can only know the world by being outside it. Enquiry must therefore always be partial in its understanding, but this partiality, because of the failure of reflexivity, is something that can never be acknowledged or accepted.

The interpretive/hermeneutic paradigm is the basis of a number of approaches to research such as phenomenology, ethnomethodology and grounded theory. It has been popular within adult education because, in emphasising the need to take the social actor's situated perspective and standpoint as paramount, it seems to be both a more fruitful and more 'human' way of doing research. It foregrounds agency, intentionality and meaning, and because of this it appears to avoid the scientism and objectivism of positivist explanations and the determinism and theoreticism of structural explanations (such as Critical Theory, to which we shall turn in a moment). Having said this, however, it is not entirely clear that adult educators who use interpretive approaches fully realise the implications of the underlying epistemology. It is not clear, for example, whether they would readily embrace the notion of the hermeneutic circle or the notion of background tradition, since to do so would render problematic the powerful belief in innate self-direction that is prevalent in adult education. Others are unhappy about other aspects; that, for example, hermeneutic knowledge is directed towards understanding rather than changing the world. They would argue that this merely serves to perpetuate the hierarchy of knowers and doers, theory and practice, and therefore serves merely to reconfigure research whilst still leaving it as supportive of the *status quo*. It is to the implications of this for an alternative paradigm of research to which we now turn.

RESEARCH THROUGH CRITICAL THEORY

Critical Theory is critical in the sense that it challenges both the positivist/empiricist and hermeneutic/interpretive paradigms of research (although it is fair to say that it is perhaps more critical of the former than of the latter). The term 'critical' in this context refers to the detecting and unmasking of beliefs and practices that limit human freedom, justice and democracy. In Critical Theory, the starting-point is that in capitalism, the fundamental social needs of labour (work) and communication are systematically distorted. Habermas (1972) argues that different knowledge/research traditions are linked with particular social needs or interests (the 'social' is emphasised here because it is important to distinguish this from the needs or interests of particular individuals).

According to Habermas (1972), the natural sciences and the dominant tendencies in the social sciences (the empirical/analytic sciences) employ a technical-instrumental reasoning where ends are pre-given and achieved by following known rules and pre-given means. Because of its instrumental means/ends character, Habermas describes this kind of knowledge as guided by a technical interest and oriented towards rational, purposive action and control. The hermeneutic sciences, e.g., history as well as some forms of the social sciences, employ practical modes of reasoning. Here neither ends nor means are pre-given and there is no rigid adherence to pre-defined methodical rules. This interest is oriented towards understanding the systems of language, rules and norms that constitute society.

Empirical/analytic science is linked with the positivist/empiricist research tradition and with prediction and control; hermeneutic science or knowledge with the hermeneutic/interpretive research tradition and with understanding, illumination and communication. Neither, however, has an interest in research and knowledge that changes the world in the direction of freedom, justice and democracy. Habermas, therefore, isolates a third type of 'knowledge-constitutive' interest, which he links with critical science or theory. This knowledge interest is emancipatory. It is oriented to the unmasking of ideologies that serve to maintain the *status quo* by restricting the access of groups to the means of gaining knowledge, and through this to raising of consciousness or awareness about the material and structural conditions that oppress them. It seeks to empower by unmasking and removing the distortions and constraints imposed by capitalism upon the need for work and communication. It is important to note here that empowerment does not mean individual self-assertion, upward social mobility or increased disposable income or even the psychological experience of feeling self-realised. What it means is an understanding of the causes of powerlessness, recognising systemically oppressive forces and acting individually and collectively to change the conditions of life. Given this, therefore, the main approach in Critical Theory is *ideology critique*, unmasking or consciousness-raising; allied to this is the *organisation of enlightenment*, taking action in the light of raised consciousness.

In Critical Theory, there is a rejection of the assumption that there is 'objectivity' in the positivist/empiricist sense because, it is argued, there is no neutral or disinterested perspective, the Archimedean point from which objective knowers can know the world objectively. Every knower is socially located, in and of the world, and knowledge will always be shaped by social interest – related to a technical, 'making' interest, a practical, communicative interest or a critical emancipatory interest. The question that follows from this therefore is 'If knowledge is grounded in this way, then which knowledge is "best", and what are the criteria that define "best"?'

In *Knowledge and Human Interests* (1972) Habermas writes about 'systematically distorted communication' and how this can be overcome. Two arguments of his are crucial here. The first is the idea of *validity claims* – the idea that all human communication (including the process of research) involves speakers implicitly making such claims. What this means is that in any communicative transaction the following claims are being made:

- what is being said is intelligible or meaningful;
- the propositional content of what is being said is true;
- the speaker is justified in what she or he is saying;
- the speaker is speaking sincerely.

On the basis of this, Habermas argues that undistorted communication is the use of language where speakers are able to defend and justify all four validity claims; where what is said can be shown to be meaningful, justified, true and sincere. The implication then is that transactions should be of such a nature for it to be possible for the parties involved to make successful validity claims.

The second argument Habermas puts forward is that of the *ideal speech situation*. This is bound up with his conception of truth. For him, truth is not a matter of correspondence with the world. Rather, truth can be understood only in relation to processes of argumentation. When we say something is 'true', we mean we can back it up – that we can warrant what we are claiming. Truth, therefore, refers to agreement or consensus reached by such warrants. For Habermas, truth is rational agreement reached through critical discussion, and it is possible to distinguish an agreement of this kind from one based on experience, custom, faith or coercion.

This means that a claim to truth can only be acceptable if it is based on situations where, first, all the relevant evidence has been brought into play, and second, where nothing apart from reasoned argument counts. This what Habermas (1989) means by an ideal speech situation. It is one where there are, first, no external or extraneous constraints on technical understanding in the sense that participants understand the technical issues involved in any action, second, participants have a procedural understanding in the sense that they have the methodological skills to act, and third, they have a participative competence in the sense that each participant has an equal and open chance of participating. Where these three types of understanding are present, then all validity claims are successful. Truth that is reached in this way can become the condition of human emancipation. Referring back, therefore, to the question asked earlier, this also means that the 'best' knowledge is that which emerges in the ideal speech situation where all validity claims have been fully met.

The ideal speech situation defines what a society would look like which truly fulfils the need for labour and communication. Habermas accepts that this situation is counterfactual, i.e., that most actual conditions of social interaction and everyday life are not like this, and he points to the distortive influence of the unconscious and of ideology as factors that prevent an ideal speech situation from being actualised. Thus, the notion of an ideal speech situation is really more a *regulative* ideal in so far as it supplies a critical measure of the inadequacies of empirically existing forms of social interaction. Actual situations can, therefore, be researched to find out the degree to which they deviate from an ideal speech situation; this knowledge then becomes an important means for changing the situation to bring it closer to the ideal.

Both the hermeneutic/interpretive and the Critical Theory paradigms would argue that being 'objective' is not a matter of having the right method but more a matter of having the right arguments and of being prepared to subject them to the scrutiny of critical dialogue. This requires a dialogic situation, that is, one where researchers are able to bring their pre-understandings into contact, through dialogue, with the pre-understandings of the researched and other researchers. But the condition for this is that dialogue must be free and unconstrained by structural/ ideological and personal (induced by the influence of the unconscious) inequalities and distortions. It is only in this way that an ideal speech situation can be achieved, and it is because of the failure to incorporate these constraints and distortions that Critical Theory finds itself most at odds with the hermeneutic/interpretive tradition.

If these conditions are not present (as invariably they will not be), then the question arises, 'Should we as researchers try to do something to bring them about?' This is the question with which Critical Theory is concerned. In other words, if research is not to be either an instrument simply for the further dominance of technical-rationality or for the important but limited task of furthering human understanding and communication, then it must involve *praxis* (informed, committed action to change the world). Dialogue is a necessary but not a sufficient condition for emancipation – action of a certain kind is also required. In Critical Theory, therefore, research and praxis become coterminous. Researchers need, at the very least, to take action to ensure that the right conditions for dialogue are present in their own practice. Furthermore, if dialogue is not enough, what action is required if the research is to fulfil its purpose of bringing about emancipation – if, in other words, research is not to be merely a matter of 'finding out' about the world, but of changing it in the name of justice and democracy.

It is not too difficult to see why Critical Theory and its approach to research has resonated with adult educators. Its discourse of basic social needs, of distortions and false consciousness, of critical dialogue, and its foregrounding of praxis, provide an appealing foundation of theory and practice for radical adult educators committed to social action. Its aim of emancipation and empowerment provides a purposive goal for educational activity. Its refusal to separate theory (research and knowledge) from practice (action) demolishes the debilitating tension between theory and practice and provides an answer to the question 'What is knowledge for and how can it best be used to not only understand but to change the world?' Above all, it offers a critical standard by which the present can be evaluated, and in the sense that the empirically existing world is never going to match up to that standard it provides a never-ending source of activity for adult educators.

However, Critical Theory is not without its problems. One major problem is that, although it aims to unmask distortions and constraints, it can itself be seen as offering a very partial and therefore distorted view of human experience. Critical Theory is, in the final analysis, founded on a very modernist conception of rationality. Not only is it a very rationalistic theorisation but it privileges the place of rationality in human experience and social interaction. To that extent, it marginalises the 'irrational', the contingent, affective, poetic dimensions of life. Desire has no place. It is cast simply as false consciousness, ideological delusion, an aspect of the distortions of capitalism which needs to be rooted out.

Another major problem with Critical Theory is its grounding of social life in basic needs, needs which are essentialist and invariant, and its self-proclaimed commitment to emancipation, where emancipation is cast as a universal value. Here, Foucault's argument that everything is dangerous (Foucault 1980) is a salutary reminder that essentialist and universalising discourses may not always have the emancipatory effect intended – that the drive for emancipation may itself become oppressive. Gore (1993: 61), for example, deploys notion of a regime of truth to argue that 'Critical Theory has its own power–knowledge nexus which in particular contexts and in particular historical moments, will operate in ways that are oppressive and repressive to people within and/or outside'.

In this chapter our concern has been to examine in some critical depth mainstream research traditions and paradigms in the social sciences generally and in education in particular. All have to varying extents influenced both the practice and self-understandings of research in the field of adult education. It could be argued that, to some extent, these influences have not always been to the benefit of the field as they have enmeshed adult education even further in oppressive discourses. In the next chapter we will critically discuss alternative and more marginalised approaches to research which, despite their often oppositional and powerless status, may none the less be more appropriate for the state in which adult education currently finds itself and the current variety of contexts in which adult learning takes place.

Chapter 9

Overstepping the limits
New approaches to research

In this chapter we will examine two alternative but in some ways linked approaches to research which have a significant impact on contemporary adult education research. Both these approaches, in an important sense, overstep the implicit yet powerful limits set by more mainstream research traditions/paradigms. Emancipatory research does so by rejecting both the idea of research being politically neutral and the view that its purpose is to simply find out about the world. Instead, it understands itself as explicitly political, as being about acting to change the world rather than just knowing it, or to know it in the service of changing it. We then turn to a postmodern approach to research – an approach which can also be understood as overstepping the limits in that it identifies the process of research as itself constructing and constructed with a consequent need for a problematising reflexivity (what it itself is doing in researching) as an integral part of the process.

EMANCIPATORY RESEARCH

As we have noted in the preceding chapter, Critical Theory has had a strong influence on and attraction for adult educators whose concern is with education's social purpose in terms of a commitment to social change. This latter emphasis is also the main characteristic of emancipatory research which, by its very name, immediately suggests that it is a way of doing research whose objective is to bring about social change. It has a clear ontological starting-point, namely, the existence of a world characterised by socio-economic and cultural inequalities, where researchers have a part to play, indeed they have an obligation to endeavour to emancipate oppressed groups, those who suffer from the greatest inequality and a lack of social justice. The epistemological commitments demanded are not those of the detached and disinterested pursuit of knowledge but the generation of knowledge in the service of emancipation. The validity of knowledge, therefore, is not a function of its generalisability and its capacity for predictive control, nor even of its power in furthering under-standing and intersubjective communication, but rather of its usefulness or efficacy in enabling the empowerment of oppressed groups. As Beder puts it:

> The desired outcome of transformative research is emancipatory social change – change in which the subordinated are empowered to take control of their lives and to change the conditions which have caused their oppression.
>
> (Beder 1991: 4)

Despite these clear objectives and explicit ontological and epistemological standpoints, emancipatory research encompasses a broad and eclectic approach to research which manifests itself in a diversity of similarly grounded research practices. Its most widely acknowledged and recognised forms are perhaps participatory research and transformative research. In relation to the former, the primary reference point has been the global inequality and continuing economic and cultural imperialism of the North over the South. Within this context, participatory research has focused more particularly on the process of research and the question of ownership. These concerns have been brought together in a refusal to accept, and a striving to dissolve, both the epistemological dichotomy between subjects and objects, researchers and researched, and the separa-tion of ethical from epistemological and methodological issues. Transfor-mative research, on the other hand, is located to a greater extent within the growing economic, social and cultural inequality amongst those living and working mainly in the economically wealthier North. Its aim is to develop a greater awareness of the relationships between power, research and social and political movements and to promote social action to trans-form the inequalities and divisions arising from the effects of poverty and racial and sexual discrimination and marginalisation.

For the very reason that it mounts a fundamental challenge to the *status quo*, to the extent that it oversteps the limits of 'normal' research and 'normal' science and therefore can only take place where there is sufficient 'subversive space' in which to operate, the varying practices of emancipa-tory research have always tended to be located on the margins. One of the purposes of this chapter is to point towards ways of moving from the margins into the mainstream in relation to adult education research and to explore wider lessons and learning points arising from the various tra-ditions and practices of emancipatory research, particularly in the context of a rapidly changing postmodern world.

However, our approach to emancipatory research will not be altogether uncritical. While we have earlier rejected the binary oppositions apparent in conventional approaches to research, we want also to review and chal-lenge some of the prevailing assumptions and founding polarities within the discourse of emancipatory research, as well as drawing lessons from the allied but different discourses of feminist and postmodern research. In so doing, we hope to find a way of developing a dialectical rather than dichotomised approach to the dualities of, for example, subject–object, structure–agency, political–personal, macro–micro, theory–data, rigour–relevance and, indeed, emancipation–domestication, perhaps the most fundamental polarity of all in this context. In doing this, we will seek where possible to exemplify our main points with concrete research practice.

Before trying to explore the promise and potential of emancipatory and other 'radical' research approaches within the mainstream of adult education research, it would be useful briefly to characterise and review some of the main values that have underpinned the practice of emancipatory research. Earlier, we noted the explicit stance taken by emancipatory research, and it is clear that this stance is unabashedly *political*. Emancipatory research seeks to address directly issues of power within an unequal world. Following a Freirian epistemology, there is a rejection of any notion of education or educational research as being politically neutral – if educational research is not dedicated to the empowerment of the powerless, then it is likely only to serve the maintenance of injustice and inequality.

Closely allied to this political stance is an emphasis on the *critical*. A commonly held position is that it is necessary not only to be critical of oppressive conditions, coercive structures and barriers to participation (in other words, of the material conditions of oppression) but also to be critical of the systematic distortions which are ideological or discursive in nature. Another key value, which we noted earlier, is need for research to be *ethical*. As we saw then, in mainstream paradigms of research, ethics is usually separated from and disprivileged in relation to methods or methodical procedures – the assumption being that ethical considerations do not affect the quality and validity of knowledge claims. The privileging of ethical issues is in a sense, therefore, a direct reaction to the supposed value-free objectivity of more mainstream paradigms. In arguing for an ethical dimension to Transformative Research, Deshler and Selener emphasise that:

> the research process should be conducted in the public interest with attention to human rights, social justice, conciliation, and preservation of environmental sustainability.

(Deshler and Selener 1991: 10)

Such an ethical position also underpins the discourse of Participatory Research (Hall 1981) and is consistent with an explicit respect for different cultures and the rights of indigenous peoples. Of course, any ethical stance raises questions about both the ends and the means of research, and here broader issues of the relation of cultural difference to universal ethical standards have considerable implications for the specific methods/ approaches to be used in conducting emancipatory research.

Related to the ethical is the belief that emancipatory research should be *holistic*. This involves identifying and emphasising relationships between the part and the whole, the subjective and the objective, the local and the global. Thus, links are acknowledged, explored and questioned between poverty and exploitation at a local level; and politics and policies at a national and an international level. One important example of this might be the restrictive and destructive impact of multinational policies on local economies throughout the developing world or the environmental damage inflicted on indigenous peoples by the destruction of rainforests in both South America and Southeast Asia (Deshler and Selener 1991).

The holistic emphasis of emancipatory research is demonstrated in another very important way in the rejection by those involved of traditional academic divisions into separate disciplines and bounded fields of work. Budd Hall describes participatory research as 'at the same time, an *approach* of social investigation, an *educational* process, and a *means* of taking action' (Hall 1981: 455; emphases in original). This illustrates a key characteristic of emancipatory research which has clear implications for adult educators. It highlights the role of educational processes in developing emancipatory research approaches and influencing practice.

Central to the whole approach of emancipatory research is that there is a commitment to *praxis*, informed committed action or, as Freire describes it, 'reflection and action upon the world in order to transform it' (Freire 1972: 28). This moves away from the purely technical or methodologically neutral considerations of conventional research as well as avoiding the extremes of past Marxist preoccupations with theoretical rigour. In research terms, it involves a translation of broad values into specific contexts through a dynamic and dialectical relationship with research subjects.

What emancipatory research promotes is the resurrection of relevance alongside a less positivistic conception of theoretical and/or empiricist rigour. Indeed, this concern with relevance is implicated both in the epistemological claims of emancipatory research and the methods and approaches it espouses. What matters most is the relevance of any research approach to the lived experience and interests of those involved in the research process. Hal Beder thus suggests a reconfiguration of rigour:

> Praxis is an ongoing, dialectical process in which the validity of the research is assessed according to the value of its outcomes rather than by its adherence to sets of empirically derived rules.
>
> (Beder 1991: 4)

While the outcomes for research participants are clearly of central importance, we believe that emancipatory research, both as research and as an educational process, cannot afford to set up such a clear opposition between research outcomes and research rigour. In focusing on outcomes, it needs also to consider and resolve issues of theory, method and empirical accountability, albeit not necessarily in the same way as in conventional research approaches. This will involve a critical engagement with questions of empowerment, with the relationship of theory to data and with alternative methods and approaches.

Emancipatory research is constructed as *research for empowerment*, defined as a form of research 'where groups, through a process of conscientization . . . define, conduct, interpret, and take action on their own research' (Deshler and Selener 1991: 14). At this stage, it may be useful to deconstruct research for empowerment, with a view to identifying key issues and learning points for broader research practice. Emancipatory research approaches focus closely on questions of knowledge and power – knowledge for whom, for what and in whose interests; knowledge that demystifies the whole nature of the research process; the development of empowering approaches to knowledge; an emphasis on knowledge generation which, in contrast to more conventional approaches to research, starts from what research subjects know rather than what they do not. Following Freire again, emancipatory research sets out to produce 'reflective knowledge which helps people to "name" their world and, in so doing, to change their world' (Beder 1991: 4).

The place of rhetoric is a central issue here. Critics of radical or emancipatory approaches have often identified the problem of the wide gap between rhetoric and reality. However, the creation of such a dualism may not be altogether productive. While there is a clear danger of educators and researchers indulging in empty rhetoric that does not connect sufficiently with the existential social and political reality of the oppressed, there is equally a need to highlight the dynamic and generative role of rhetoric in helping subordinated groups to re-envision and so reconstruct their lives. This is what Giroux means when he talks of moving from the language of critique to a 'language of possibility' (Giroux 1992: 10). While a tendency to be over-rhetorical needs to be acknowledged and guarded against, it should be seen alongside the alternative danger of becoming locked into quietism and an uncritical acceptance of a 'reality' aligned too readily with the *status quo*.

The language of empowerment has undoubtedly penetrated mainstream educational discourse and practice, where it is now firmly sited and widely cited. In response to this, emancipatory educators have rightly identified the obvious danger of reductionism, whereby social and critical empowerment has often been reduced to an unproblematic matter of method or technique, whether constructed as a humanistic, introspective Rogerian approach or as the unreflexive instrumentality of technical-rationality (Allman 1987; Collins 1991a; Macedo 1994).

What is palpably missing in such reductionist approaches is a crucial socio-economic critique that hinges on the notion of empowerment, such as, for example, that presented by Freire and advocates of critical pedagogy. However, there may also be problems in privileging the critical without sufficient attention being paid to the process or specific local circumstances of research for empowerment. A key issue here is the place of 'conscientisation' within the research process. It is one thing to acknowledge the hegemonic influence of dominant discourses, to advocate critical awareness and to promote critical consciousness within any research process. However, this may need to be counter-balanced by both a self-reflexivity and commitment by the researcher to a more systematic research rigour and theorisation so as to avoid the dangers inherent in a top-down, deterministic, blanket attribution of 'false consciousness'. In this context, Cadena (1991), for example, in developing popular education and transformative research in Latin America, stresses the need for 'systematisation', a more systematic and reflective engagement with the experience of learners and a more dialectical understanding of the relationship between theory and practice, as a way of ensuring that critical consciousness does not lapse into false consciousness.

In analysing and learning from emancipatory research geared to social change, it may be useful to pick up on more recent feminist and postmodernist perspectives on pedagogy and research in reconsidering assumptions about power and knowledge, highlighting the 'voice' of research participants and looking critically at the idea of the 'transformative intellectual' (Aronowitz and Giroux 1985).

Mechthild Hart identifies the danger of vanguardism and the dominance of 'authoritative voices':

> the term, "emancipatory learning" resonates with the elitism of a well-informed "objective" professional educator who has figured out how to use learning methods to educate the ill-informed masses who are in the grip of domination.
>
> (Hart 1995: 1)

This could equally well apply to research. The danger is that, in the name of emancipation, researchers (explicitly or implicitly) impose their own meanings on situations rather than negotiate these meanings with research participants. From a feminist and to some extent postmodern position, Jennifer Gore (1992) points out that, whereas an alternative set of values such as those contained in emancipatory research offers a necessary challenge to that of more conventional and mainstream approaches to research, these are still universal and to some extent totalising values. Hence, there is still the risk that yet another 'regime of truth' will be imposed upon research subjects – the promise of 'speaking for oneself' can still be frustrated.

Gore also offers a useful critique of top-down approaches to a pedagogy of empowerment, a critique which may point to alternative ways forward in the research process. She challenges the assumed central role of the agent of empowerment, questions the notion of power as property (to be bestowed on the people) and problematises the macro 'vision' and desired end-state of the whole empowerment process. Such an approach may help to encourage researchers to acknowledge more humbly the limits of subject agency (including their own), re-emphasise the local context and 're-view' the power–knowledge relationship. This prompts a rethinking of empowerment as the exercise of power in an attempt to help others to exercise power, so connecting with a wider postmodern emphasis, within the research process, on who speaks rather than what is said (Lather 1991: 47). Lather argues that empowerment does not mean individual self-assertion, upward mobility and the psychological experience of feeling powerful. Rather, it means understanding the causes of powerlessness, recognising systemic oppressive forces and acting individually and collectively to change the conditions of life.

An instructive example of an emancipatory adult education approach to questions of power and knowledge which acknowledges the above points can be illustrated in the research carried out by Sallie Westwood with the Black Mental Health Research Group in Leicester. Drawing upon the discourses of both transformative research and postmodernism, and so integrating the perspectives on power/knowledge of both Freire and Foucault, Westwood worked over time and in some depth with research group members in framing the whole research process, both ideologically and conceptually. In deciding to focus on 'narratives of sickness . . . the ways in which . . . black people reconstructed their biographies; the onset and experience of mental illness; and their treatment by psychiatry' (Westwood 1992: 196), the group was able not only to give voice to those previously silenced but also to challenge and confront the objectification of their experience as a conventional psychiatric case, a classic example of an institutional knowledge/power nexus.

The Westwood/Black Mental Health Group research succeeded in empowering black people within the contexts of surveillance by the state and the oppressive impact of racism on their everyday lives, and in contributing to a contestation of a broader knowledge/power complex. Significantly, in documenting this research project and its outcomes, and in highlighting the role of research in challenging the abuses of, for example, racism and sexism, Westwood stresses the need for self-reflexivity in research alongside engagement with fundamental issues for change (the big issues).

In trying to develop self-reflexivity within emancipatory research, Patti Lather advocates the need for reciprocity, a mutual negotiation of meaning and power. This highlights two vital relationships: those between researcher and researched and those between *data and theory* (Lather 1991: 57). In both instances, the imperative is that researchers make every effort to make sense of research data through a co-investigation and problematisation of the lived experience, self-understandings, identified problems and aspirations of research participants. Of course, research data need not be confined to participant experience. Significantly, Westwood and the Black Mental Health Group did not neglect more conventional empirical data, but worked to connect participant experience and voice to effective use of more conventional statistical evidence which demonstrated the overrepresentation of black people within mental health institutions and categorisations of mental illness.

At the same time and just as important, researchers need also to be prepared to expose to mutual exploration and interrogation their own theories and constructions of research. Dialectical theory-building would appear to involve a greater reflexivity and democratic commitment than that suggested in 'teach[ing] the masses clearly what we have learnt from them confusedly' (Mao, quoted in Freire 1972: 66) – it implies that all research processes should be conducted in an interactive and dialogic manner. This has been demonstrated in an adult education context by Westwood's lengthy process of negotiation and dialogue with the Black Mental Health Group regarding theory, data and methods.

In the process of negotiating the use and interrelationship of theory, data and methods, the hegemonic power of conventional research cannot lightly be disregarded. In another attempt to develop emancipatory adult education research, Wildemeersch set out to have a protracted participation and collaboration with grassroots community groups in a thematic investigation of the many economic, social and ecological problems of a depressed region of Belgium (Wildemeersch 1992a). Interestingly, although he was successful in developing participatory dialogue and investigation and in giving voice to research participants in the process of constructing a codification/video of 'Anger and Hope in the Rumpelstreek', Wildemeersch is also self-critical in 're-viewing' his role as a researcher. In retrospect, he admits that, notwithstanding his emancipatory intent, he was still 'infected' by the positivist tradition of research. Thus, at a crucial stage and in the interests of developing a respectable methodology and achieving academically meaningful outcomes, he was influential in separating out, in the final analysis, action and research objectives, in taking 'an 'objectifying' rather than a 'performative' stance towards the 'objects' of research' (ibid.: 52). In this way, Wildemeersch admits to having been instrumental in limiting the final impact of the research on practice in the field.

Wildemeersch's self-critical analysis poses important questions about the relationship of emancipatory research to more mainstream research and we will return to this later in the chapter. It also highlights the importance within emancipatory research of a commitment to a *democratic methodology*. Budd Hall and the advocates of participatory research emphasise, first of all, participation, involving a shift in focus from the North to the South, the expatriate to the local researcher and, crucially, the increased involvement of the poor and exploited in the research process itself (Hall 1981: 450–1). Equally important, Hall identifies a number of vital prerequisites for this participation to take place, for example, the need for sufficient time and space in order to avoid the temptations and logic of an expertist 'quick fix' and the use of alternative and creative research methods. Indeed, here there are a number of documented examples where researchers in the North have productively adapted and developed alternative research methods pioneered in the South, e.g., the decoding of photographic representations (Kirkwood and Kirkwood 1989), the use of people's theatre (Duffield 1992) and collective expression and analysis of problems and issues through song, oral history, audio and video recordings (see Wildemeersch 1992; Newman 1995). There is a link here with our earlier discussion of the significance of performativity in postmodern critical practices. Indeed, it could be argued that these practices embody participatory research approaches, given the emphasis both on performative methods and on the generation of knowledge for performing, i.e., for realising efficacious action in relation to specific life problems. Certainly, a focus on performative methods may offer one possibility for adult education researchers to make productive connections with the approaches and agendas of 'new social movements'.

Central to all the above is the issue of *voice*. The development of voice is an essential ingredient of many emancipatory research approaches, in that the idea is to 'name' and by so doing foreground the oppressive weight of a 'culture of silence'. Naming serves as a kind of guarantee against any replication, albeit in emancipatory guise, of the oppressive and alienating social conditions of more conventional research approaches and discourses. Of course, the development of voice for those who have been silenced is far from an unproblematic process, as has been illustrated in a teaching/seminar situation by Ellsworth (1992), as reported earlier in this book.

There is perhaps a crucial difference here between a classroom situation and the broader context of research. Indeed, it is possible that the longer timescale and more systematic nature of a research process could serve either to further diminish or enhance the development of voice, depending on the contingent circumstances of the particular research process. Critical factors here would appear to be the need to facilitate appropriate preconditions and foster sufficient space, infrastructure and confidence for people to speak – in this process, the nature, use and ownership of language is a vital consideration for those who have been silenced at a number of different levels and may well offer prospects for more emancipatory research praxis both on the margins and more closely related to the mainstream. Kathleen Weiler documents the achievements of the Jamaican women's theatre group, Sistern, in working on 'memory work' and exploring their experience collectively through writing their life stories and sharing, exploring and analysing them further in their own creative theatre work (Weiler 1994: 31). This points to one way where participant voice can be fostered and developed through collective and participatory research. It is clear what the promise of auto/biography is for both emancipatory and more mainstream research approaches, in developing countries and in the more developed world. The following chapter will investigate this further in the context of more mainstream research.

The discourse of emancipatory research highlights the direct engagement of research with the world and with social change. In this process, it offers a challenge to the values of mainstream research paradigms and identifies a variety of alternative, innovative and productive approaches for engaging with research subjects. In identifying the very political nature of research, it reasserts the importance of values, ethics and outcomes for participants.

The discussion in this chapter, drawing on feminist and postmodern perspectives on research, has stressed the importance of the way values are translated and negotiated in particular contexts of practice, and it is perhaps this which offers the greatest prospects and stimulus for developing more emancipatory research approaches in relation to adult learning. This is also the most useful learning point for adult education practitioners doing research in broader 'mainstream' research contexts.

Research is clearly a very political process. Nevertheless, in the broad and diverse context of adult learning, researchers will often have sufficient relative autonomy, even sometimes 'subversive space' to promote research as praxis, to take account of the complexity of the power/knowledge complex, to problematise the relationship between theory and data, to use democratic methods and to provide time and space to promote participant voice. However, in identifying with the critique of emancipatory research and maintaining a broad commitment to the values it stresses while, at the same time, trying to move from the margins to the mainstream, a number of problems may need to be confronted and issues considered.

As we have seen, emancipatory research oversteps the limits of research traditions in instructive and productive ways. However, in attempting to move from the margins to the mainstream whilst also maintaining an emancipatory interest and commitment, it may be necessary to look again at *limit situations* within research. In his advocacy of praxis, Paulo Freire recognises the need to identify and explore 'limit situations', temporary but not unsurmountable barriers, and link this to a commitment to undertake 'limit acts', those directed at overcoming, rather than passively accepting the given (Freire 1972). Such a focus may help researchers move away from the disabling implications for research praxis of polarities like domestication versus liberation. For example, the 'questions for participatory research' identified below need not be seen as moral absolutes or a badge of purity but rather can be used as important reference points for researchers with emancipatory intent.

QUESTIONS FOR PARTICIPATORY RESEARCH

Initiation and control
  Who initiates?
  Who defines the problem?
  Who pays?
Critical content
  What is studied?
  Why?
  By whom?
Collective analysis
  How is information gathered?
  By whom?
  How is data analysed?
  By whom?
Learning and skills developed
  What is learnt?
  Who develops what skills?
  What are the products and by-products?
Uses for action
  How are results disseminated?
  Who uses them?
  How are they used?
  Who benefits?

(International Participatory Research Network 1982)

Clearly, these questions need to be mediated by the political context of the research in question and the particular views and circumstances of research participants. Nevertheless, such questions could well be used in a similar way to Habermas' 'ideal speech situation', as an analytical framework and reference point for researchers and research participants trying to move towards a more empowering research praxis. They could form a goal for the development of a wider 'stakeholder research'.

Even in relatively restricted research contexts, the idea of 'limit situations' would appear to have some relevance to research praxis. In policy-oriented research, it is certainly difficult to move away from the 'adaptive hermeneutics' which appears so central to current research analysis and the circumscribed process of making research bids. However, in this context, a critical problematisation and re-engagement with the power/knowledge relationship within research may point towards ways of moving some way along the continuum from 'adaptive' to more 'transformative hermeneutics'. This, in turn, may allow more radical researchers to develop research as praxis within what relative autonomy exists and exploit the possibilities of unexpected outcomes. In this process and with this aim in mind, it is perhaps reassuring to note how, according to Stephen Ball, the history of educational policy making points to:

> Multicausal[ity], pluralistic conflict, administrative complexity and historical inertia as having equal theoretical and conceptual relevance in understanding policy-making processes as does the logic and development of the capitalist mode of production.
>
> (Ball 1990: 14–15)

A final limit situation to be considered for research in the context of adult learning is that of the academic context and the academic mode of production. In reflecting on the possibilities and problems of developing transformative research from a university base, Zacharakis-Jutz *et al.* ask the crucial question:

> can a state-supported institution . . . conduct research that supports and even stimulates collective action which leads to a changed society?
>
> (Zacharakis-Jutz *et al.* 1991: 24)

Paradoxically, the very world-wide trend towards increasing research specialisms and the search for research niches could operate to provide sufficient space and insulation for continuing radical and participatory approaches to research. In an increasingly pluralistic world where, at the same time, there is a re-emerging concern for community and social cohesion, there are examples from Chicago, Leeds, Southampton, Leiden and Sydney (see Zacharakis-Jutz *et al.* 1991; Johnston 1992; Wildemeersch 1992a; Ward 1996; Newman 1995) where university adult educators have been able to work in partnership with community groups in developing research, predominantly in their interests. Of course, much depends on the relationship of the researchers both to the mainstream university and to local communities. Compromises may have to be made in the use of different forms of representation of the research conducted and the effect of this should not be underestimated. This will be dealt with later in this chapter. Nevertheless, there might be sufficient relative autonomy for more radical researchers to undertake 'limit acts' in research which acknowledge explicitly the different stakeholders in the research process and highlight the key issue of research ownership. In this way, it may be possible to develop research that 'does not view the community as "objects" of study but as co-researchers engaged in the task of

comprehending the causes of unemployment, oppression and poverty'
(Zacharakis-Jutz *et al.* 1991: 26).

Emancipatory research approaches focus on the position that research
can empower those involved in it. At the same time, however, research
can disempower, even when it seeks to empower. It is this paradox to
which a postmodern approach is oriented. This highlights one of the key
differences between emancipatory research and a postmodern perspective
on research. Whereas the two approaches have much in common, for
example, a recognition and celebration of difference, opposition to the
defining power of research traditions and to oppressive structures, they
differ somewhat in their attitude to oppression. Emancipatory research, in
focusing on the need to empower the powerless within external oppressive
structures, stresses alternative emancipatory goals and directions for
research. In contrast, a postmodern approach is suspicious of all kinds of
totalising discourses, whether deemed 'emancipatory' or not, and sees
oppression as existing at both an external and internal level.

SOME FEATURES OF A POSTMODERN APPROACH

We have seen in the previous chapter how social and educational phenomena are more aptly understood as indeterminate and open-ended. Postmodernism challenges the powerful and virtually taken-for-granted view
that there is a determinate world which can be definitively known and
explained. It argues that the social sciences are sciences of indeterminacy,
where theories do not succeed by predicting unique and determinate outcomes. Furthermore, it argues that all research, even 'scientific' research,
is a product of certain kinds of social, historically located practices. This
means that research can itself be examined as a social product, a social
construct embedded in local and specific cultures.

In contemporary times there is a general postmodern scepticism about
epistemology and in particular of the epistemological aim of distinguishing
true, certain knowledge by means of a logic of enquiry which defines the
limits of knowledge. As we have seen in the previous chapter, it has traditionally been the task of epistemology to privilege scientific method as
the methodological guarantee of a true and certain knowledge. It sought
to formulate universal rules as to what could be counted as scientific
knowledge, a set of universal characteristics that qualified a practice as
scientific and a theory or explanation as adequate.

Postmodernism takes one step further the critique of this dominant
epistemology which sought to set the standard and provide the model for
all knowledge. As we have seen the critique of this epistemology has
challenged the assumptions that:

- observation is value-neutral and atheoretical;
- experience is a 'given';
- a univocal and transparent language is possible;
- data is independent of its interpretations;
- there are universal conditions of knowledge and criteria for deciding between theories.

In the postmodern, there is a questioning of whether knowledge is established through systematic empirical observation and experiment mediated by reason or whether a necessary first step requires a shifting of the way the world is seen and the construction of a new world to investigate. In other words, in the postmodern, ontology precedes epistemology (McHale 1992).

On the other hand, a postmodern approach does not simply embrace alternatives such as hermeneutic/interpretive or critical theory paradigms and research traditions, since it sees these as still implicitly operating within the terms and discourse of the positivist/empiricist paradigm – for example, the hermeneutic/interpretive emphasis on the 'subjective' instead of the 'objective' can be seen as merely a reversal of an opposition where 'objective/subjective' is still retained as a defining and definitive polar opposition. Instead, a postmodern approach seeks to subvert this dichotomy, to show that apparently mutually exclusive polar opposites are, in effect, mutually implicated, and to suggest alternatives which radically challenge and critique dominant epistemological paradigms and discourses in all their various forms.

A significant starting-point is the actual historically located practices of the various sciences, natural as well as social. This historical approach which, as we have seen, informs the work of Kuhn (1970), displaces the essentialist and transcendental view of science which is to be found in both the positivist/empiricist and hermeneutic/interpretive paradigms and instead argues that all sciences are social practices. Here, there is obviously some affinity with the critical theory paradigm. The emphasis on the actual practice of a science highlights its specificity and situatedness and the practice-constituted criteria for judging the validity of knowledge claims and theory choice. This serves to highlight both the constructed nature of research and its constructive or 'world-making' power.

The postmodern displacement of epistemology and the foregrounding of ontology has two important consequences. The first is bound up with the 'world-making' that occurs through the necessary implication of research in language, discourses and texts. Postmodernism sees knowledge-generation as a practice of 'languaging', a practice of textual production. Here, language is not conceived as a mirror held up to the world, as simply a transparent vehicle for conveying the meaning of an independent external reality. In language, as an always already existing structure of significations, the referent is the effect rather than the source of the sign system. Thus, it is language, discourse and text which enables the world to be known. No form of knowledge can be separated from language, discourses and texts at work within culture. These are both the carriers and creators of a culture's epistemological codes – the way we as researchers know the world and the way we are located within culture.

The structures, conceptuality and conventions of language, embodied in discourses and texts, language as a meaning-constituting system, governs what can be known and what can be communicated. This means that knowledge is always partial and perspectival, always shaped by language and discourse, always situated within specific cultures which provide meaning and significance. Thought and experience – the positivist/empiricist bedrock – and actions and meanings – the hermeneutic/interpretive bedrock – are never independent of socio-cultural contexts and practices. All epistemological paradigms and research traditions are coded by language and discourse in terms of binary oppositions, e.g., masculine/feminine, subject/object, rational/irrational – oppositions that constitute identity through powerful and oppressive hierarchies which are their consequence.

The second aspect of the postmodern (which was discussed in Chapter 5) is a decentring of the knowing subject, the epistemological subject attributed with a universal and essential human nature – unitary, rational, consciousness-centred and the originary point of thought and action. This essential nature is conceived as allowing subjects to be autonomous of the world and to occupy an Archimedean point that transcends their own subjectivity, history and socio-cultural location. This stance of 'objectivity', where the subject is a pure experiencer and reasoner transcending particularity, partiality and contingency, defines who can be a knower (and traditionally this has been the white, middle-class male) and is at the same time the condition for the interchangeability of knowing subjects and hence the public verifiability of scientific knowledge (Code 1993).

Postmodernism challenges and displaces this abstract, transcendental subject, arguing instead that subjects cannot be separated from their subjectivity, history and socio-cultural location. In the postmodern, there are no Archimedean points, the subject is, instead, decentred, enmeshed in the 'text' of the world, constituted in intersubjectivity, discourse and language. Equally, the separation of subject and object, objectivity and subjectivity, is itself a position maintainable only so long as the knower is posited as abstract and decontextualised and the object known posited as the 'other' unable to reflect back on and affect the knower (Acker *et al.* 1991).

The need to take account of the status of knowers-researchers and their socio-cultural contexts, the intimate inseparability of knower and known, the known and the means of knowing, the impossibility of separating the subjects and objects of research, subverts the epistemological assumption of an 'objective' world and the foundational systems of thought which secure, legitimate and privilege 'objective' ways of knowing that world. Knowledge, it is argued, is never absolute and universal. In the post-modern, there is a foregrounding of complexity, uncertainty, heterogeneity and difference. There is a questioning of the powerful notion that there is 'one true reality', stable and ordered, that exists independently of knowers, which can be experienced 'as it really is' and which is best represented in scientific models of research. Instead, postmodernists argue that the 'real' is unstable, in flux and contingent. Although we can experience the real, knowing it (in the sense of experience having meaning and significance) is only possible by representing it through a culturally located signifying system. But, in representation, the real is not simply being reflected 'as it really is' but is being constructed or shaped in a way particular to the codings of the signifying system. As we have seen earlier, these codings take the form of binary, hierarchical oppositions.

Postmodernism highlights the need for science to be much more varied and self-reflexive about its limitations. Science assumes a knowing subject, a known object, and an unambiguous knowledge. The postmodernist argu-ment is that none of these can any longer be taken for granted, all are subject to incredulity. Science's claim to authority has been premised on its appeal to experience mediated by purportedly value-neutral, logical-empirical method which promised the growth of rational control over ourselves and our world. Practices of control and prediction were rooted in unreconcilable polar opposites, for example:

- linearity/chaos
- teleology/historical contingency
- representational language/constitutive language
- 'innocent' knowledge/power/knowledge
- facts as given/facts as constructed by the questions asked.

In every case, one pole of the opposites is privileged over the other, e.g., linearity over chaos, facts as given over facts constructed. In other words, these polar opposites are not 'natural' or existing in reality but are them-selves social constructs and cultural codes, organised in hierarchical forms and possessing normative power because they were considered 'natural', i.e., found in the world.

As we have already noted, the implication of this is that social events, processes and phenomena are indeterminate. Knowledge in the form of predictive generalisations requires a closure which itself requires a deter-minate, orderly 'real'. If closure can only be *imposed*, then the very status of this knowledge becomes questionable. Closure involves violence, since to close the real is an act of power involving the drawing of boundaries, policing and excluding, given that the real is not 'naturally' closed, i.e., it is not of itself fixed, determinate and orderly. However, acts of power are not supposed to figure in 'scientific' research. But, once they do become relevant, then the 'objectivity' of the research process becomes highly problematic.

The need to take account of the dimension of power challenges the possibility of 'disinterested' research and value-free knowledge. Science is both constituted by a particular set of values and itself is value-constituting, yet the scientific attitude is one that continually attempts to suppress the place of values and conceal the workings of power. As we have argued already, it is impossible to escape the value-ladenness of research, since ways of knowing are inherently culture-bound and will therefore reflect the dominant values of the particular culture in which they are located. The striving for value-neutrality and the striving for detachment from the world is itself a value-position located in the particular culture of Western society as it has developed since the European Enlightenment. What this implies, therefore, is that there is a need to be self-reflexive, to be aware of how researcher values permeate research both in its methods and outcomes.

Research can be seen as an enactment of power relations between researchers and researched or between researchers and the world. Who does the interpreting, who are the sense-makers, who decides what the 'data' means? It is by denying the place of values and power that science can become a form of mystification and a source of oppression. As Foucault has argued, power is always present in any attempt to know; indeed, power works its effects through its intimate interconnection with knowledge. It is for this reason that a postmodern approach to research highlights the need to consider not only outcomes and methods but also the implication of research with power and unspoken values and the *effects*, or politics, of research.

The dependence of knowledge on socio-cultural practices and contexts, unacknowledged values, tacit discourses and interpretive traditions means that research is embedded in unconscious fore-structures of understanding, the 'unsaid' and 'unsayable' that is the condition of any methodical knowing. Postmodernism argues that all knowledge of the real is textual, i.e., always already signified, interpreted or 'written' and, therefore, a 'reading' which can be 'rewritten' and 'reread'. Hence, there is neither an originary point of knowledge nor a final interpretation. However, as we have already noted, some readings are more powerful than others. The most powerful readings are those imposed by the violence of closure and the 'metaphysics of presence', i.e., the powerful 'way of seeing' enshrined in traditional epistemology that the world can be known in an unmediated way by a rational 'objective' self through the use of a neutral scientific method. Yet, given that all readings are subject to contingency and the historical moment in which they are read, and given that the object of scientific research is always open to contest, then all claims to presence, to an unmediated self and an unmediated knowledgeability, are always problematic.

Postmodernism challenges foundationalism, the position that knowledge is founded in disciplines, and the consequent boundary-defining and maintenance that is characteristic of disciplinary knowledge and discipline-based research. There are two aspects to this. The first is that social scientists, located as they are in the modernist epistemological project, want to give 'reasoned', connected and totalising accounts. But, as we have seen, the world they investigate and seek to explain is not one that can readily be *reflected* in their theories and accounts. It is, in other words, not organised naturally into disciplinary compartments. They are always, therefore, as Acker *et al.* (1991: 149) point out, in the business of attempting to systematically 'reconstruct social reality and to put these reconstructions into the form of a social theory'.

The social sciences conceive of themselves as representing the real, whereas, it can be argued, what they are actually doing is 'writing' it. Social reality does not exist as an extra-discursive context, rather the real and the discursive are intimately interwoven, 'the social is written . . . there is no extra-discursive real outside cultural [i.e. meaning] systems . . . the social world does not consist of ready-made objects that are put into representation' (Game 1991: 4). If disciplinary research and theorising is itself a practice of writing then theory cannot be tested directly against the real. The question then becomes by what discursive strategies does a discipline maintain its claims to the status of knowledge. In the case of the social sciences, this is done through a privileged representation of social reality based on the binary opposition 'real/representation'. The assumption here is that there is a 'real' separate and distinct from its representation but that representations generated by research accurately (truthfully) reflect the real. The failure to recognise that the real and its representation are inseparably intertwined leads to the repression of the fictionality or textuality of the social sciences. Research, therefore, comes to be seen as the discovery rather than the inscription of the real.

The lesson here is that a postmodern approach to research is not part of an alternative paradigm for research, let alone a new method for doing research. What it is, if it is anything at all, is an injunction to be constantly vigilant, to take nothing for granted in doing research. By being vigilant we are reminded to always ask not only 'What is my research finding out?', but also 'Where is it coming from?', 'What is it doing?'; and 'What is it implicated in?' In this way, we become aware that research is not a transcendental activity or merely the application of an invariant technical process. Most of all, we become aware that research is both a 'constructed' and a 'constructing' activity. Furthermore, in seeing things this way we can better understand research as a kind of storytelling – as 'constructed' and 'constructing'. An advantage of this approach is that it foregrounds the illuminative, insightful and emancipatory possibilities of research. But what is also revealed is that storytelling can be 'power-ful', oppressive and dangerous. There are always two sides to the text of social research.

As an example of a postmodern approach to research we will outline work carried out by Patti Lather and reported in a chapter entitled 'Staying Dumb: Student Resistance to Liberatory Curriculum' (Lather 1991). The research was a three-year enquiry into student resistance to a liberatory curriculum in an introductory women's study course. She not only describes the research, its purpose, methods and outcomes but also explores what it means to do research differently – in this case, in a postmodernist way. Although, on the face of it, the research is conventionally empiricist with data collected from interviews, research reports and the entries from her own reflective diary, her aims in doing the research were rather different from most empiricist educational research; as she puts it, it was a question of what one does with data after encountering postmodernism! Certainly, for her, the encounter meant that she could no longer produce a conventional research text, let alone ignore demands such as:

(a) To make a space from which the voices of those not normally heard could be heard.
(b) To move outside conventional research texts, outside the textual devices which are found in 'scientific' research.
(c) To ask questions about the way she as the 'author' constructs her research text and organises meaning – and in this way to highlight the performativity or constructive nature of language.
(d) To challenge the myth of a found or already existing world in research and its communication outside the intrusion of language and an embodied researcher.
(e) To explore a complex and heterogeneous reality which does not fit neatly into pre-established categories.
(f) To be concerned with the politics of research – in particular, to examine how any categorising is an act of power which always marginalises.
(g) To put the researcher back into the picture. The researcher is a social subject in relation with others. The specificity of the researcher, for example Patti Lather's interest in emancipatory pedagogy, shapes the process and product of her enquiry.

As a consequence, in the course of analysing her data she found herself asking questions not normally asked in empiricist research. Instead of focusing exclusively on questions about the validity of outcomes and methods, she asked:

i Given that she was purporting to do 'scientific' research, what is it that confers scientificity?

ii Is research simply a matter of 'finding out' or do we need to also consider what it is we want research to do?

iii What is the relationship between method and findings and is it the case that a particular method privileges certain findings?

iv What is the place of research procedures in the claims we make about validity?

v What does it mean to recognise the limits of exactitude and certainty whilst respecting the empirical world?

vi How is the research to be reported – is the linear way of writing, the style of narrative realism, the attempt to demonstrate mastery of language the only way to write the research text? Or is it possible to use textuality against itself and construct a text without linearity and with an openness and ambivalence?

Of course, these are not the only questions that could have been asked. But these were the questions that Patti Lather as both an empirical and postmodernist researcher felt needed to be asked. Moreover, they are questions that can be asked of any research, whatever its locating paradigm.

Research approaches inherently reflect our beliefs about the world we live in and want to live in. When we do research what we see reflected is ourselves located in our biography and culture. Postmodernism reflects a decline of absolutes – no longer does following the correct method guarantee true results. Instead of only one truth and one certainty, we are more ready to accept that there are many truths and that the only certainty is uncertainty. The questioning of what scientific, rigorous research is, and what its effects are, is part of a contemporary condition which Habermas refers to as a 'crisis of legitimation' and others have called 'postmodernity'. Here, the formerly secure foundations of knowledge and understanding are no more. The quest for a 'God's-eye view', a disembodied and disembedded timeless perspective that can know the world by transcending it, is no longer readily accepted. What has taken its place is a loss of certainty in ways of knowing and what is known. What we are left with is not an alternative and more secure foundation but an awareness of the complexity, historical contingency and fragility of the practices through which knowledge is constructed about ourselves and the world. The orthodox consensus about how to do research scientifically has been displaced. As we have seen, there are many research traditions each with its own epistemology. Postmodernism, however, is not an alternative tradition, although it does foreground the epistemological commitments which are implicit in all research traditions.

To do research in a postmodernist way is to take a critical stance towards the practice of sense-making and sense-taking which we call research. What it focuses on, however, is not the *world* which is constructed and investigated by research but the way in which that world is written in the research *text*. This is an unfamiliar process, because generally what we think we are doing as researchers is producing a text which accurately represents the world that has been researched. We also assume that the appropriate and correct use of methods ensures that the representation is accurate. Furthermore, we tend to believe that once we have done this then no more questions need be asked about the text itself.

To take a postmodernist approach to research involves more than generating accurate representations. It is to focus on our text and ask certain questions about it of the kind that Patti Lather asked about her research. As we have noted, this is an essentially *reflexive* or self-referential task. We ask: 'Why do we do research?', 'How has our research been constructed?', 'What is it silent about?', 'What gives our text its narrative authority?', 'What are the gender, race and class relations that produce the research and how does the text reproduce these relations?'

Research practices inscribe certain kinds of legitimation. When we think of research as a practice rather than a technology we can see more readily how research becomes authoritative *because* it is embodied in particular kinds of text. Although research is always an attempt to represent the world, representations are not themselves neutral. Research is an example of how meanings are framed within an authorial context; in other words, the researcher is an author who is also an 'authority'! For the postmodernist, therefore, 'objectivity' is a textual construction, i.e., it is achieved through the way the text is framed and organised by the use of certain textual devices, e.g., narrative realism, that create the 'objective' researcher or 'scientific self'. Hence, we can study the way in which research is *written* in terms of the way in which the social relations of the research process are enacted in the research text.

These are all reflexive questions. They are autobiographical, but not in a purely individualistic sense. As researchers, we all have an individual trajectory which shapes the research we do, the questions we ask and the way we do it. But, as researchers, we are also socio-culturally located, we have a social autobiography and this has an equally if not more important part to play in shaping our research and directing the kinds of reflexive questions which need to be asked but rarely are. It is towards a further elaboration of these questions in relation to the micro-politics of the research process that the next chapter is directed.

Chapter 10

Writing and learning about research

The purpose of research is to go 'beyond the limits' of what is known, to offer new 'facts' and explanations and, in the case of postmodern approaches, to question their grounding in conventional epistemologies and practices of enquiry. In this chapter, we revisit the idea of research as a practice in which the self is engaged as a reflective practitioner. In the light of our previous analysis of a) how the self has been configured in theories of adult learning and b) the effects of discourse and the nature of practice as inscription, research can be viewed as the practice of writing and rewriting selves and the world. Personal and social change which occurs through learning, as well as being brought about by natural means such as ageing, is accompanied and consolidated by discursive shifts, i.e., in the ways in which we talk and write about ourselves and others. So-called 'new paradigm' research in the educational field – of which action research, collaborative and participatory research can be considered examples – represents a practical change in the conduct of research and a potential liberation from the technical-rationality model which scripts both investigators and their subjects in restrictive ways. It has contributed significantly to the rewriting of educational research as a practice in a number of domains. At the same time, new research voices have to find their place in a world of competing voices – including those of conventional researchers, adult learners, teachers and policy-makers.

In a postmodern context, action research and associated modes of enquiry foreground the idea of 'voice', together with the related ideas of research as a practice which is both scripted (i.e., dependent on existing discourses) and inscribing (i.e., potentially producing new discourses). Subjects can be shaped (i.e., 'in-formed' and perhaps even 'trans-formed') by such research. We want here to try and open up some action spaces and practice possibilities for researchers and reflective practitioners who are committed to change in the service of educational values. We build on a previous analysis of adult education research (Usher and Bryant 1989) which criticised conventional methodologies for reproducing the voices of foundational disciplines, especially behaviourist psychology and empirical sociology, thus constituting the adult learner in particular ways and downgrading the voices of 'ordinary experience'. At the same time, we have seen how the concept of experience itself is problematic. To be consistent with this critique, and to be reflexively so, it is necessary to take account of the everyday practices of doing research such as those examined by Woolgar, Steier and colleagues (Woolgar 1988; Steier 1991) and in the emerging field of critical ethnography (Atkinson 1990; Long and Long 1992; Law, 1994).

Our analysis extends the idea of the 'self' as a researcher who is culturally and historically configured and is situated within a nexus of relationships which have to be negotiated, to include the idea of an experiential 'trajectory' as a dynamic component in the conduct of enquiry. In such a trajectory, there is an important affective dimension. How the self is disposed as an engaged enquirer is a neglected dimension of reflective research practice, one which can influence the conduct of research as either impediment or resource. Given that all practices are scripted and inscribing activities, it follows that research as a writing of the self and the world has a biographical and temporal dimension. This will allow us to link the ideas of 'voice' to that of 'time', and the construction of a research account as a plausible narrative – in short, a 'story' (Ricoeur 1991; Usher 1993) which has to hold its own alongside other possible stories.

Research as a process of coming to understand and to make claims about what one has discovered is only possible on the basis of pre-understandings which provide the conceptual furniture which is used to inhabit the world. Pre-understanding is an essential ingredient of the habitus of practice; it cannot be theorised away in the service of some misplaced notion of objectivity nor can the already existing narrativity of the self be 'purified'. In addition, the practical problems of conducting research have tended to be theorised as impedimenta which prevent one from arriving at 'the truth', and which can be overcome via technical rational means. Since the best that research can do is only to produce a discourse of truth, which may either become incorporated into an existing regime of truth or exist more or less successfully as a counter-discourse, we would wish to claim that learning about research is learning how to produce a discourse which 'works' for the audience intended, and here to include in the audience the self as author. In this process, another narrative of the self is written. We conclude by presenting examples of ways of teaching about research in a reflective practice mode. These examples are grounded in the foregoing analysis and the belief that teaching about research, and research training in an academic context generally, is more than the transmission of technical expertise. Teaching about research as writing the self and the world should encourage the production of a text which is alien neither to author nor audience.

METHODOLOGY AND THE POWER OF THE TEXT

We have already seen that, within the disciplines taken to be foundational for educational practice, research typically embodies and reproduces a technical-rationality model for the conduct of enquiry. In this model, particular methodologies are warranted as the appropriate means to produce the ends of obtaining certified knowledge of some aspect of reality – psychological, social, historical, etc. A means–ends approach is adopted to the discovery and explanation of things 'out there', existing as entities which are independent of the ways in which they are described. This is the stance of epistemological realism that conventional research takes in identifying instances of variables and determining their relationships by employing a transparent language – ideally one of conjecture and refutation (Popper 1963), in practice more likely one of assertion and confirmation.

Methodologies are more than just the defining characteristics of academic disciplines; they are central to the operation of power/knowledge in disciplines, whereby the subjectivities of researchers and researched are 'in-formed'. Conventional methodology textbooks train successive generations of researchers in a linear, algorithmic approach to conducting investigations, emphasising a fairly standard and well-worn sequence of research activities designed to produce warrantable findings about the world. Researchers are thereby constituted as analytical machine processors. Indeed, in quantitative, and increasingly now in qualitative research, the machine processing of findings is becoming commended in the name of objectivity and data manageability. Such texts typically warn of the dangers of data being contaminated by subjective incursions; subjectivity is problematised as an issue of validity. There is a strange tension here. Subjectivity is 'written into' guidelines for the conduct of research as something to be avoided almost, it seems, at all costs. At the same time, it is 'written out' of research when it comes to reporting one's results. Methodological prescriptions and research reports discursively and jointly confirm the power of the technical-rationality model.

In offering ways of getting at the 'truth', no methodologies are innocent. Critical research practice requires a consideration of the constitutive nature of the production of text upon the researcher as an author. Of whatever type, methodology texts provide a vehicle for inducting practitioners into particular research paradigms. It is something of a paradox that, in explicitly scripting the practice of research in approved ways, methodology *as text* does not draw attention to itself. Research as a practice is depicted in ways which ignore the reflexivity of the researcher as a sense-making agent. Even when claiming to address the 'real world' problems of research (e.g., Robson 1993), such texts do not normally incorporate the researcher as part of that world. This is so even for eclectic methodology texts, despite their recognition of the legitimacy of alternative approaches to generating data and explanations.

In the reporting practices of researchers, attention is rarely given to the circumstances in which reports get written. Joint authorship, for example, rarely accounts for the negotiations between contributing partners. The register for reports is ideally impersonal. The self is decentred in agentless prose. It is normally not considered appropriate to write the researcher into the report as one who is developing her/his own understanding, clarifying personal uncertainties, etc.

A central problematic for any researcher is that of validation. Validity is prescribed and textually confirmed in the practices of writing and reading research. We see validity as being primarily concerned with the production of a 'rigorous' text – one which works within the community of readers to which it is offered and is attuned to the habitus of its audience. Of course, since readers are not required to interpret research texts in the ways intended by their authors, the validity of research is always open to question. In relation to research as a scripted practice and the practice of writing, there are three aspects of this:

1 *Pre-validation:* this occurs at that stage of the research proposal when an acceptable account of the intentions of an investigation has to be provided as a prerequisite for securing the conditions to engage in research in the first place. This is an especially important issue in relation to funding proposals, in which one can see the discursive construction of the self as a 'credible' researcher. Formats for research proposals are expected to follow particular technical-rational conventions, often highly circumscribed. This is one of the reasons why action research/ reflective practice types of enquiry have difficulty in securing funding; they need to be contrived as practices which can gain assent at the 'pre-validity' stage by playing a particular discursive game which may be alien to them. Conventional academic research has to demonstrate, in the text of its proposal, that it fits into the canon and can contribute to the furtherance of 'normal science'.

2 *Internal validation:* this refers to the actual conduct of the research itself as following the precepts of appropriate practices with respect to devising indicators, data collection and analysis. The key here is the production of a text which is self-validating in so far as it follows the formal rules of enquiry.

3 *Post-validation:* the research text must prove acceptable to a community of readers. It seeks to inhabit a particular disciplinary domain and is the product of a particular habitus. Research is, therefore, scripted to be acceptable to anonymous referees (experienced practitioners acting as guardians of the domain) and thereby to the canon as a whole. In post-validation, the audience both is and is not anonymous. The

researcher knows the kind of community to which it is offered, even if she/he can not anticipate who will be the actual readers.

Through all the above processes, the researcher is both a scripted and scripting practitioner and also a risk-taker and stakeholder. S/he has a personal interest in the outcomes of research in terms of how it is read by others. One can, therefore, say that researchers are contributing, through their own practice, to their own discursive formation and confirmation as particular kinds of practitioner – a nice Foucauldian example of the disciplining of the self through self-discipline. In a particular sense, one knows that this is the case, yet the central activity of research as writing the self and thereby inscribing a practice is neglected. In conventional research, one writes about one's subjects and not about the self as a writer of the world under investigation, at least not concurrently but just possibly as a *post hoc* reflection. The downplaying of the self as a writer is a crucial aspect of the neglect or outright denial of the importance of reflexivity in research. Scripting the researcher, the researched and their relationship in impersonal ways is the means by which technical-rationality reproduces itself in conventional research.

It is important to recognize here that we are not suggesting that it is only research conducted within a positivist/empiricist paradigm that is open to the charge of being unaware of its textual practices. In a sense, this type of research is an easy target since one of the defining characteristics of the paradigm is the very absence of reflexivity and a critical scrutiny of practice. But a similar charge can be brought, as we have seen in our discussion of Schon's work, against those who offer alternative understandings of research and practice. We can also see, for example, in Knowles's influential theory of adult education as andragogy, how uncritical notions of 'learner-centredness' and 'self-directedness' can easily spawn technical-rational applications of tools such as the so-called 'Learning Readiness Scale' to disempower learners in the name of autonomy (Collins 1991a). Other adult education research traditions, whether humanistic or critical, need also to interrogate their own productions as authored works which 'in-form' the subjects on whose behalf they are claiming to work.

RELOCATING THE SELF IN RESEARCH

In *The Captive Triangle*, we were concerned that one of the effects of conventional research reporting in adult education was that, notwithstanding an express commitment to learner-centredness among teachers, adult education researchers had unreflectively followed the conventions of writing themselves as learners out of the investigative process. Until the emergence of so-called 'new paradigm' research, there was little appreciation of researchers as sense-making agents involved in developing understanding through dialogue. The theorising of subjects and researchers as collaborative agents or co-learners engaged in mutual understanding was underdeveloped. In arguing for the merits of action research and reflective practice which engaged all participants in enquiry, we foregrounded the notion of the 'self' as a questioning practitioner within the research arena. Having identified the importance of seeing practices as scripted and of research as the practice of generating a convincing narrative, we can proceed to link this to the idea of the self as an author.

Previously, we have theorised the enquiring self as one who is engaged in a variety of exchanges. The metaphor of the research arena (Usher and Bryant 1989: 150 ff.) was suggested by symbolic interactionist accounts of selves as agents who are required to negotiate with significant others. As a metaphor, it is heuristically useful, though limited. Interestingly, many readers of our analysis took the metaphor rather too literally, suggesting that it was somewhat combative and did not represent for them what research was 'really like'. There is an important implication here for the readership of texts to which we will return. For the moment, suffice it to say that, at the time, we found the metaphor illuminative in highlighting a number of practical questions about the conduct of negotiations in collaborative, participatory and action research contexts, and would still maintain that such questions need to be unpacked and cannot be addressed as purely technical matters. Indeed, it is just such routine practical matters concerning the propriety of action which raise questions of fine judgement and resist technical-rational solutions that are foregrounded in these types of research.

The problem with a symbolic interactionist account of the self as a researcher is that it emphasises the structural aspects of relationships (reinforced by the metaphor of the arena) at the expense of seeing enquiry as a process of (self-)understanding. Considering research as the practice of writing, as the pre-eminent means by which one develops understanding rather than as a transparent medium for reporting the already understood, is now central to the project of extending our own understanding of research as reflective practice. Critical reflective practice cannot be modelled in a conventional way and requires the interrogation of practice as scripted. It is legitimate to say that our own practice as academic analysts of adult education research was trapped in a contradiction; it had been scripted in a conventional way to the extent that we adapted a formal, foundational theory of interpersonal relations predicated on a particular epistemology of the self, i.e., symbolic interactionsim, in contradiction to the anti-foundational argument that we were trying to develop at the time.

To supplement and perhaps unwittingly to try and 'save' the model of the self in the research arena, we incorporated an understanding of how selves are constructed in dialogue by drawing on the discourse-analytic approach of Potter and Wetherell (1987). This approach emphasises the self as a knowledge claimant engaged in constructing plausible accounts within the arena about what is going on and, in action terms, what should be done. We would thus maintain that, at the time, the combined symbolic interactionst/discourse analytical approach gave us a better purchase on understanding the problematics and possibilities of generating knowledge through action research and reflective practice than any other theories of the self as a researcher then available. However, neither approach, alone or in combination, is sufficiently reflexive. The process of coming to know and thereby to 'in-form' the self through writing and rewriting is absent. And co-implicated with the issue of writing the research text is that of how the text is to be *read*. We will consider later how a critical interrogation of the authorship and authority of knowledge claims within adult education as a field of study and practice can be conducted along the lines suggested by Brookfield (1993b).

There are both practical and theoretical problems concerning how to write the self into the research process. As we have seen, the conventional 'solution' to these problems is to write the self out of the process altogether. If, however, one takes the view that in conducting research in a reflective practice mode one needs to provide textual exemplification of, as Schon puts it, 'reflection-in-action', then how can this be represented within the conventionalities of standard research texts? Can one write about reflexivity in a self-exemplifying and non-subversive manner? Possibly. Would such writing be generally acceptable to the research community? Probably not. There are also problems associated with the rendition of experience and the tacit dimensions of practice, both of which are acknowledged as key aspects of reflective practice. After all, one of the defining characteristics of the 'tacit' is that it cannot be written. One possible solution might be that of employing an allusive rather than a realist genre for reporting research. Another is to mix reporting styles, to give narrative space to different voices and to set conventional texts alongside less conventional counterparts.

It seems to us that a precondition for deciding how to (re)write research which engages with the problematic of reflexivity, and which might suggest some practical answers to the above questions, is to further develop our understanding of the self as a situated practitioner – not one who is merely located structurally within an arena of negotiated relationships but also on a dynamic personal trajectory of evolving understanding.

THE RESEARCH TRAJECTORY

Conventional models of investigation write research as a formal sequence of stages, each with its own operational imperatives – starting with the construction of a proposal, through developing an enquiry design, collecting data, analysing findings and reporting results. Each stage is scripted in terms of various technical problematics such as focusing, sampling, coding, testing, theorising, displaying results, etc. Methodologies are authored and authorised accounts of appropriate investigative practices to given circumstances, and represent the theorisations of a technical trajectory of research. At the same time, a research trajectory is a path along which individuals travel in order to meet their own requirements for understanding as well as attempting to satisfy the transpersonal goals of enquiry. Even within a model of research that is apparently unilinear, there will be a good deal of recursion, with operational decisions taken at a later stage having implications for revising and recasting previous decisions. We do not discount the importance of the technical trajectory of research. To be recognisable as systematic enquiry rather than just aimless searching, research needs to be procedurally appropriate and therefore follow certain rules of practice. One may question the requirement to follow any given rule, but of the necessity for investigative rules of some sort there can be no doubt. Many of these will be technical in nature. The matter is one for debate and judgment: which rules to follow and under what conditions? In any kind of research and, in particular in the kinds of research now commended as appropriate in adult education to achieving change through learning, this will be a judgment of affordance ('What is possible?') and propriety ('What is desirable?') or developing contextually appropriate criteria for the use of rules – metarules, if you like. In this domain, these are matters of interpersonal negotiation and reflexive consideration within a dialectical exchange which necessarily foregrounds researchers as knowledge claimants and sense-making selves. Reflexive research is a practice which embodies a critique of its own situatedness.

Any kind of research is concerned with making sense of and making claims about the world. Yet in the representations of conventional research, except in cases where the 'self' is a direct object of enquiry (e.g., in studies of personality), selves as individuals or parties in negotiation are written out of the research process. In attempting to satisfy the transpersonal canons of objectivity and generalisability, the self is regarded as a subjective contaminant. In scientific research, collaborative authorship is now the norm (Gibbons *et al.* 1994), yet the interpersonal dialectics of research do not get reported. Authors are an 'absent presence' in the scientific literature; both corporate and individual research is de-authored by the same textual device of indirect prose. The resulting accounts follow and privilege a technical trajectory in which selves as authors, authorisers and authorities are absented. In this way, science maintains its own fiction as a practice without practitioners, an agentless and therefore universally valid enterprise.

In maintaining that researchers are sense-making selves (and what else could they be?) our problematic is how one should write about the self in a non-conventional figuration of research. We want to retain the heuristic features of the symbolic interactionist and discourse analytic approaches to research at the same time as acknowledging the importance though not the exclusivity of technical considerations in a trajectory of enquiry. We also need an understanding of research as simultaneously the writing of one's own practice and the world that can assist would-be researchers, and especially educational research students, to engage reflexively and productively with their chosen enquiries. The metaphor of research as the texts of personal journeys which readers as potential fellow-travellers are invited to a) follow imaginatively in thought and b) possibly retrace themselves in action, offers valuable insights into how 'real-world' enquiries (with their frequent detours and false trails) are actually carried out. It represents an experiential view of research, one in which 'experiences' are not taken as given but provisional, i.e., subject to continuing critical review by all parties. It is closer to the enacted realities of participants and therefore has better claims to contextual validity than technical-rational models.

Drawing on the acknowledged importance of personal experience as an adult learning resource and the inherent situatedness of all understanding, including that which results from systematic research, we can map an experiential trajectory onto the technical trajectory of research in order to restore and reposition the self in the research process (see Figure 10.1). Selves are both situated and dispositional entities. These qualities need more than a notional recognition, but to be actively written into the conduct of research if it is to embody reflexivity. Reflective practice is the public recognition and interrogation of the *effects* of *affect* within action. Yet, even within the reflective practice literature, we have seen how affect tends to be theorised as a cognitive problem – one which it is suggested without irony gets in the way of effective practice and which could be resolved by some technical-rational means of straightening out our personal theories of action.

To recognise the existence of an experiential trajectory within research helps to relocate the enquiring self as someone who is guided by both dispositional and situational factors which change over time. Among the former may be counted such personal factors as tolerance for ambiguity/uncertainty, enthusiasm and energy, anticipation, frustration, etc. These are aspects of the researcher's self which are frequently acknowledged in private as important, but which are rarely documented. They may occasionally be alluded to in methodology texts, but are almost never publicly acknowledged in formal research reports. At the same time, the experiences of research supervisors attest to the importance of managing the advice given to graduate students in recognition of the formative influence

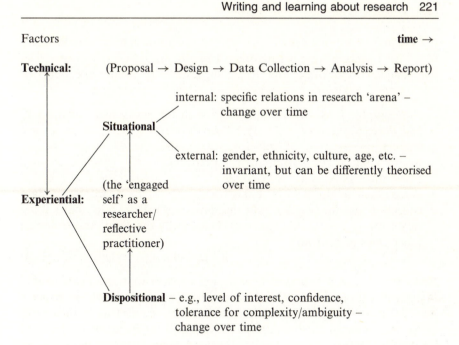

Figure 10.1 Dimensions of the research trajectory

of such factors in the conduct of research. The problem is that, although there is a nascent literature on the dispositional aspects of research (see for example, Schratz and Walker 1995), as such it is textually segregated from that on formal methodology and has a subordinate status. Mapping affect into a research trajectory allows us, as Schneider (1988: 81) notes, to engage practically with the following questions: 'Which highlights are there?', 'What has bored me, made me excited, irritated, frustrated, enjoyed, hurt and why?', 'Which theories can I make friends with?', 'How do I select appropriately, where do I get lost?', etc.

Situations within action research are rarely stable and require continuous rereadings and re-scriptings in recognition of the contingencies of action. Conventional research which uses experimental or survey methods is 'easier' to write in the sense that it is already 'pre-scribed' through the prior manipulation of the objects of enquiry, for example, by selective sampling and explicit controls. It is characterised by stability and closure. Reporting is expected to conform to the particular compositional rules which mirror the structure of the investigation itself. Convention thus reproduces itself through the relative ease by which it is scripted. In addition, normal science holds that the situatedness of the researcher is in principle of no relevance to the research results obtained, and the texts of normal science uphold the principle rather than the privately acknowledged practice (cf. Law 1994). We have argued for the necessity to address

the situatedness of practice in both teaching and research and would therefore wish to incorporate a situational trajectory within a model of reflective enquiry following the lines suggested by Ball. Speaking of
ethnographic fieldwork in educational research, he notes that:

> ethnographic fieldwork relies primarily on the engagement of the self,
> and that engagement can only be learnt enactively. . . . It requires a
> studied presentation of self (or selves) and the adaptation of the
> research self to the requirements of the field. It is much more like
> going on a blind date than going to work . . . the social process of
> engagement in the field [is linked] with the technical process of data
> collection and the decision that that linking involves. I call that linking
> *reflexivity* . . . reflexivity connects dialectically the social and technical
> trajectories of fieldwork.
>
> (Ball 1993: 33; emphasis in original)

Ball's model does not, however, incorporate disposition as an experiential
ingredient within the dynamic of investigation. Experiences interweave
personal dispositions and situations and can be mapped as a trajectories
which interact with the operational or technical trajectory of research, to
produce a dynamic structure for reflecting-in-action while doing research.
Such a model would allow one to identify one's needs as a self and
researcher in relation to various personal and technical 'sticking points' in
enquiry and suggest how these might be addressed by contextually appropriate (i.e., both operationally and experientially relevant) actions. The
implication for research supervisors and trainers is that their effective practice requires attending to both the researcher's experiential (dispositional
and situational) trajectories as well as the operational imperatives of any
investigation. This suggests that supervisors need to act as exemplars of
how they work through their own equivalent research experiences and to
share their feelings about research and that trainers need to provide
research trainees with contextually (i.e., experientially as well as formally)
appropriate resources. Our remodelling of the research process points to
the threefold requirements in writing and learning about research of
technical competence, contextual sensitivity and dispositional attentive-
ness. In short, an experiential trajectory helps to set the advisory context
for supervision and training, since one cannot judge the efficacy of advice
except in terms of the circumstances in which it is received and acted
upon by students.

RESEARCH AS NARRATIVE

Writing is the essence of research. It is a practice which demands to be
written, one of inscribing the world by constructing a plausible account
of how it works. Having emphasised the temporal and textual aspects of

research, we can now consider the narrative form of research along the lines suggested by Atkinson (1990) and Ricoeur (1991). This will give us an additional if somewhat slippery handle on reflexivity. As Atkinson notes:

> In principle, the notion of reflexivity recognizes that texts do not simply and transparently report an independent order of reality. Rather the texts themselves are implicated in the work of reality-construction.This principle applies not only to the spoken and written texts that are produced and interpreted by social actors, but to the texts of social analysts as well.
>
> (Atkinson 1990: 7)

By attending to the narrativity of research, we note a number of structural features that are rarely made explicit in theories of reflective practice. The first is that, in providing an account of some aspect of the world, research is telling a story which to be convincing has to follow certain conventions of storytelling acceptable to a particular readership. Only certain kinds of account will do. In that sense we are not talking about 'just stories' but depictions which follow certain narrative rules for the formation of accounts. Second, narrativity links the idea of authorship to that of agency, i.e., the researcher as an active teller of plausible tales of discovery and invention and not simply – as conventional conceit would have it – a passive witness and reporter of events. We have seen how the narratives of normal science are constructed as agentless, disembodied descriptions to which anyone in principle can attest. At the same time, narratives are authorised by means of a readership and re-authorised by the readers themselves acting as writers in the production of further texts, through processes of citation.

> Explicit citations of cultural knowledge blend almost imperceptibly with implicit reliance on everyday knowledge of a diffuse sort. . . . The apparatus of citations and similar sorts of reference thus help to establish the credentials and the credibility of a given text.
>
> (ibid.: 41, 45)

This is the intertextuality of practice to which Usher (1993) refers, in which all practices (but academic research most explicitly through its reporting and referencing conventions) show the presence of other texts within an interpretive culture. By an invitation 'to participate in its own process of reality construction' (Atkinson 1990: 54), the text implicates its readers in going along with the writer's story through appeals to what can be commonly assumed.

Drawing on arguments from Aristotle's *Poetics*, Ricoeur contrasts the theoretical understanding to which science aspires with *narrative under-standing* 'which is much closer to the practical wisdom of moral judgment'

(Ricoeur 1991: 23). He introduces the concept of 'emplotment' to show that it is only possible to follow stories because they are constructed in particular ways. We have certain templates for how to read them and certain expectations about their outcomes. To that extent, writers and readers have a shared frame of reference. Stories have their temporal elements (first . . . then . . . then . . ., etc.) which are completed in the anticipations of readers:

> the sense or significance of a narrative stems from the intersection of the world of the text and the world of the reader . . . it is the *act* of *reading* which completes the work, transforming it into a *guide* for reading, with its zones of indeterminancy, its latent wealth of interpretation, its power of being reinterpreted in new ways in new historical contexts.
>
> (ibid.: 26, 27; emphasis in original)

Experiences are rewritten in any new historical context, such as that signalled by postmodernism. It is narratives which put temporal experiences into order and thereby generate self-understandings which, in turn, are always open to new readings. Ricoeur's message is that although matters can never be finally settled by texts alone, narrators can be empowered as authors of their own stories, if not of their own lives.

If research reports are stories about the world, then they are also stories, which are more or less disguised, about the self. They are accounts of events in the life of the investigator. Research can therefore be considered as a form of autobiography, a consideration which is recognised in experiential learning and reflective practice circles by the recommendation that learners and practitioners keep a personal journal. Yet even here it is rare to find extensive references to 'private' texts in accounts intended to be read by others. At best, it is considered somewhat risky to incorporate personal researcher narratives into public accounts. In addition, within the storied accounts of researchers in the human sciences there are, of course, the stories of research subjects themselves. It is here that we can locate the problem of 'voice', not only in relation to authorship ('How shall one write about research?') but also in relation to the subjects of research ('How can they be given "voice"?'). For both researchers and researched there is an overriding problem of how the uncertainties of voice can be reported, given that the ideal to which modernist research aspires is the narration of ultimate certainties by means of the singular voice of the 'grand narrative'. Of course, the postmodern lesson is that there is no one story to end all others, no grand narrative of all-encompassing explanation, no final theory of everything (Lyotard 1984). Narratives are therefore forced to compete and to find an accepting readership where they can. Lyotard's 'solution' to the failure of grand narratives is to refuse transcendent standards of judgment, and to encourage the proliferation of critical practices through local voices which would challenge their pretentions.

How in practice might this work? Atkinson has drawn attention to the different ways in which the voices of ethnographical research subjects can be reported, ranging from the indirect discourse of the summary or paraphrase through to what he calls 'free [sic] direct discourse, used to represent first-person speech' (Atkinson 1990: 123–4). It is important to recognise here, however, that research subjects are not given 'voice' in the sense of being empowered to speak for themselves merely through the device of direct quotation. This is still likely to be a (re)presentation within an overall text that is unavailable for critical scrutiny by those who are quoted. We have seen in the previous chapter how emancipatory research highlights the problem of voice and requires the opportunity to name one's experiences for oneself and not leave this to the formal theories of foundational disciplines. Empowerment in this context requires that people are a) able to access *all* of the text which discursively constructs their experiences and b) have the opportunity to rewrite them. In his critique of andragogical approaches to research, Collins recommends that:

> Instead of deploying intrusive research designs based on independent learning project protocols, [adult educators] might invite willing individuals to engage in exploratory conversations, as part of a pedagogical and hermeneutic process, to discover with what meanings adults endow their own learning experiences. This could be enacted without having recourse to pre-designed explanatory frames of reference.
>
> (Collins 1991b: 114)

Schratz and Walker (1995) develop an approach to questioning the self in the research context which engages co-participants in 'collective memory work', as shown in Figure 10.2.

This type of research involves 'ways of thinking about the self, and changing the self, that are socially rather than individualistically located' (ibid.: 61), and is an example of collaborative research as teaching and learning through scripting and exchange (see also Bryant 1992).

Of all the possible texts that could be written in relation to adult education research, the overarching critical question for readers is 'Why is it that only certain kinds of texts get to be written?' An important dimension of reflective practice which is critically reflexive is that of critical readership which engages with this question. Brookfield identifies four sets of questions (methodological, experiential, communicative, political) for adult educators who, as practitioners, may look to the literature of the field as a guide to action (Brookfield 1993b). To paraphrase, he includes the following:

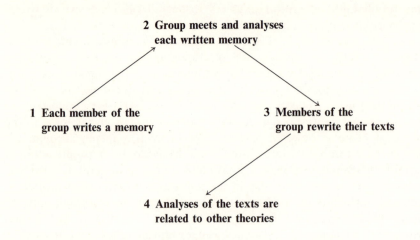

Figure 10.2 Phases in the memory-work process

Source: Schratz and Walker 1995

- Are culturally specific assertions about adult learners presented as universal?
- Are descriptive and prescriptive claims conflated?
- How are experiences constructed? Do they resonate with the reader's own experiences?
- Are ethical issues acknowledged, uncertainties and dilemmas given due weight?
- Whose voices are heard (and not heard)?
- Is the language accessible (with reasonable effort) to readers?
- Does the language connect to practice in opening up potential action spaces?
- Does the text serve to empower particular interests?
- Do texts represent individuality at the expense of community?
- Do evaluations reinforce or challenge the *status quo*?

We endorse these as key questions to be asked of any type of literature in the field, but would wish to extend the interrogation to a critical examination of practice itself (and not just the research literature) as a 'text' to be read along the lines suggested.

In Chapter 3 we have seen how empirical research in the service of management feeds into information systems which hijack experience and exercise control through categorization and enumeration. Other types of research text, while acknowledging the importance of personal, subjective dimensions, nevertheless discursively construct learners' experiences in uncritical and restricting ways. Following Foucault, and from our pre-vious discussion of research methodology, we can see that whatever proce-dures are adopted for capturing and telling the experiences of researchers and researched, the research process itself is always implicated in power/knowledge formations. The power/knowledge nexus reminds us that research as a critical, reflective practice cannot attend to the one without also considering the other. Research is neither innocently concerned with the detached production of knowledge, nor is the self as a researcher trans-parently 'given'; s/he is a power-fully informing and informed agent – both a narrator and narratee. We can see the power of the technical-rationality model in how the practice of producing acceptable research is problem-atised. In raising questions about the roles of author and reader of research texts, we have moved beyond the limits of thinking about these matters simply as problems about 'how to write up your research' or 'how to conduct a literature search'. To approach these as technical matters of editorship or bibliographic retrieval may result in the reproduction of texts which fit into the canon of normal science (and in dissertation exam-inations this is usually what is expected), thereby adding strength to its own voice at the expense of others. What is missing is a critical question-ing of how the identities of researchers and researched are framed within a particular (academic) culture and tradition.

IMPLICATIONS FOR TEACHING ABOUT RESEARCH AS REFLECTIVE PRACTICE: TWO EXAMPLES

We have emphasised the centrality of writing to research practice and developed some ideas about the self as a scripted and scripting agent on a trajectory of enquiry, a model which attends to the dispositional and situational features of personal experience as well as to technical require-ments. It follows that teaching about educational research is more than a matter of providing graduate students with the right formal tools for enquiry, though these are clearly important. One implication of the model is that supervisors and research trainers need to address the question of affect in the research process. How, then, can the idea of a research trajec-tory incorporating disposition and situatedness be built into a curriculum for teaching about research as a textual practice?

The first of the two examples is intended to demonstrate that scripting oneself as an *a*ffective researcher can assist one to become an *e*ffective researcher, especially in an action research/reflective practice context, and that dealing with the textuality of research evidence gives an additional interrogative handle on the surface data of practice. The second example shows how experienced practitioners can be introduced to some ideas about reflective practice in a formal context with no opportunity at the time to explore collaboratively how these ideas might be incorporated within their own practice.

Example 1: incorporating 'affect' into action research

One of the present authors teaches an elective course within his faculty's research training programme entitled 'Action Research and Reflective Practice'. Reflecting on his own rather disappointing first experience in attempting to convey what action research was all about by initially having students consult the literature in this area, he recognised a contradictory attempt to introduce the idea of action research by trying to get students to respond to someone else's text rather than engage directly in action and produce a text of their own. The problem was redefined as how to establish the conditions for real action research within the confines of the classroom and timetable. At the same time, he was aware that the research students – fifteen in all, of both sexes, different ages and from different cultures – swapped stories and talked informally among themselves outside the class about their research, including how they were feeling about the particular stage that each had reached (the students were at various stages on the trajectory).

At the next class, the teacher made no announcement that he was going to engage the students in some action research, but invited the class to divide into three groups of five students each. He then handed all the students in each group a small blank card. Then he asked each individual to write *one word only* that best described her/his current feelings about doing research at the stage they were then at (whether just beginning or some way along the trajectory). Each group of five cards was then collected, shuffled, and handed back to members of the same group, ensuring that nobody received their own card. Each student then read aloud the word on the card and gave their own interpretation to the group of what it meant. That interpretation was then checked against what the author of the word had meant, after which others were invited to comment, and so on around the group. Each group then reported to the class as a whole on what it had discovered about the way its members felt about doing research. A list of personal feelings and their meanings was then compiled, for review by the whole class. The class had generated data, collaboratively explored its meaning, and suggested further lines of enquiry to follow (in this case, were the affective responses and/or their interpretations cultured or gendered, and if so how?)

The teacher then announced that the students had been engaging in action research.

A number of features of this exercise are worthy of note:

1 It was difficult to identify feelings under the 'one word only' rule, yet nobody questioned the right of the teacher to impose this.

2 The act of writing, and the subsequent exchange of comments on the 'text', helped to authenticate each student's experience through unfolding personal stories (e.g., about how and why they came to be doing research) in the context of others doing the same.

3 The opportunity for shared comment (which in principle could build another text) extended the limits of participants' understanding about the role of feelings in research.

4 Voice and action are co-implicated in this exercise; participants were empowered through ownership of the processes of writing, reading and exchanging their experiences. The groups and the class as a whole began to develop a constructively critical edge which questioned the givenness of experience by looking at a number of alternative ways in which different experiences could be rendered.

Example 2: four aspects of practice

The same present author was invited to give a formal talk on the subject of action research and reflective practice to an audience of 100 senior nurses. He was informed by the organiser that such a presentation was expected, that he had half an hour only to speak and that he could not assume that the audience knew anything about the topic. The invitation was accepted and he then wondered, rather too close to the event for comfort, what to do. He decided that in the time available and with such a group it was not possible to exemplify action research as in Example 1. What was needed in the circumstances was a 'quick fix' on researching one's practice that anyone could relate to. Elaborate theorising was out. The key was a realisation that the event itself was a scripted occasion, with a common formal agenda but which participants were likely to experience and to read in different ways. They would subsequently be able to tell 'different' stories about the 'same' event (e.g., in terms of its interest or value to them as practitioners). Why not try and turn the occasion itself into an object of reflection?

The speaker scripted the following presentation, in which the audience was invited to consider four related aspects of practice which can be addressed by participants in any event.

Settings

In our everyday familiar practices, settings are tacitly appreciated and rarely questioned. However, there are also occasions when events confound expectations. The practitioner calls into question routine assumptions and asks 'What is going on here?' How might such a question be dealt with? It suggests a natural follow-on question of the form, 'What is/ are he/she/they doing?' At this point, one might be satisfied with an answer in terms of other people's behaviour. Prudently, one might wish to check one's own reading of the situation with colleagues or others. Reflectively, one might ask oneself, 'How am I reading this situation, and are there alternative readings available?' This leads to a general affirmation about reflective practice. There are many possible interpretations of settings; the reflective practitioner is one who has a range of readings to hand, those which point to others but also readings which point to oneself as an interpreter.

Play

Another way in which we could ask a question about settings is 'What game is being played here?' (or 'What game is she/he playing?'). Practice can be viewed as play within a game, but not just in the frivolous sense or the negative sense of 'power plays'. All games imply rules that are both enabling and constraining. So, another way of looking at practice is in terms of the rules which permit and proscribe different activities. They create the action spaces that characterise what we do. Actions are guided not just by formal requirements but also by personal standards – one's own rules. These are in principle more flexible. Inventiveness within the formal rules is commended; outside the rules it may lead to the equivalent of a 'red card' or possibly even a new game. Thinking of practice as a game allows us to open up new action spaces, to be inventive within the rules or to create new 'play' with alternatives. At a mental level, thought experiments can rehearse practice alternatives virtually in the absence of formal rules; good brainstorming sessions attest to this. At an action level, gaming needs to be more prudent and to consider its own standards in relation to others. At the very least, the reflective practitioner will call some rules into question and may wish to take the risk, at an action level, of trying to change the rules or to start another game.

Scripts

Another aspect of play is that of performance. Action research involves the monitoring of performance when practice 'gets stuck' or 'goes wrong'. Practice is also activity which is scripted, such as the script which is being followed for the event we are all now attending, in which we have the pre-senters' performances. In the performative sense of 'play', actions follow the script or score but at the same time allow considerable latitude in interpretation. Like rules, scripts both define and enable our practices; they are the texts which mark out but which do not completely define performance. They do not come to life except by being enacted, and we all know that a meeting is more than its formal, written agenda. Professionals are often required to produce scripts in their public roles, but anyone also can be a private author of his/her own practices by keeping a journal or diary as a medium for and record of reflection. The reflective practitioner is someone who reads practice as script and who also builds a public and personal practice through the creation and interplay of scripts.

Communication

Practice problems are often put down to 'difficulties of communication', as if all that was needed to put things right is the clarification of meaning and intent. Can one ever be sure that meanings are shared and commonly understood? No, because of the ever-present possibility of different interpretations. This illustrates an inherent problem with all language and not just a local difficulty with reading a particular message. The meaning intended may not be the one received, including any message in this presentation. And this goes for everything that is said, has ever been said, or ever can be said. Because language is performative, communication works to persuade as well as to inform. It has a rhetorical quality whose power lies in the fact that it is often hidden. This presenter's message is intended to persuade you, the audience, of the value of certain ideas about action research and reflective practice. The rhetoric of the inclusive register 'we' may only be obvious when attention is drawn to it (as now), but other rhetorical features may not be so clear. Perhaps you expected a presentation based on 'facts', which would be persuasive because of the association of 'facts' with 'things that are true'. The intended message is that there are no facts, just questions and a moral: be wary of anyone who says, 'these are the facts', which often carries with it the implication that 'there is nothing more to be said'. In action research and reflective practice, there are more questions than answers, and perhaps the most important message is that there is always more to be said.

The above case is offered to show that even within a formal, non-collaborative context it is nevertheless still possible to offer some 'hooks' into research as reflective practice without engaging in elaborate theorising, by asking some fairly simple and direct questions which engage the attention of participants. Of particular note are the following points:

1 In attempting to find a common denominator through co-presence at a particular event, the presenter appealed to what could be assumed among fellow professionals (e.g., that the participants had prior experience of attending formal meetings and occasions similar to the present one).

2 In circumstances where it is not practicable to negotiate a learning agenda, it is still possible to offer an invitation in the form of some open questions which can subsequently be taken up in a less formal context; these provide entry points for researching one's own practice.

3 'Facts' are presented in the guise of questions for engagement. On different occasions after this formal presentation, the speaker was contacted by some of those who were present in the audience, and who affirmed that the questions posed were indeed useful hooks into thinking more critically and productively about their practice.

CONCLUSION

We have seen how postmodernism problematises the representation of research, which is supposed to go beyond the limits of what is known but is trapped by the limits of its own traditions, the conventions of its own texts. In this chapter, and throughout the whole of this work, we have given our own 'voice' as academic adult educators to an understanding of the nature of these limits, within a text which is itself inevitably limiting. This is the conundrum of reflexivity, which we try to practise in our own teaching and research. Critical reflexivity acknowledges the conundrum. It is for readers to decide whether this text offers valuable conceptual resources for them to transcend the limits of their own practice. In focusing here on the writing and reading of research, we have brought to the fore the idea of a research trajectory which provides a dynamic template for understanding the storied nature of research. In reading research, one is exploring the horizons of its author(s) within the ambit of one's own. A personal research trajectory of critically reflective practice is one which continually interrogates the possibilities and limitations of its own horizon of understanding. We now invite our readers to contribute to that critique.

References

Abel Smith, B. and Titmuss, K. (eds) (1987) *The Philosophy of Welfare: Selected Writings of Richard M. Titmuss*, London: Allen & Unwin.

Acker, J. *et al.* (1991) 'Objectivity and Truth: Problems in Doing Feminist Research', in M. Fonow and J. Cook (eds), *Beyond Methodology*, Bloomington, Ind.: Indiana University Press.

Allman, P. (1987) 'Paulo Freire's Education Approach: A Struggle for Meaning', in G. Allen and I. Martin (eds), *Community Education: An Agenda for Educational Reform*, Milton Keynes: Open University Press.

Althusser, L. (1977) 'Ideology and Ideological State Apparatuses', in B. Brewer (trans.), *Lenin and Philosophy, and other Essays*, London: NLB.

Apple, M.W. (1993) *Official Knowledge: Democratic Education in a Conservative Age*, New York: Routledge.

Argyris, C. and Schon, D.A. (1974) *Theory in Practice: Increasing Professional Effectiveness*, San Francisco, Ca.: Jossey-Bass.

Aronowitz, S. and Giroux, H. (1985) *Education Under Siege*, South Hadley, Mass.: Bergin & Garvey.

—— (1991) *Postmodern Education*, Minneapolis, Minn.: University of Minnesota Press.

Ashcroft, B. and Jackson, K. (1974) 'Adult Education and Social Action', in D. Jones and M. Mayo (eds), *Community Work One*, London: Routledge & Kegan Paul.

Atkinson, P. (1990) *The Ethnographic Imagination: Textual Constructions of Reality*, London: Routledge.

Ball, S. J. (1990) *Politics and Policy Making in Education*, London: Routledge.

—— (1993) 'Self-doubt and Soft Data: Social and Technical Trajectories in Ethnographic Fieldwork', in M. Hammersley (ed.), *Educational Research: Current Issues*, London: Open University/Chapman.

Baudrillard, J. (1988) *Selected Writings*, Cambridge: Polity Press.

Bauman, Z. (1992) *Intimations of Postmodernity*, London: Routledge.

Becher, T. and Kogan, M. (1992) *Process and Structure in Higher Education*, London: Routledge.

Beckett, D. (1995) 'Adult Education as Professional Practice', unpublished D.Phil. thesis, University of Technology, Sydney.

Beder, H. (1991) 'Mapping the Terrain', *Convergence* XXIV, 3: 3–7.

Benhabib, S. (1992) *Situating the Self,* Cambridge: Polity Press.

Bernstein, J (1986) *Philosophical Profiles*, Oxford: Polity Press.

Boud, D. (1989) 'Some Competing Traditions in Experiential Learning', in S.W. Weil and I. McGill (eds), *Making Sense of Experiential Learning*, Milton Keynes: SRHE/Open University Press.

Boud, D., Cohen, R. and Walker, D. (1993) 'Introduction: Understanding Learning from Experience', in D. Boud, R. Cohen and D. Walker (eds), *Using Experience for Learning*, Milton Keynes: SRHE/Open University Press.

Bourdieu, P. (1984) *Distinction: A Social Critique of the Judgment of Taste*, Cambridge, Mass.: Harvard University Press.

—— (1991) *Language and Symbolic Power*, Cambridge: Polity Press.

Bourdieu, P. and Passeron, J. (1977) *Reproduction: In Education, Society and Culture*, London: Sage.

Bourdieu, P. and Wacquant, L.J.D. (1992) *An Invitation to Reflexive Sociology*, Cambridge: Polity Press.

Bowles, S. and Gintis, H. (1976) *Schooling in Capitalist America*, New York: Basic Books.

Brady, J. (1994) 'Critical Literacy, Feminism and a Politics of Representation', in P. McLaren and C. Lankspear (eds), *Politics of Liberation: Paths from Freire*, London: Routledge.

Brah, A. and Hoy, J. (1989) 'Experiential Learning: A New Orthodoxy?' in S.W. Weil and I. McGill (eds), *Making Sense of Experiential Learning*, Milton Keynes: SRHE/Open University Press.

Bright, B. (1989) *Theory and Practice in the Study of Adult Education: The Epistemological Debate*, London: Routledge.

Broadfoot, P. (1986) *Profiles and Records of Achievement*, London: Holt, Rinehart & Winston.

Brookfield, S. (1983) *Adult Learners, Adult Education and the Community*, Milton Keynes: Open University Press.

—— (1992) 'Developing Criteria for Formal Theory Building in Adult Education', *Adult Education Quarterly* 42, 2: 79–93.

—— (1993a) 'Through the Lens of Learning: How the Visceral Experience of Learning Frames Teaching' in D. Boud, R. Cohen and D. Walker (eds), *Using Experience for Learning*, Milton Keynes: SRHE/Open University Press.

—— (1993b) 'Breaking the Code: Engaging Practitioners in Critical Analysis of Adult Education Literature', *Studies in the Education of Adults* 25, 1: 64–91.

Brubaker, R. (1993) 'Social Theory as Habitus', in C. Calhoun *et al.* (eds), *Bourdieu: Critical Perspectives*, Cambridge: Polity Press.

Bryant, I. (1992) 'Subverting Theory in Adult Education' in Erben, M. (ed.), *Occasional Papers in Education and Interdisciplinary Studies I*, Southampton: School of Education, University of Southampton.

—— (1994) 'Hijacking Experience and Delivering Competence: Some Professional Contradictions', *1994 SCUTREA Conference Proceedings*, University of Leeds.

Burbules, N. (1995) 'Postmodern Doubt and Philosophy of Education', unpublished paper, Philosophy of Education Society Annual Conference, San Francisco.

Burchell, G., Gordon, C. and Miller, M. (eds) (1991) *The Foucault Effect: Studies in Government*, London: Harvester Wheatsheaf.

Butler, L. (1993) 'Unpaid Work in the Home and Accreditation', in M. Thorpe, R. Edwards and A. Hanson (eds), *Culture and Processes of Adult Learning*, London: Routledge.

Cadena, F. (1991) 'Transformation through Knowledge – Knowledge through Transformation', *Convergence* XXIV, 3: 62–70.

Candy, P. (1987) 'Evolution, Revolution or Devolution; Increasing Learner Control in the Instructional Setting', in D. Boud and V. Griffin (eds), *Appreciating Adults Learning*, London: Kogan Page.

Carr, W. and Kemmis, S. (1986) *Becoming Critical: Education, Knowledge and Action Research*, London: Falmer Press.

Cervero, R. (1992) 'Professional Practice, Learning and Continuing Education: an Integrated Perspective', *International Journal of Lifelong Education* 11, 2: 91–101.

Challis, M. (1993) *Introducing APEL*, London: Routledge.

Claxton, G. (ed.) *Psychology and Schooling: What's the Matter?*, London: Institute of Education.

Code, L. (1993) 'Taking Subjectivity into Account', in L. Alcoff and E. Potter (eds), *Feminist Epistemologies*, London: Routledge.

Collins, M. (1991a) *Adult Education as Vocation*, New York: Routledge.

—— (1991b) 'On Contemporary Practice and Research: Self-directed Learning to Critical Theory', in R. Edwards, A. Hanson and P. Raggatt (eds), *Boundaries of Adult Learning*, London: Routledge/Open University.

Cowburn, W. (1985) *Class, Ideology and Community Education*, London: Croom Helm.

Crane, J.M. (1991) 'Moses Coady and Antigonish', in P. Jarvis (ed.), *Twentieth Century Thinkers in Adult Education*, London: Routledge.

Curt, B.C. (1994) *Textuality and Tectonics*, Milton Keynes: Open University Press.

Dale, R. (1989) *The State and Education Policy*, Milton Keynes: Open University Press.

Derrida, J. (1978) *Writing and Difference*, London: Routledge.

Deshler, D. and Selener, D. (1991) 'Transformative Research: in Search of a Definition', *Convergence* XXIV, 3: 9–21.

Donald, J. (1992) *Sentimental Education*, London: Verso.

Dreyfus, H. and Rabinow, P. (1993) 'Can there be a Science of Existential Structure and Social Meaning?', in C. Calhoun *et al.* (eds), *Bourdieu: Critical Perspectives*, Cambridge: Polity Press.

Duffield, A. (1992) 'The Social Theatre of Empowerment: Drama in Education as an Approach to Adult Education', unpublished MA (Ed.) dissertation, University of Southampton Faculty of Educational Studies.

Duke, C. (1992) 'Introduction' in C. Duke (ed.), *Liberal Adult Education – Perspectives and Projects*, Warwick: Continuing Education Research Centre, University of Warwick.

—— (1992) *The Learning University: Towards a New Paradigm?* Milton Keynes: SRHE/Open University Press.

Durkheim, E. (1956) *Education and Sociology*, Glencoe: Free Press.

—— (1961) *Moral Education*, Glencoe: Free Press.

—— (1964) *The Division of Labour in Society*, Glencoe: Free Press.

—— (1992) *Professional Ethics and Civic Morals*, London: Routledge.

Edwards, D. and Potter, J. (1992) *Discursive Psychology*, London: Sage.

Edwards, R. (1994) 'From a Distance? Globalisation, Space–Time Compression and Distance Education', *Open Learning* 9, 3: 9–17.

Edwards, R. and Usher, R. (1994) 'Disciplining the Subject: The Power of Competence', *Studies in the Education of Adults* 26,1: 1–14.

Elliott, J. (1991) *Action Research for Educational Change*, Milton Keynes: Open University Press.

Elliot, J., Francis, H., Humphreys, R. and Istance, D. (eds) (1996) *Communities and their Universities: the Challenge of Lifelong Learning*, London: Lawrence and Wishart.

Ellsworth, E. (1992) 'Why Doesn't this Feel Empowering? Working Through the Repressive Myths of Critical Pedagogy', in C. Luke and J. Gore J (eds), *Feminisms and Critical Pedagogy*, New York: Routledge.

Featherstone, M. (1991) *Consumer Culture and Postmodernism*, London: Sage.

Field, J. (1994) 'Open Learning and Consumer Culture', *Open Learning* 9, 2: 3–11.

Fieldhouse, R. (1992) 'Tradition in British University Adult Education and the WEA' in C. Duke (ed.), *Liberal Adult Education: Perspectives and Projects*, Warwick: Continuing Education Research Centre, University of Warwick.

Flax, J. (1990) *Thinking in Fragments*, Oxford: University of California Press.

—— (1993) *Disputed Subjects*, London: Routledge.

Foucault, M. (1972) *The Archaeology of Knowledge*, New York: Pantheon.

—— (1974) *The Archaeology of Knowledge*, London: Tavistock.

—— (1979) *Discipline and Punish: The Birth of the Prison*, Harmondsworth: Penguin.

—— (1980) *Power/Knowledge; Selected Interviews and Other Writings*, Brighton: Harvester Press.

—— (1981) 'The Order of Discourse', in R. Young (ed.), *Untying the Text*, London: Routledge & Kegan Paul.

—— (1988) *Technologies of the Self*, Boston: University of Massachusetts Press.

—— (1991a) 'Questions of Method', in G. Burchell *et al.* (eds), *The Foucault Effect: Studies in Governmentality*, London: Harvester Wheatsheaf.

—— (1991b) 'Governmentality', in G. Burchell *et al.* (eds), *The Foucault Effect: Studies in Governmentality*, London: Harvester Wheatsheaf.

—— (1993) *Language, Counter-Memory, Practice*, Ithaca, NY: Cornell University Press.

Freire, P. (1972) *Pedagogy of the Oppressed*, Harmondsworth: Penguin.

—— (1993) in P. Mclaren and P. Leonard (eds), *Paulo Freire: A Critical Encounter*, New York: Routledge.

Gadamer, H-G. (1975) *Truth and Method*, London: Sheed & Ward.

Galbraith, J.K. (1992) *The Culture of Contentment*, New York: Sinclair-Stevenson.

Game, A. (1991) *Undoing the Social*, Milton Keynes: Open University Press.

Gibbons, M., Limoges, C., Nowotny, H., Schwartzman, S., Sott, P. and Trow, M. (1994) *The New Production of Knowledge: The Dynamics of Science and Research in Contemporary Societies*, London: Sage.

Gilbert, R. (1992) 'Citizenship, Education and Post-Modernity', *British Journal of Sociology of Education* 13, 1: 51–69.

Giroux, H. (1989) *Schooling for Democracy: Critical Pedagogy in the Modern Age*, London: Routledge.

—— (1992) *Border Crossings: Cultural Workers and the Politics of Education*, New York: Routledge.

Giroux, H. and McLaren, P. (1994) *Between Borders: Pedagogy and the Politics of Cultural Studies*, London: Routledge.

Gore, J. (1992) 'We Can Do For You? What *Can* We Do For You? Struggling Over Empowerment in Critical and Feminist Pedagogy', in C. Luke and J. Gore (eds), *Feminisms and Critical Pedagogy*, New York: Routledge.

—— (1993) *The Struggle for Pedagogies: Critical and Feminist Pedagogies as Regimes of Truth*, London: Routledge.

Gramsci, A. (1971) *Selections from the Prison Notebooks*, London: Lawrence and Wishart.

Gunew, S. (ed) (1990) *Feminist Knowledge: Critique and Construct*, London: Routledge.

Habermas, J. (1972) *Knowledge and Human Interests*, London: Heinemann.

—— (1974) *Theory and Practice*, London: Heinemann.

—— (1989) *Theory of Communicative Action*, Boston: Beacon Press.

Hall, B. (1981) 'The Democratization of Research', in P. Rowan and J. Reason (eds), *Human Inquiry: A Sourcebook of New Paradigm Research*, Chichester: Wiley.

Hall, S. and Held, D. (1990) 'Citizens and Citizenship', in S. Hall and M. Jacques (eds), *New Times: The Changing Face of Politics in the 1990s*, London: Lawrence & Wishart.

Hammersley, M. (1992) 'Reflections on the Liberal University: Truth, Citizenship and the Role of the Academic', *International Studies in the Sociology of Education* 2, 2: 165–83.

Hampton, W.A. (1983) *Existing Provision and New Developments in Political Education for Adults*, Leicester: Advisory Council for Adult and Continuing Education.

Hart, M.U. (1992) *Working and Educating for Life: Feminist and International Perspectives on Adult Education*, London: Routledge.

—— (1995) 'Education and Social Change', in Newman, M. (ed.) *Social Action and Emancipatory Learning*, Sydney: School of Education, UTS Seminar Papers.

Harvey, D. (1991) *The Condition of Postmodernity: An Enquiry into the Origins of Social Change*, Oxford: Basil Blackwell.

Henriques, J., Holloway, W., Urwin, C., Venn, C. and Walkerdine, V. (1984) *Changing the Subject: Psychology, Social Regulation and Subjectivity*, London: Methuen.

Hill, D.M. (1994) *Citizens and Cities*, London: Harvester Wheatsheaf.

Hirst, P. (1974) *Knowledge and the Curriculum*, London: Routledge & Kegan Paul.

Hitchcock, G. (1986) *Profiles and Profiling*, London: Longman.

Hoskin, K. (1990) 'Foucault Under Examination: The Crypto-Educationalist Unmasked', in S.J. Ball (ed.), *Foucault and Education: Disciplines and Knowledge*, London: Routledge.

Hughes, (1980) *The Philosophy of Social Research*, London: Longman.

International Participatory Research Network (1982) *An Introduction to Participatory Research*, Toronto: Participatory Research Group.

Jackson, K. (1980a) 'Some Fallacies in Community Education and their Consequences in Working-Class Areas', in C. Fletcher and N. Thompson (eds), *Issues in Community Education*, Lewes: Falmer.

—— (1980b) 'Foreword' to J.L. Thompson (ed.), *Adult Education for a Change*, London: Hutchinson.

Jensen, T. and van der Veen, R. (1992) 'Reflexive Modernity, Self-reflexive Biographies: Adult Education in the Light of the Risk Society', *International Journal of Lifelong Education* 11, 4: 257–86.

Jeffs, T. (1992) 'The State, Ideology and the Community School Movement', in G. Allen and I. Martin (eds), *Educatiion and Community: The Politics of Practice*, London: Cassell.

Johnson, R. (1988) 'Really Useful Knowledge 1790–1850', in T. Lovett (ed.), *Radical Approaches to Adult Education*, London: Routledge.

Johnston, R. (1992) 'Education and Unwaged Adults: Relevance, Social Control and Empowerment', in G. Allen and I. Martin (eds), *Education and Community, The Politics of Practice*, London: Cassell.

—— (1994) 'Jobs, Unemployment and Education for Work', *Studies in Continuing Education* 16, 1: 37–52.

Keddie, N. (1980) 'Adult Education: An Ideology of Individualism', in J.L. Thompson (ed.), *Adult Education for a Change*, London: Hutchinson.

Kemmis, S. (1989) 'Metatheory and Metapractice: Educational Theorising and Research', unpublished paper.

Kenway, J. with Bigum, C. and Fitzclarence, L. (1993) 'Marketing Education in the Postmodern Age', *Journal of Education Policy* 8, 2: 105–22.

Kirkwood, G. and Kirkwood, C. (1989) *Living Adult Education*, Milton Keynes: Open University Press.

Knapper, C. and Cropley, A. (1985) *Lifelong Learning and Higher Education*, London: Croom Helm.

Knowles, M. (1978) *The Adult Learner: A Neglected Species*, Houston, Tex.: Gulf Publishing.

—— (1985) *Andragogy in Action*, San Francisco, Ca.: Jossey-Bass.

Kuhn, T. (1970) *The Structure of Scientific Revolutions*, Chicago, Ill.: University of Chicago Press.

Kvale, S. (ed.) (1992) *Psychology and Postmodernism*, London: Sage.

Lacan, J. (1977) *Ecrits: A Selection*, London: Tavistock.

Lash, S. (1990) *Sociology of Postmodernism*, London: Routledge.

Lather, P. (1991) *Feminist Research In Education*, Geelong: Deakin University Press.

Law, J. (1994) *Organising Modernity*, Oxford: Blackwell.

Long, N. and Long, A. (eds) (1992) *Battlefields of Knowledge: The Interlocking of Theory and Practice in Social Research and Development*, London: Routledge.

Lovett, T. (1975) *Adult Education, Community Development and the Working Class*, London: Ward Lock Educational.

Lovlie, L. (1992) 'Postmodernism and Subjectivity', in S. Kvale (ed.), *Psychology and Postmodernism*, London: Sage.

Lyon, J. (1994) *Postmodernity*, Milton Keynes: Open University Press.

Lyotard, J-F. (1984) *The Postmodern Condition: A Report on Knowledge*, Manchester: Manchester University Press.

Lukes, S. (1973) *Emile Durkheim: His Life and Work: A Historical and Critical Study*, Harmondsworth: Penguin.

Macedo, D. (1994) 'Preface' to P. McLaren and C. Lankshear (eds), *Politics of Liberation: Paths from Freire*, New York: Routledge.

McHale, B. (1992) *Constructing Postmodernism*, London: Routledge.

McLaren, P. and Lankspear, C. (eds) (1994) *Politics of Liberation: Paths from Freire*, London: Routledge.

Marcuse, H. (1970) *One Dimensional Man*, London: Sphere.

Marshall, J.D. (1989) 'Foucault and Education', *Australian Journal of Education* 33, 2: 99–113.

—— (1990) 'Foucault and Educational Research', in S.J. Ball (ed.), *Foucault and Education: Disciplines and Knowledge*, London: Routledge.

Marshall, T.H. (1950) *Citizenship and Social Class*, Cambridge: Cambridge University Press.

Michelson, C. (1996) 'The usual suspects: experience, reflection and the engendering of knowledge', *International Journal of Lifelong Education*, forthcoming.

Miller, P. and Rose, N. (1993) 'Governing Economic Life', in M. Gane and T. Johnson (eds), *Foucault's New Domains*, London: Routledge.

Morss, J. (1995) *Growing Critical*, London: Routledge.

Mouffe, C. (1988) 'The Civics Lesson', *New Statesman and Society*, 7 October.

Mulkay, M. J. (1985) *The Word and the World: Explorations in the Form of Sociological Analysis*, London: Allen & Unwin.

Newman, M. (1995) 'Locating Learning in Social Action', *Social Action and Emancipatory Learning*, Sydney: School of Education, UTS Seminar Papers.

O'Reilly, D. (1989) 'On Being an Educational Fantasy Engineer', in Weil, S. and McGill, I. (eds) *Making Sense of Experiential Learning*, Milton Keynes: SRHE/ Open University Press.

Parker, I. (1989) *The Crisis in Modern Social Psychology*, London: Routledge.

Peters, J.M. and Bell, B. (1991) 'Horton of Highlander', in P. Jarvis (ed.), *Twentieth Century Thinkers in Adult Education*, London: Routledge.

Plant, S. (1995) 'Crash Course', *Wired*, April: 44–7.

Polanyi, M. (1958) *Personal Knowledge: Towards a Post-Critical Philosophy*, London: Routledge.

Polkinghorne, D. (1992) 'A Postmodern Epistemology of Practice', in S. Kvale (ed.), *Psychology and Postmodernism*, London: Sage.

Popper, K. (1963) *Conjectures and Refutations: The Growth of Scientific Knowledge*, New York: Harper.

Potter, J. and Wetherell, M. (1987) *Discourse and Social Psychology*, London: Sage.

Rabinow, P. (ed.) (1984) *The Foucault Reader*, Harmondsworth: Penguin.

Richards, B. (1989) *Images of Freud*, London: J.M. Dent.

Ricoeur, P. (1991) 'Life in Quest of Narrative', in D. Wood (ed.), *On Paul Ricoeur: Narrative and Interpretation*, London: Routledge.

Ridley, F.F. (1983) 'What Adults? What Politics?', in *Political Education for Adults*, Leicester: Advisory Council for Adult and Continuing Education.

Robson, C. (1993) *Real World Research: A Resource for Social Scientists and Practitioner-researchers*, Oxford: Blackwell.

Rogers, A. (1992) *Adults Learning and Development*, London: Cassell.

Rogers, C.R. (1967) *On Becoming a Person*, London: Constable

—— (1983) *Freedom to Learn in the '80s*, Columbus, Oh.: Charles E. Merrill.

Rorty, R. (1980) *Philosophy and the Mirror of Nature*, Oxford: Blackwell.

—— (1989) *Contingency, Irony, and Solidarity*, Cambridge: Cambridge University Press.

Rose, N. (1990) 'Psychology as a "social" science', in I. Parker and J. Shotter (eds), *Deconstructing Social Psychology*, London: Routledge.

—— (1994) *Governing the Soul: The Shaping of the Private Self*, London: Routledge.

Rosenau, P.M. (1992) *Postmodernism and the Social Sciences*, Princeton, NJ: Princeton University Press.

Ryle, G. (1949) *The Concept of Mind*, London: Hutchinson.

Sampson, E. (1993) *Celebrating the Other*, Hemel Hempstead: Harvester Wheatsheaf.

Schneider, U. (1988) 'Studienreflexion in Tagebuchform als Prufungsmethode', (cited in Schratz, M. and Walker, R. 1995) *Research as Social Change*, London: Routledge.

Schon, D.A. (1983) *The Reflective Practitioner: How Professionals Think in Action*, Aldershot: Avebury.

—— (1987) *Educating the Reflective Practitioner*, San Francisco, Ca.: Jossey-Bass.

Schratz, M. and Walker, R. (1995) *Research as Social Change*, London: Routledge.

Sheridan, A. (1980) *Michel Foucault: The Will to Truth*, London: Tavistock.

Shotter, J. (1989) 'Social Accountability and the Social Construction of "You"', in J. Shotter and K.J. Gergen (eds), *Texts of Identity*, London: Sage.

—— (1993) *Conversational Realities*, London: Sage.

Steier, F. (1991) *Research and Reflexivity*, London: Sage.

Stubbs, M. (1983) *Discourse Analysis*, Oxford: Blackwell.

Taylor, R. (1986) 'Problems of Inequality: The Nature of Adult Education in Britain', in K. Ward and R. Taylor (eds), *Adult Education and the Working Class*, London: Croom Helm.

Taylor, R. and Ward, K. (1986) 'Adult Education and the Working Class: Policies, Practice and Future Priorities for Community Adult Education', in K.Ward and R. Taylor (eds), *Adult Education and the Working Class*, London: Croom Helm.

Taylor, R., Brookhill, K. and Fieldhouse, R. (1985) *University Adult Education in England and the USA*, London: Croom Helm.

Thompson, J.B. (1991) 'Editor's Introduction' to P. Bourdieu, *Language and Symbolic Power*, Cambridge: Polity Press.

Thompson, J.L. (1980) 'Adult Education and the Disadvantaged', in J.L. Thompson (ed.), *Adult Education for a Change*, London: Hutchinson

—— (ed.), (1980) *Adult Education for a Change*, London: Hutchinson.

—— (1993) *Learning Liberation: Women's Responses to Men's Education*, Beckenham: Croom Helm.

Thorpe, C. (1993) 'Course Profiling: An In-house Method of Validating Adult Education Courses', unpublished MA (Ed.) dissertation, University of Southampton Faculty of Educational Studies.

Urry, J. (1994) 'Time, Leisure and Social Identity', *Time and Society* 3, 2: 131–50.

Usher, R. (1985) 'Beyond the Anecdotal: Adult Learning and the Use of Experience', *Studies in the Education of Adults* 17: 59–74.

—— (1989) 'Locating Adult Education in the Practical', in B. Bright (ed.), *Theory and Practice in the Study of Adult Education*, London: Routledge.

—— (1991) 'Theory and Metatheory in the Adult Education Curriculum', *International Journal of Lifelong Education* 10, 4: 305–15.

—— (1992) 'Experience in Adult Education: A Postmodern Critique', *Journal of Philosophy of Education* 26, 2: 201–13.

—— (1993) 'From Process to Practice: Research, Reflexivity and Writing in Adult Education', *Studies in Continuing Education* 15, 2: 98–116.

Usher, R. and Bryant, I. (1989) *Adult Education as Theory, Practice and Research: The Captive Triangle*, London: Routledge.

Usher, R. and Edwards, R. (1994) *Postmodernism and Education*, London: Routledge.

—— (1995) 'Confessing All? A "Postmodern" Guide to the Guidance and Counselling of Adult Learners', *Studies in the Education of Adults* 27, 1: 9–23.

Vincent, C. (1993) Education for the Community', *British Journal of Educational Studies* 41, 4: 366–77.

Walkerdine, V. (1985) 'Psychological knowledge and educational practice: producing the truth about schools', in G. Claxton (ed.), *Psychology and Schooling: What's the Matter?*, London: Institute of Education.

Ward, K. (1995) 'Community, Generation and Social Exclusion; Some Current Policy Issues', *UCACE Conference Proceedings*, Swansea.

—— (1996) 'Community regeneration and social exclusion: some current policy issues for higher education', in Elliot, J., Francis, H., Humphreys, R. and Istance, D. (eds), *Communities and their Universities: the Challenge of Lifelong Learning*, London: Lawrence and Wishart.

Weedon, C. (1987) *Feminist Practice and Post-structuralist Theory*, Oxford: Basil Blackwell.

Weil, S. and McGill, I. (1989a) 'A Framework for Making Sense of Experiential Learning', in S. Weil and I. McGill (eds), *Making Sense of Experiential Learning*, Milton Keynes: SRHE/Open University Press.

—— (1989b) 'Continuing the Dialogue: New Possibilities for Experiential Learning', in S. Weil and I. McGill (eds), *Making Sense of Experiential Learning*, Milton Keynes: SRHE/Open University Press.

Weiler, K. (1994) 'Freire and a Feminist Pedagogy of Difference', in P. McLaren and C. Lankspear (eds), *Politics of Liberation*, Routledge: New York.

Welton, M. (1995) 'The Disinteration of Andragogy, the Emergence of the Social Learning Paradigm, the Demise of Adult Education?', in *Educating the Adult Educator: The Role of the University*, Saskatoon: University of Saskatchewan.

Westwood, S. (1991) 'Constructing the Future: A Postmodern Agenda for Adult Education', in S. Westwood and J.E. Thomas (eds), *Radical Agenda? The Politics of Adult Education*, Leicester: NIACE.

—— (1992) 'When Class Became Community in Adult Education', in A. Rattansi and D. Reeder (eds), *Rethinking Radical Education*, London: Lawrence & Wishart.

Wildemeersch, D. (1992a) 'Ambiguities of Experiential Learning and Critical Pegagogy', in D. Wildemeersch and T. Jansen (eds), *Adult Education, Experiential Learning and Social Change: The Postmodern Challenge*, Belgium: VUGA Gravenhage.

—— (1992b) 'Transcending the Limits of Traditional Research: Towards an Interpretative Approach to Development Communication and Education', *Studies in Continuing Education* 14, 1: 42–55.

Williams, R. (1961) *The Long Revolution*, London: Chatto & Windus.

Woolgar, S. (ed.) (1988) *Knowledge and Reflexivity: New Frontiers in the Sociology of Knowledge*, London: Sage.

Wright Mills, C. (1959) *The Sociological Imagination*, Oxford: Oxford University Press.

Zacharakis-Jutz, J., Heaney, T. and Horton, A. (1991) 'The Lindeman Centre: A Popular Education Center Bridging Community and University', *Convergence* XXIV, 3: 24–9.

Index